Death and Personal Survival

Death and Personal Survival

The Evidence for Life After Death

Robert Almeder

Littlefield Adams Quality Paperbacks

LITTLEFIELD ADAMS QUALITY PAPERBACKS

a division of Rowman & Littlefield Publishers, Inc.
4720 Boston Way, Lanham, Maryland 20706

British Cataloging in Publication Information Available

Library of Congress Cataloging-in-Publication Data

Almeder, Robert F.
Death and personal survival : the evidence for life after
death / Robert Almeder.
  p.   cm.
Includes bibliographical references and index.
1. Future life—Case studies.   2. Spiritualism—Case studies.
3. Reincarnation—Case studies.   I. Title.
BF1311.F8A55   1992
133.9'01'3—dc20   92–7911 CIP

ISBN 0–8226–3016–8 (pbk. : alk. paper)

Printed in the United States of America

For their honesty, good humor, selfless integrity, and uncompromising thirst for excellence in the art of philosophizing, this book is warmly dedicated to my respected colleagues and friends,

Milton Snoeyenbos and James Humber

Acknowledgments

For their permission to quote from appropriate materials, we would like to thank the following:

The Atlanta Constitution, January 18, 1982, G. G. Rigsby and Tommy Clack

International Association for Near-Death Studies, Inc.

Vital Signs, December 1981, Reinée Pasarow

Ian Stevenson, Children Who Remember Previous Lives (Charlottesville: University Press of Virginia, 1987)

Ian Stevenson, Twenty Cases Suggestive of Reincarnation (Charlottesville: University Press of Virginia, 1980)

Rhea White, Journal of the American Society for Psychical Research

Bernhard Haisch, Journal of Scientific Exploration

Arthur S. Berger, Aristocracy of the Dead: New Findings in Postmortem Survival (Jefferson, N.C.: McFarland, 1987)

Scottie Twine, American Society for Psychical Research

Karlis Osis, American Society for Psychical Research

Donna McCormick, American Society for Psychical Research

Contents

Preface

My 1987 book *Beyond Death: Evidence for Life after Death* offered a brief defense of personal survival and concluded that the evidence garnered from the *best* case studies on reincarnation, possession, apparitions of the dead, near-death experiences, out-of-body experiences, and trance mediumship is collectively compelling in ways not yet appreciated either by the public at large or by the scientific, religious, and academic community. More precisely, the book asserted that we now have, for the first time in our history as a species, compelling empirical evidence for belief in some form of personal survival after death. Given the general importance of the conclusion, I wrote the book for a generally literate audience and argued the case as simply as possible without doing violence to the complexity of the issues involved. It was a thin book intended for a large popular audience.

Although the first chapter of *Beyond Death* was a defense of the belief in personal reincarnation, no sooner had the book gone to press than new evidence emerged along with a number of spirited and sustained attacks on the belief in reincarnation—attacks that raised many objections and arguments not considered at all in the first chapter of *Beyond Death*. For example, in 1987 the magazines *Free Inquiry* and the *Sceptical Inquirer* collectively published no fewer than 100 journal pages, authored by at least three sceptics, devoted to showing either the falsity or the absurdity of belief in reincarnation. Unfortunately, as a matter of policy, neither of those magazines would allow a response of more than 2,000 words (approximately eight pages) to the essays they published. During this time also, Geddes MacGregor's *Reincarnation in Christianity* came to my attention as an argument urging, persuasively, that the belief in reincarnation was legitimate for all Christians. Because I had argued earlier that Christianity had been and probably would continue to be the primary reason for the suppression of the belief in the West, it seemed that this topic deserved a fuller discussion than it received in *Beyond Death*.

Also, between then and now, I found more persuasive evidence and more interesting discussions on the topics of apparitions of the dead, possession, out-of-body experiences, near-death experiences, and the validity of mediumship as a source of evidence for personal postmortem survival. As a result, this book seeks to offer a much stronger defense of personal survival based on a more careful assessment of the available empirical evidence than was intended or accomplished in *Beyond Death*. Given the breadth of the changes, the scope of the critical discussions, and the new material covered, it would be a serious mistake to classify this effort as a second edition of *Beyond Death*. The conclusion is the same, and some of the case studies are the same; but this book is quite different. Hopefully, the reader will find this book a much stronger and considerably more persuasive argument for reincarnation and personal survival.

A word about the case studies is in order. My primary concern in selecting case studies has been to present the most compelling cases—most compelling in terms of the kind and force of evidence needed to counter the sceptical response. I have been forced, therefore, to exclude a number of cases that are extremely interesting and entertaining, because they did not have the appropriate logical features to be compelling in the way of evidential strength. In selecting particular case studies as offering the best evidence for personal survival, the entertainment value of the studies was not a relevant factor.

When asked whether I believe in reincarnation, my answer is that it makes little difference what anyone in fact believes in this matter; the question, rather, should be this: "If a person were to believe in reincarnation or in any case some form of personal postmortem survival, for the reasons defended in this book, would that person's belief be a rational belief?" My answer to this question is yes, and this book is a defense of that answer. As a matter of fact, my answer is even stronger because it goes on to assert that it would be irrational to withhold belief in the presence of the data and arguments presented here. Even so, on some days, like many people, I find it difficult to believe in much of anything.

Of course, the plain and awful truth of the matter may be that some of us are not interested in finding rationally compelling answers on this issue. We seem more interested in being supported in beliefs we find congenial, even if they are unwarranted. There are many who have a strong emotional interest in believing that reincarnation—or any form of personal survival—must be absurd, silly, rationally indefensible, or just plain boring. Where the emotional investment is deep, the fear of being wrong determines what one will see, or can see, as evidence. The only rational antidote for such fear is confrontation with the evidence. And, as we all know, if the fear is deep enough, a calm philosophical confrontation is impossible.

Even so, there is an undetermined number of people who are interested, able, and willing to confront their biases, just as there is an undetermined number of people who can be persuaded by the superior force of evidence and sound argument. This book is for them and is inspired by the American philosopher Charles Peirce's belief that the truth, sooner or later—however frequently crushed to earth and ignored—will arise and flourish just because it is the truth. So, in the end it makes little difference whether the world is persuaded by the truth in the short run. But it makes a world of difference that we find out what the truth is. And that is the only point to this book.

I am very indebted to a number of people who have encouraged this project. Ian Stevenson took time from his busy schedule to share his research and his insight. As a matter of fact, he read carefully every line and footnote of an earlier version of this manuscript, made a long and detailed list of compelling suggestions and criticisms, and offered the use of his library. Such generosity and seriousness is a rare and enviable trait. As a result of taking his criticisms and suggestions fully into account, writing this book took at least a year longer, but hopefully the product is better thereby than it would otherwise have been. Similarly, Stephen Braude no less graciously gave the manuscript a hard reading and provided a number of very helpful criticisms and suggestions. In the end, while I still disagree with some of Braude's basic views on the role of ESP in accounting for data that dualists regard as evidence for postmortem personal survival, his comments were extremely pointed and required a good deal of attention and extensive rewriting. Rhea White kindly spent many long, and presumably frustrating, hours editing final copy and correcting my many stylistic and footnoting infelicities. Ian Stevenson, Stephen Braude, and Rhea White provided me with considerably more hours of work than I had desired or originally intended. Bowen Johnson encouraged a fuller philosophical treatment of the issues, and provided very specific recommendations to that end. Mark Woodhouse was always there with friendly criticism and supportive suggestions. Finally, Emily Williams Cook was very helpful in often sending crucial research materials sorely needed at crucial junctures. In this labor of love, each of these people has provided something very special for which I am sincerely grateful. Hopefully, the final product is as worthy of their efforts as it is of mine. Finally, the nice people at the Hambidge Center in Rabun Gap, Georgia, provided the protected solitude necessary for finishing this project.

1

Reincarnation

It is no more surprising to be born twice than it is to be born once.
Voltaire

Do human beings reincarnate? To think that one's personality could survive biological death (which would imply that the body is not essential to one's full personality) and then subsequently "take up" a new body for some purpose or other seems philosophically fantastic. Nevertheless, in 1982 a Gallup poll found that nearly one in four Americans believed in reincarnation; in 1980 the *London Times* had reported the results of their own poll in which 29 percent of the British population surveyed expressed a belief in reincarnation. The emerging popularity of the belief, however, is no clear sign that there is any truth to it. Such growing popularity only *raises the question* of its truth. After all, the National Science Foundation recently conducted a national poll and announced that approximately 30 percent of all the American adults surveyed either did not know or agreed with the statement that the sun goes around the earth.

Even so, serious philosophers no less famous than Plato, Nietzsche, Schopenhauer, Giordano Bruno, and Cicero have argued for reincarnation on purely philosophical grounds. Of course, most people who believe in reincarnation do so primarily for religious, rather than scientific or philosophical, reasons; and this sort of motivation is apparent as far back as the ancient Pythagoreans, for whom belief in reincarnation (or transmigration of souls) was simply a matter of religious faith.

1

Quite apart from the religious context, however, belief in reincarnation has not prompted much serious philosophical discussion since Plato. This is not surprising. The most interesting evidence warranting such a discussion did not appear until quite recently. But even so, philosophers have still not yet noticed this evidence. They have been preoccupied with what they consider the more pressing question in the area of inquiry surrounding death, namely, whether we can successfully identify human personality with the corruptible body. There is, of course, no logically necessary connection between the answer to this question and reincarnation. Presumably, even if human personality should turn out to be identified with some nonphysical and naturally incorruptible principle (like a soul), the truth of reincarnation would not follow from that fact alone. One's personality could in some way survive one's biological death and yet *not* reincarnate. So, even if contemporary philosophers of mind do establish the falsity of mad-dog materialism, the most that would thereby be granted is the *possibility* of reincarnation as one of the ways in which human personality might survive biological death.

Curiously and interestingly enough, however, the belief in reincarnation offers the best available *scientific* explanation for certain forms of observable behavior not capable of explanation by appeal to any current scientifically accepted theory of human personality. In the conclusion to this chapter, one of the points that will emerge strongly is that, from a philosophical point of view, the belief in reincarnation is certainly as well established as (if not better than), say, the belief in the past existence of dinosaurs.

Anyway, in this chapter we will assume at the outset something we shall see proven in the conclusion of this book, namely, that belief in personal survival after death is certainly neither logically absurd nor factually impossible. Given this assumption, let us examine the best evidence for reincarnation. For reasons we shall explore later, many philosophers and scientists manage to bypass this evidence while seeking to determine whether human beings are more than just physical bodies.

Stevenson's Argument for Reincarnation, and Some Compelling Cases

The strongest argument for reincarnation has been offered by Ian Stevenson, primarily in his book *Twenty Cases Suggestive of*

Reincarnation.[1] Throughout most of this chapter, we shall review that argument, say why it is convincing, and confront various objections to it.

Basically, Stevenson's argument is that the belief in personal reincarnation offers the best available explanation for a large body of data that, until recently, has been generally ignored or rejected for various unacceptable reasons. The body of data consists in a number of case studies (described in great detail in *Twenty Cases Suggestive of Reincarnation* and elsewhere), many of which typically and ideally share at least the following core features:

A. A young person, usually between the ages of three and nine, claims to remember having lived an earlier life as a different person, and provides his (or her) parents with a *detailed* description of his alleged earlier life—a description including, but not restricted to, where and when he lived, his name, the names and characteristics of his various relatives, highly selective historical events that could be known only by the person he claims to have been in that earlier life, the way he lived, and the specific details of the way in which he died.

B. These memory claims consist of two types: (1) those that admit of simple verification in terms of available information; and (2) those that admit of verification but not in terms of available information. For example, if a young person from Evanston, Illinois, claims to remember having lived an earlier life as one Lazarus Smart, born in approximately 1630 in Boston, Massachusetts, and the son of Mary and Abraham Smart who lived on Boylston Street during the Boat Fire of 1642, then the fact that one Lazarus Smart did exist under this description could be verified easily in terms of available birth records, historical documents, and other information publicly accessible. But if the same person claims to recall having secretly buried a silver spoon with the initials L.S. in the concrete pier under the northwest corner of the Boylston Street Church when it was rebuilt in 1642, then this is the sort of claim that would be verifiable but not in terms of known or existing information.

C. The person claiming to remember having lived a past life, as well as the person's immediate (present) family members, are interviewed (with near-verbatim notes taken and some tape recordings) at great length, and asked to provide information one would expect to emerge if indeed the subject did live that earlier life. Although the majority of the person's memories are involuntary and spontaneous (and hence not often the direct response to questions of the interviewers), the relevant memory claims and information are provided during the interviews.

D. Investigators independently confirm both the spontaneous and the solicited memory claims; and in some cases (those cases in which the person's claims refer to extant past-life family members with whom he was intimate), past-life family members are interviewed and led to confront the subject, who proceeds to remind them of various nonpublic details of the life they spent together.

E. The person claiming to remember having lived a past life also manifests certain skills (such as speaking fluently a foreign language or dialect, or playing an instrument) that the person in the alleged earlier life had, but that the person claiming to have lived the earlier life could not have acquired or learned in this life. For example, if a person claims to remember having lived a life in medieval Sweden, and in a hypnotic trance he begins to speak and describe his earlier life in a difficult but clear dialect of medieval Swedish, then that person (assuming we can document that he has not learned or been exposed to the study of medieval Swedish) manifests a skill not acquired in this life.

F. Deception, or the real possibility of deception, by way of fraud or hoax on the part of the person claiming to have lived a past life cannot be substantiated.

Stevenson's basic argument says that for cases with characteristics A through F the only available explanation that plausibly fits the data is belief in reincarnation. Before discussing all available objections to this argument, however, we need to examine a few particular cases (some of them Stevenson's) that have the characteristics A through F.

Memory Evidence and Acquired Skills

Certainly some of the most compelling evidence for reincarnation occurs in cases that, as described in Stevenson's ideal-typical characteristics, offer detailed memory claims substantiated by extant past-life family members. The first case we will examine—the Bishen Chand case—involved just such evidence. The second—the Mrs. Smith case—is more problematic in that the past life remembered took place centuries ago. However, historical records (some of them extremely obscure or only recently available) have been used to verify many of the surprising memory claims of the subject.

Both cases exhibit another of Stevenson's ideal-typical characteristics, namely, the manifestation of skills acquired by the past-life person but not acquired by the present-day subject in this life. As explained later in this chapter as well as in Chapter 3 in our discussion of possession, this characteristic carries a great deal of evidential weight in replying to those sceptics who see these cases as evidence of paranormal knowledge rather than reincarnation.

The Bishen Chand Case

Bishen Chand Kapoor was born in 1921 to the Gulham family living in the city of Bareilly, India. At about one and a half years, Bishen began asking questions about the town of Pilibhit, some 50 miles from Bareilly. Nobody in his family knew anybody in Pilibhit. Bishen Chand asked to be taken there, and it became obvious that he believed he had lived there during an earlier life.[2]

As time passed, Bishen Chand talked incessantly of his earlier life there in Pilibhit. His family grew increasingly distressed with his behavior. By the summer of 1926 (when he was five and a half years old), Bishen Chand claimed to remember his previous life quite clearly. He remembered that his name had been Laxmi Narain, and that he had been the son of a wealthy landowner. Bishen claimed to remember an uncle named Har Narain, who turned out to be Laxmi Narain's father. He also described the house in which he had lived, saying it included a shrine room and separate quarters for women. Frequently, he had enjoyed the singing and dancing of nautch girls, professional dancers who often functioned as prostitutes. He remembered enjoying parties of this sort at the home of a neighbor, Sander Lal, who lived in a "house with a green gate." Indeed, little Bishen Chand one day recommended to his father that he (the father) take on a mistress in addition to his wife.

Because Bishen Chand's family was poor (his father was a government clerk), Bishen Chand's memories of an earlier and wealthier life only made him resentful of his present living conditions with the Gulham family. He sometimes refused to eat the food, claiming that even his servants (in his former life) would not eat such food.

One day Bishen's father mentioned that he was thinking of buying a watch, and little Bishen Chand said, "Pappa, don't buy. When I go to Pilibhit, I shall get you three watches from a Muslim watch dealer whom I established there." He then provided the name of the dealer.

His sister Kamla, three years older than he, caught Bishen drinking brandy one day (which finally explained the dwindling supply of alcohol kept in the house for medicinal purposes only). In his typically superior way, the child told her that he was quite accustomed to drinking brandy. He drank a good deal of alcohol in his earlier life. Later, he claimed to have had a mistress (again showing he knew the difference between a wife and a mistress) in his former life. Her name, he said, was Padma; and although she was a prostitute, he seemed to have considered her his exclusive property, because he proudly claimed to have killed a man he once saw coming from her apartment.

Bishen Chand Kapoor's memory claims came to the attention of one K. K. N. Sahay, an attorney in Bareilly. Sahay went to the Kapoor home and recorded the surprising things the young boy was saying. Thereafter, he arranged to take Bishen Chand, along with his father and older brother, to Pilibhit. Not quite eight years had elapsed since the death of Laxmi Narain, whom this little boy was claiming to have been in his earlier life.

Crowds gathered when they arrived at Pilibhit. Nearly everyone in town had heard of the wealthy family and its profligate member

Laxmi Narain who had been involved with the prostitute Padma (who still lived there), and how in a jealous rage Laxmi Narain had shot and killed a rival lover of Padma's. Although Laxmi Narain's family had been influential enough to get the charges dropped, he died a few months afterward of natural causes at the age of 32.

When taken to Laxmi's old government school, Bishen Chand ran to where his classroom had been. Somebody produced an old picture, and Bishen recognized in it some of Laxmi Narain's classmates, one of whom happened to be in the crowd. When the classmate asked about their teacher, Bishen correctly described him as a fat, bearded man.

In the part of town where Laxmi Narain had lived, Bishen Chand recognized the house of Sander Lal, the house that he had previously described (before being brought to Pilibhit) as having a green gate. The lawyer Sahay, when writing the report later for the national newspaper *The Leader* in August 1926, claimed to have seen the gate himself and verified that its color was green. The boy also pointed to the courtyard where he said the nautch girls used to entertain with singing and dancing. Merchants in the area verified the boy's claims. In the accounts published by *The Leader,* Sahay wrote that the name of the prostitute with whom the boy associated in his previous life was repeatedly sought by people in the crowd (following the boy). When Bishen Chand mentioned the name "Padma," the people certified that the name was correct.

During that remarkable day, the boy was presented with a set of *tabla,* a pair of drums. The father said that Bishen had never seen tabla before; but to the surprise of his family and all assembled, Bishen Chand played them skilfully, as had Laxmi Narain much earlier. When the mother of Laxmi Narain met Bishen Chand, a strong attachment was immediately apparent between them. Bishen Chand answered the questions she asked (such as the time in his previous life when he had thrown out her pickles), and he successfully named and described Laxmi Narain's personal servant. He also gave the caste to which the servant belonged. He later claimed that he preferred Laxmi's mother to his own. Laxmi Narain's father was thought to have hidden some treasure before his death, but nobody knew where. When Bishen Chand was asked about the treasure, he led the way to a room of the family's former home. A treasure of gold coins was later found in this room, giving credence to the boy's claim of having lived a former life in the house.

Finally, Bishen Chand's older brother testified that Bishen could, when he was a child, read Urdu (written in Arabic script) before he had been taught this language. Bishen Chand's father, in a sworn statement about the case, stated that Bishen had (as a child) used some Urdu words that he could not have learned in the family—words such as *masurate* and *kopal* (for "women's quarters" and "lock," respectively), rather than the usual Hindi words *zenana* and *tala*. Laxmi Narain was reasonably well educated and quite capable of speaking Urdu.

In examining this case, Ian Stevenson urges that it is especially significant because an early record was kept by a reliable attorney when most of the principals were still alive and capable of verifying Bishen Chand's memory claims.[3] Many of the people who knew Laxmi Narain were still alive and well when Bishen Chand Kapoor was making his claims. They verified nearly all the statements Bishen made before he went to Pilibhit. Moreover, according to Stevenson, the possibility of fraud is remote because Bishen Chand's family had little to gain from association with the Laxmi Narain family.[4] It was well known that the latter had become destitute after Laxmi Narain had died. As in most cases similar to this, the events could not be explained in terms of anticipated financial gain.

Let us turn to our second case, a more recent and local one.

The Mrs. Smith Case

In his book *The Cathars and Reincarnation,* a British psychiatrist named Dr. Arthur Guirdham describes in detail a particular case that compelled him to accept the belief in reincarnation.[5] The woman in the case, Mrs. Smith, was his patient; and he met her in 1961 when he was chief psychiatrist at Bath Hospital in England. Mrs. Smith's problem was that she had persistent nightmares during which she shrieked so loud that she and her husband feared it would wake the whole neighborhood.

Dr. Guirdham examined her closely for neuroses but found she had none. After a few months, Mrs. Smith told Guirdham that, when she was a girl, she had written her dreams down. She had also written things that came spontaneously to her mind as recollections—things she could not understand that had to do with people, and specific names she had never heard. She gave the papers to the doctor, and he examined them.[6]

Dr. Guirdham was surprised to find that what she had written as a schoolgirl were verses of songs in medieval French and in langue d'oc, the language spoken in southern France in the twelfth and thirteenth centuries. The doctor ascertained that she had never studied these languages in school and that there was no source available to her for learning them. He sent a report of her story to Professor René Nelli of Toulouse University, and asked for the professor's opinion on the matter. Nelli responded that her writings gave an accurate account of the Cathars in Toulouse in the thirteenth century. The Cathars were a group of Christian dissidents of the extreme dualist persuasion, whose religious beliefs were close to the Albigensians and centered on the belief in reincarnation. They were persecuted and destroyed during the Inquisition.

Only gradually did Mrs. Smith admit having had an intensive uprush of memory in her early teens[7]—memories of a past life with a Cathar priest named Roger de Grisolles, whom she loved very much, and who taught her Cathar rituals and religious principles.[8] Guirdham states that, apart from her dreams, Mrs. Smith had experienced a number of these spontaneous recollections, and she told him in horrid detail her recollection of the massacre of the Cathars.[9] She also told him that in her dreams and recollections of a previous life she had been kept prisoner in a certain church crypt. Guirdham notes that, at first, experts said this church crypt had never been used for that purpose, but later research showed that so many religious prisoners were taken on one occasion that there was no room for all of them in regular prisons. Some had been kept in that very crypt.

Guirdham visited the south of France in 1967 to investigate the case. He read thirteenth-century manuscripts (available to only a limited number of scholars), and these manuscripts showed that Mrs. Smith's account was accurate. She had given Guirdham names and descriptions of people, places, and events, all of which turned out to be accurate to the last detail. Guirdham claims that there was no normal way in which Mrs. Smith could have known about these things. He even found in the manuscripts four of the songs she wrote as a child. They were correct, word for word.[10]

Guirdham notes that, although his subject claimed never to have read any books on the subject of thirteenth-century life, she made correct drawings of old French coins, jewelry worn at the time, and the layout of buildings—to say nothing of the intricate details of Cathar ritual.

Guirdham attests that Mrs. Smith was able to name and place accurately in their family and social relationships people who do not appear in the textbooks, but who were ultimately traced by going back to the dog-Latin records of the Inquisition. These minor characters are still traceable owing to the antlike industry of the Inquisitors and their clerks. Mrs. Smith remembered members of the Fanjeaux and Mazzarolles families, in particular giving their first names and the roles they played. She recollected treating her friend Roger de Grisolles with sugarloaf as a tonic. However, the experts called this into question: the existence of sugar at this time in Europe was doubted. Further investigation disclosed that sugar in loaf form was derived from Arab medicine and did indeed exist at this period in France.[11]

Even more remarkable was Guirdham's patient's description of her death when she was burned at the stake. This she both dreamed and subsequently claimed to remember. The description, conveyed by Guirdham as part of his case, reads as follows:

> The pain was maddening. You should pray to God when you're dying, if you can pray when you're in agony. In my dream I didn't pray to God. . . . I didn't know when you were burnt to death you'd bleed. I thought the blood would all dry up in the terrible heat. But I was bleeding heavily. The blood was dripping and hissing in the flames. I wished I had enough blood to put the flames out. The worst part was my eyes. I hate the thought of going blind.

. . . In this dream I was going blind. I tried to close my eyelids but I couldn't. They must have been burnt off, and now those flames were going to pluck my eyes out with their evil fingers. . . .

The flames weren't so cruel after all. They began to feel cold. Icy cold. It occurred to me that I wasn't burning to death but freezing to death. I was numb with the cold and suddenly I started to laugh. I had fooled those people who thought they could burn me. I am a witch. I had magicked the fire and turned it to ice.[12]

Finally, in a lecture entitled "Reincarnation and the Practice of Medicine," Dr. Guirdham reflected on certain crucial details of the case, many of which were also discussed in his book.

Twenty five years ago, as a student, a school girl at the age of 13, she was insisting that Cathar priests did not always wear black. You will find the statement that they did in any book on the subject written in any language until 1965. Yet she said that her friend in the thirteenth century wore *dark blue*. It now transpires that at one sitting of the Inquisition (the Inquisition of Jacques Fournier, who was Bishop at Palmiers), it came out ten times in one session that Cathar priests sometimes wore dark blue or dark green. But that fact had been lying in the archives in Latin for long enough, and was only accessible to the public in 1965 when Duvernoy edited the record of the said Inquisitors that was published in Toulouse in 1966. But this woman knew this in 1944 as a school girl.

Again she could describe rituals in a house, a kind of convent. . . . Professor Nelli, the greatest living authority on the Troubadors—who definitely are connected with the Cathars—wrote to me and said, "This is almost exactly Cathar ritual, making allowance for local deviation." He also added later that he could tell me where the place was, the Convent of Montreal. By way of future advice, he added that, in case of doubt, one should "go by the patient." Professor Nelli is the most meticulous and sceptical assessor of evidence.

When I first wrote to another specialist, Professor Duvernoy of Toulouse, he said, "Get in touch with me about anything you want. I am astonished at your detailed knowledge of Catharism." I couldn't say, "I've got this by copying down the dreams of a woman of thirty-six or seven which she had when she was a grammar school girl of thirteen. He's found out since, but he's all the more keen to supply me with the evidence. . . .

If the professors at Toulouse are amazed at the accuracy with which an English girl can produce details of Catharism known to few, that is good enough for me. . . . [A]ll I have done in this matter is to listen to the story, act as an amateur historian, and try to verify from many sources the details she had noted. I believe this to be a unique and entirely valid experience.[13]

Let us proceed to other recent cases of a different sort.

Responsive Xenoglossy

Xenoglossy refers to an alleged ability to speak—and often also to understand—a foreign language that has not been learned by the speaker in any normal way. This phenomenon has occurred in cases similar to the cases noted above, and constitutes a special kind of evidence in favor of reincarnation—evidence beyond that offered by memory of people and places and acquired skills. In *Xenoglossy* Ian Stevenson presents the case of Lydia Johnson;[14] and in *Unlearned Language* he presents the case of Gretchen, along with another one called the Sharada case.[15] In this chapter, we shall examine Stevenson's reports of the Lydia Johnson and Gretchen cases. Each case is a well-documented instance of *responsive* xenoglossy, rather than *recitative* xenoglossy. The recitative type occurs when a person can actually speak or write in a language not previously taught to her or him, without knowing what the words mean or how to respond in the language; whereas responsive xenoglossy occurs when the person can respond in the language, thus showing an ability to understand the language spoken.

We have already seen an instance of recitative xenoglossy in the Mrs. Smith case. Mrs. Smith wrote in a medieval language she could not have been taught, but she did not claim to understand what she wrote. Of the three cases we shall now examine, the case of Shanti Devi is an alleged instance of responsive xenoglossy, but it is somewhat different from the other two in that the subject speaks and understands an unlearned language spontaneously and not under conditions of regression and hypnotic suggestion. Also unlike the other two, it took place long ago, and there are reasons to think we should not include it as a well-established case of responsive xenoglossy. This is primarily because we have no well-documented verification of the responsive xenoglossy—of which there are very few authentic instances. Even so, it will do no real harm to include the Shanti Devi case and anticipate what it would be like to come across an ideal authentic case of spontaneous responsive xenoglossy combined with a rich set of memory claims supportive of belief in reincarnation. Since the case is not well documented, we will not actually appeal to it as a well-established case later on in our discussions.

The Lydia Johnson Case

In 1973, Lydia Johnson agreed to help her husband with his experiments in hypnotism. As it turned out, she was an excellent subject because she could easily slip into a deep trance. Doctor Harold Johnson (not his real name) was a respected Philadelphia physician. He had taken up hypnotism in 1971 to help some of his patients in treatments they were receiving. As his experiments with his wife were working so well, he decided to try a hypnotic regression, taking her back in time. In the middle of the regression, she suddenly flinched (as if struck) and screamed. She clutched at her head. He ended the session immediately, but his wife had a headache that would not go away. Twice Johnson repeated the session and the result was the same. Each time Lydia awoke from the trance, she said she had visualized a scene with water in which old people were seeming to be forced into it to drown. She had felt herself being pulled down, and then the blow, her scream, and the headache. As a result of all this, Doctor Johnson then called in another hypnotist, one Doctor John Brown (not his real name). Doctor Brown repeated the regression; but before the pain could strike again, he told her, "You are ten years younger than that." And then it happened.

She began to talk—not in sentences, but in words and occasional phrases. Some of it was in broken English, but much of it was in a foreign language that nobody at the session could understand. Her voice, moreover, was deep and masculine. Then from the mouth of this 37-year-old housewife came the words "I am a man." When asked her name, she said, "Jensen Jacoby." It was during this trance that Lydia began, in halting English punctuated with foreign words, to describe a past life. In this session (and in others that followed) she told, in her low masculine voice, of living in a small village in Sweden some three centuries ago. The sessions were tape-recorded, and careful notes were kept. Swedish linguists were called in to translate Jensen's statements. In the later sessions he spoke almost exclusively in Swedish, a language totally foreign to Lydia. When asked "What do you do for a living?" he answered in eighteenth-century Swedish, "A farmer." "Where do you live?" He answered, "In the house." And when asked "Where is the house?" he answered, again in Swedish, "In Hansen." These questions, by the way, were also *asked* in Swedish.

Judging by what Jensen said, he had a simple personality quite consistent with the peasant life he described. He showed little knowledge of anything beyond his own village and a trading center he visited. He raised cows, horses, goats, and chickens. He ate goat's cheese, bread, milk, salmon, and poppy-seed cakes made by his wife Latvia. He had built his own stone house, and he and Latvia had no children. He was one of three sons, his mother had been Norwegian, and he had run away from home.

Certain objects were brought in while Lydia was entranced. She was asked to open her eyes and identify the objects. As Jensen, she identified a model of a seventeenth-century Swedish ship, which she correctly identified in Swedish; so too a wooden container used then for measuring grain, a bow and arrow, and poppy seeds. She did not, however, know how to use modern tools—for example, pliers.

All the data in this case came from Jensen's statements and associated behavior. The principal investigator was Ian Stevenson.[16]

The Gretchen Case

Similar to the Lydia Johnson qua Jensen case is the Gretchen case. In both, the responsive xenoglossy was induced by hypnosis. After periods of an hour or so, the communicating personalities were dismissed by the hypnotist; and in both cases, while the communicating personalities could speak their languages responsively, they did so only haltingly and with imperfect grammar and vocabulary. Ian Stevenson began to investigate the Gretchen case in 1971.[17]

In the late 1960s Carroll Jay (hereafter C.J.), who was a Methodist minister and a hypnotist, began experimenting with suggestions that his subjects should regress to "previous lives." C.J. one day hypnotized his wife Dolores (hereafter D.J.) in order to relieve her from a backache. In the course of doing this, he asked her if her back hurt. She responded, *"Nein."* This occurred on May 10, 1970. A few days later (on May 13), he hypnotized her again, and the new trance personality identified herself by saying, *"Ich bin Gretchen"* (I am Gretchen). Over the next few months, further sessions were held, and Gretchen gradually emerged more fully and gave more details about herself. Stevenson notes that, with but rare exceptions, Gretchen spoke only German words. Both of the Jays stated that—other than the few words that every American knows—they knew absolutely no German at the time the case developed. Naturally then, C.J. did not understand any of what Gretchen was saying. But with the help of a dictionary and some friends who knew some German, he gradually began to piece together the story Gretchen was relating. Gretchen understood simple English and, initially, she would answer in German the questions put to her in English. Shortly thereafter she began to answer, in German, questions put to her in German. The sessions were taped beginning on August 2, 1970; Stevenson offers a verbatim transcript of extracts from the tapes, in his book *Unlearned Language*.[18]

Stevenson heard of the case in 1971; and in September, accompanied by a companion, he traveled to Mt. Orab, Ohio, where the Jays lived. During a number of subsequent sessions in which the Gretchen personality emerged, Stevenson had sensible conversations in German with her, as did a number of other people who were native speakers of German or who were quite conversant in the spoken language. With one exception (a woman who wanted to leave up to the reader of the transcripts the question of whether Gretchen really understood what she said), the general conclusion accepted by all who spoke German with Gretchen was that, even though she spoke haltingly and with some mistakes in grammar, and even though she sometimes did not respond at all well to questions asked in German, nonetheless she spoke German responsively and answered quite satisfactorily some questions put to her in that language.[19]

In seeking to determine whether D.J., or Gretchen, might have learned her German in ordinary ways, Stevenson conducted a thorough examination of the early lives of C.J. and D.J. He searched for any opportunity that D.J. might have had for learning German—"perhaps adventitiously"—when she was young. With the approval of the Jays, Stevenson spent two days in Clarksburg, West Virginia, where the Jays had grown up and where members of D.J.'s family were still living. C.J. provided Stevenson with the names of people who would be qualified informants on the central question of his wife's exposure to the German language during her childhood. Stevenson interviewed all those whose names had been given him. Moreover, he took the precaution of browsing in the neighborhood where D.J. had spent her childhood, and interviewed a number of people whose names C.J. had not given him. He interviewed 19 persons in Clarksburg and some of its adjoining suburbs. He also corresponded in 1973 with Mrs. Dorothy Davis, author of *History of Harrison County, West Virginia,* concerning the settlement of German-speaking immigrants in the area of Clarksburg, which is the county seat and principal town of Harrison County. Further, on February 5, 1974, D.J. took a polygraph test for lie detection with regard to her knowledge of the German language. The test was administered, in Stevenson's presence, by a Mr. Richard Arther in his offices in New York City. According to C.J. and D.J., no one had spoken German to Gretchen (or to D.J.) before the session on May 10, 1971.

Stevenson notes that after a few more sessions with the Gretchen personality—this time at the University of Virginia—Mrs. Jay, understandably exhausted, called a halt to any further experiments. She and her husband had undergone a good number of them already, and were receiving considerable adverse criticism from members of the communities where they lived, who thought that the experiments were (as Stevenson relates), "to put it mildly, outside what might be expected of a Christian clergyman and his wife."[20] In 1977, C.J. published an account of the case in which he described some of the troubles he and his family endured during and after its development. Apart from the time spent in the actual sessions with Gretchen and in transcribing the tapes, Stevenson estimates that his interviews with the Jays on various aspects of the case lasted about 25 hours.

In conveying the results of the investigation into whether D.J. could have acquired her knowledge of German through normal processes, Stevenson established that no school D.J. had ever attended taught German, no family member (even grandparents) ever spoke German, and nobody in her neighborhood ever spoke German. She married right after high school, at 18 years of age, and settled down in the same town. Further, as Stevenson documents, the lie detector test conducted on D.J. supported her claim that neither she nor her husband ever studied or knew any German. Lastly, it was also clear that, up until the development of the case, the Jays had nothing more than what would be described as an intelligent layman's interest in paranormal phenomena; they were, at best, only moderately well informed about scientific parapsychology. They were not associated with any occultist groups of the sort that, as Stevenson puts it, "thrive on the fringes of parapsychology." Typically, C.J. used his knowledge of hypnosis to help friends and parishioners.

As to the content of her principal communications in German, Gretchen said that her name was Gretchen Gottlieb and that she lived with her father in Eberswalde, Germany. Her father, Hermann Gottlieb, was the mayor of that town. He was rather old and had white hair. Her mother, Erika, had died when Gretchen was about eight years old. She had no brothers or sisters. Occasionally she mentioned a grandparent, but more frequently referred to Frau Schilder who did the household cooking and seems to have been employed as a housekeeper. Frau Schilder did not live with the Gottliebs but came during the day, bringing several of her own children (four of whose first names Gretchen gave). Gretchen lived on Birkenstrasse; and she said that Eberswalde was a small town, with a river not far away and a forest nearby. The town had a college, a church, a butchershop, and a bakery. Stevenson goes on to characterize further the content of Gretchen's story:

Gretchen could tell little about her daily life. She appears to have passed most of the time in the kitchen playing with Frau Schilder's children and regarded herself as to some extent assisting in their care. (The youngest of these children was, she said, only three years old.) She could describe rather well the food she ate. She did not go to school and had never done so. She explained this by saying that young girls did not attend school. She said she could not read or write. Sometimes Gretchen referred to herself diffidently as being "stupid" (German: "dumm"). She seemed uninformed about the geography and current politics of the period in which she lived. She could not name any large city near Eberswalde, although Berlin, the capital of Prussia and later of the German Empire, is approximately 45 kilometers southwest of Eberswalde. She said that Darmstadt, which is more than 400 kilometers away, was "near." . . . She was, on the other hand, quite definite that the head of the church was the Pope, and when asked his name, she said it was Leo. Concerning her knowledge of Martin Luther, Gretchen made different statements at different times. . . . Almost always, however, she spoke of Luther adversely as a troublemaker and the person responsible for the strife of which she claimed to be a witness. . . .

Gretchen rarely spoke spontaneously; usually she remained silent until asked a question. She would then reply briefly and fall silent again. Her manner was always polite and a little deferential, like that of a well-behaved child. On several occasions, however, she rather firmly corrected some mispronunciation by C.J. of a German word or set straight an interviewer who had misheard what she had said.[21]

Gretchen often spoke of the trouble between the government and the church and suggested that it was not a good idea to talk about these things. She seemed fearful of being watched by the Bundesrat.

From various things Gretchen said, incidentally, Stevenson was able to piece together roughly the time (the 1870s) and general area of Gretchen's life. But owing to the difficulty of determining the precise location of Eberswalde, and to other difficulties with regard to the content of Gretchen's story, the existence of this Gretchen Gottlieb has not been verified, and so—unlike in other cases such as the Bishen Chand case—any connection between the

Gretchen personality and an actual person of past times has not been established.

As in the Lydia Johnson qua Jensen case, however, the knowledge that the Gretchen personality manifested regarding her own historical time and place is precisely what one would minimally expect of a person living then and there. Moreover, in both cases, the argument is that—even when we cannot verify the actual historical existence of Jensen and Gretchen—we have no way to explain the linguistic skills and the other knowledge that the subjects have unless we appeal to reincarnation as the most plausible hypothesis. We will touch on this again later when we examine specific objections to the Gretchen case as evidence for reincarnation.

Let us turn to the last of the language cases under consideration here.

The Shanti Devi Case

Some researchers believe, for various reasons, that the Shanti Devi case offers the best available evidence for reincarnation. However, owing to the inaccessibility of the original case study, and because of the seriously questionable methods used in gathering and corroborating the alleged facts of the case, I will not include it for *critical* discussion along with the other cases examined here.[22] But because, as noted earlier, it is an interesting case and shows what *would* be strong evidence, it is certainly worthy of our qualified consideration.

Shanti Devi was born in 1926 in old Delhi. At three, she began to entertain her family with "stories" about a former life in which she had been married to a man named Kedar Nath who lived in nearby Muttra, had two children, and died in childbirth bearing a third child in 1925.

Like Bishen Chand, she also described in detail the home in Muttra where she said she had lived with her husband and children. Shanti said her name in that life was Lugdi. She further described the relatives of her former family and those of her husband, what her former life had been like, and how she had died. Unlike Bishen Chand, however, her alleged reincarnation had occurred so quickly (one year after her death) that there was the possibility of extensive corroboration by extant relatives with fresh memories. When her parents could no longer turn her from these stories, her grand uncle Kishen Chand sent a letter to Muttra to see how much, if any, of the little girl's story might be true. He sent it to an address Shanti gave him. The letter reached a startled widower named Kedar Nath who was still grieving the loss of his wife Lugdi. Lugdi had died in childbirth in 1925. Even as a devout Hindu, he could not accept the fact that Lugdi was reborn, living in Delhi, and in possession of an accurate picture of their life together. Suspecting some sort of fraud, Kedar Nath sent his cousin Mr. Lal (who lived in Delhi) to investigate and interrogate the girl. If she were an imposter, his cousin would know. When Mr. Lal, on the pretext of business, went to Devi's home, Shanti opened the door and, after screaming, threw herself into the arms of the astonished visitor. Her mother rushed to the door. Before the visitor could speak, Shanti (now nine) said, "Mother, this is a cousin of my husband! He lived not far from us in Muttra and then moved to Delhi. I am so happy to see him. He must come in. I want to know about my husband and sons."

With Shanti's family, Mr. Lal confirmed all the facts she had testified to over the years. As a result of this, they all agreed that Kedar Nath and the favorite son should come to Delhi as guests of the Devis.

When Kedar Nath arrived with the son, Shanti showered them with kisses and pet names. She treated Kedar Nath as a devoted wife would be expected to, serving him biscuits and tea. When Kedar Nath began to weep, Shanti consoled him using endearing little phrases known only to Lugdi and Kedar Nath.

Eventually, the press featured the case, and independent investigators appeared on the scene. The investigators decided to take Shanti to Muttra and have her lead them to the home where she claimed to have lived and died in her earlier life. When the train pulled into Muttra, Shanti cried out in delight and began waving to several people on the platform. She told the investigators with her that they were the mother and brother of her husband. She was right. More importantly, however, she got off the train and began to speak with and question them using not the Hindustani she had been taught in Delhi, but rather the dialect of the Muttra district. Shanti had not been exposed to, nor had she been taught, this dialect. But she would certainly have known the dialect if, like Lugdi, she had been a resident of Muttra.

Later Shanti led the investigators to the Nath home and conveyed other information that only Lugdi could have known. For example, Kedar Nath asked her where she had hidden several rings before she died. She said they were in a pot and buried in the ground of the old home where they had lived. The investigators subsequently found the rings where she said they would be.

As the case developed, it was celebrated in the international press and became the subject of extensive speculation on the part of scholars everywhere. At last word, Shanti never returned to live with Kedar Nath, though; and she could very well still be living in Delhi with her Devi family. As far as we can tell, all those who had known Lugdi accepted Shanti fully as Lugdi's reincarnation.

Apart from the fact that cases like this are somewhat rare, the Shanti Devi case (as well as Stevenson's Sharada case, which we shall not discuss here)[23] offers an instance of responsive xenoglossy that was not induced under hypnotic regression. In this respect it obviously differs from both the Lydia Johnson qua Jensen case and the D.J. qua Gretchen case. What is important here is that there are cases of spontaneous (or uninduced) responsive xenoglossy in which the subject demonstrates a clear knowledge of historical events that neither the subject nor any interviewer could have had natural knowledge of in this life, because the truth of the claims made could be established only after the subject's testimony. For example, in the Shanti Devi case, Shanti told the investigators something nobody else knew, namely, where Lugdi had hidden several rings before she died. And, if you will remember, we have seen in the Mrs. Smith case an instance of recitative xenoglossy with this same feature: she was right when it came to the question of the color of the Cathar priests' garments—a fact not known for quite some time after her testimony. More on this later. For now, let us look at a particularly rich memory case that does not involve xenoglossy in any straightforward way, but that is persuasive for other reasons. Thereafter we will begin our discussion on the evidential strength of these cases.

Memory Evidence and Recognition: The Swarnlata Case

In 1951 an Indian man named Sri M. L. Mishra took his three-year-old daughter Swarnlata and several other people on a 170-mile trip south from the city of Panna (in the district of Madhya Pradesh) to the city of Jabalpur, also in the same district.[24] On the return journey, as they passed through the city of Katni (57 miles north of Jabalpur), Swarnlata unexpectedly asked the driver to turn down a certain road to "my house." The driver quite understandably ignored her request. Later, when the same group was taking tea at Katni, Swarnlata told them that they would get better tea at "my house" nearby. These statements puzzled her father, Mishra; neither he nor any member of his family had ever lived near Katni. His puzzlement deepened when he learned that Swarnlata was telling other children in the family further details of what she claimed was a previous life in Katni as a member of a family named Pathak. In the next two years Swarnlata frequently performed for her mother (and later in front of others) unusual dances and songs that, as far as her parents knew, there had been no opportunity for her to learn. In 1958, when she was ten, Swarnlata met a woman from the area of Katni whom Swarnlata claimed to have known in her earlier life. It was at this time that Mishra first sought to confirm the numerous statements his daughter made about her "previous life."

In March 1959, H. N. Banerjee began to investigate the case; and in 1961 (after Banerjee's investigation), Ian Stevenson went to Chhatarpur to recheck carefully the work done by Banerjee. From the Mishra home in Chhatarpur, Banerjee had traveled to Katni where he became acquainted with the Pathak family of which Swarnlata claimed to have been a member. He noted, before journeying to Katni, some nine detailed statements Swarnlata had made about the Pathak residence. These statements he confirmed on his arrival. Incidentally, before Banerjee went to Katni, the Mishra family did not know or know of the Pathak family.

Banerjee also found that the statements made by Swarnlata corresponded closely to the life of Biya, a daughter in the Pathak family and deceased wife of a man named Pandey who lived in

Maihar. Biya had died in 1939—nine years before the birth of Swarnlata.

In the summer of 1959, members of the Pathak family and of Biya's marital family traveled to Chhatarpur (where the Mishra family lived). Without being introduced to these people, Swarnlata recognized them all, called them by name, and related personal incidents and events in their various lives with Biya—events that, according to these relatives, only Biya could have known. For example, Swarnlata claimed that, as Biya, she had gold fillings in her front teeth. Biya's sister-in-law confirmed as much. The Pathaks eventually accepted Swarnlata as Biya reincarnated, even though they had never previously believed in the possibility of reincarnation.

After these visits, in the same summer, Swarnlata and members of her family went first to Katni and then to Maihar where the deceased Biya had spent much of her married life and where she died. In Maihar, Swarnlata recognized additional people and places and commented on various changes that had occurred since the death of Biya. Her statements were independently verified. Later, Swarnlata continued to visit Biya's brother and children, for whom she showed the warmest affection.

The songs and dances that Swarnlata had performed presented some problem, however. Biya spoke Hindi and did not know how to speak Bengali, whereas the songs Swarnlata had sung (and danced to) were in Bengali. Although the songs were publicly available and had been recorded on phonograph records and played in certain films, she could not have learned these songs from records or films because her parents had neither seen nor heard them and, therefore, Swarnlata—as a typical child under close surveillance of her family—had no occasion to do so. The parents were also certain that Swarnlata had not been in contact with Bengali-speaking persons from whom she might have learned the songs. Swarnlata claimed that she had learned the songs and dances from a previous life. Stevenson notes that this is a case of recitative rather than responsive xenoglossy, because she could not converse in Bengali although she could sing Bengali songs.[25]

After careful examination, Ian Stevenson concludes that it is very difficult to explain the facts of the case without admitting that Swarnlata had paranormal knowledge. After all, how other-wise could Swarnlata have known the details of the family and of the house? These details (including the fact that Biya had gold fillings in her teeth—a fact that even her brothers had forgotten) were by no means in the public domain. Moreover, how otherwise can we explain her recognition of members of the Pathak and Pandey families? How can her knowledge of the former (as op-posed to the present) appearances of places and people be ex-plained? Her witnessed recognitions of people amount to 20 in number. As Stevenson notes, most of the recognitions occurred in such a way that Swarnlata was obliged to give a name or state a relationship between Biya and the person in question. On several occasions, serious attempts were made to mislead her or to deny that she gave the correct answers, but such attempts failed.

Could there have been a conspiracy among all the witnesses in the various families (the Mishras, the Pathaks, and the Pandeys)? Might not all of them have conspired to bring off a big hoax? Well, according to Stevenson, a family of prominence such as the Pathaks, with far-reaching business interests, is unlikely to partic-ipate in a hoax with so many people involved, any one of which might later defect. If a hoax did occur, it is more likely to have come from the Chhatarpur side. But even here, Sri M. L. Mishra had nothing to gain from such a hoax. He even doubted for a long time the authenticity and truth of his daughter's statements, and he made no move to verify them for six years. Most of the people involved agreed that they had nothing to gain but public ridicule.

But even if we suppose that there *was* some attempt at fraud, who would have tutored Swarnlata for success in such recogni-tions? Who would have taken the time to do it? Sri M. L. Mishra, apart from Swarnlata, was the only other member of the family who received any public attention from Swarnlata's case. And what attention he received, he was not too happy about. Also, how could Sri Mishra have gotten some of the highly personal information possessed by Swarnlata about the private affairs of the Pathaks (e.g., that Biya's husband took her 1,200 rupees)?

Might Swarnlata have been tutored by some stranger who knew Katni and the Pathaks? As Stevenson notes, like all children in India—especially girls—Swarnlata's movements were very carefully controlled by her family. She never saw strangers in the house alone, and she never was out on the street unaccompanied.[26]

Besides the legal documentation and methods used in Stevenson's examination, what is interesting about this case is that it is one of many similar cases. Can we explain the facts plausibly without appealing to the belief in reincarnation?

The Argument Stated: What Better Explanation?

The Bishen Chand case and the Swarnlata case (and many other cases too numerous to include here) exemplify, in varying degrees, the ideal-typical characteristics A through F mentioned above in conjunction with Stevenson's argument for reincarnation. Of course, in the Bishen Chand case the interviews were not taped, but they were written down. And Swarnlata did not speak in an unlearned foreign language or, like Bishen Chand, play an instrument she had not learned to play; but she did sing in a foreign language that she had not been taught, and she did perform complicated dances that she had never seen. Both subjects provided memory information about facts that were not in the public domain and yet were subsequently verified by independent investigators. Also, the accuracy of their memory claims down to the very smallest details was much too high to be explained in terms of probability or luck or coincidence; and the large number of extant family members who provided extensive verification of the memory claims about personal and very private historical details is particularly important. Not only because of the methods employed in examining these cases, but also because of their richness of detail, I submit that, logically, these two cases typify the strongest sort of evidence for reincarnation.

The Mrs. Smith case may not match all the ideal-typical characteristics, involving as it does a long-ago past life. But the recitative xenoglossy exhibited by Mrs. Smith, and her consistent memory of previously unknown but then often verified historical facts, qualify the case as worthy of serious consideration in the context of this study.

Further, the Lydia Johnson qua Jensen case and the D.J. qua

Gretchen case certainly do not contain all the characteristics A through F. Notably, they are cases in which we have not been able to verify the historical existence of the past-life personalities the subjects manifested in regressed hypnotic states. Nor do the subjects actually claim to remember having lived a past life as Gretchen or as Jensen. Nevertheless, these cases are included here because, even without Stevenson's ideal-typical characteristics, their rich past-life content cannot be ignored. We still have no way of explaining the subjects' capacity to speak in unlearned languages and to describe successfully so many of the historical details of the past lives they depict without appealing to reincarnation. Or so it would seem.

At this point, then, the argument for reincarnation is very simple. It is this. What would be a better or more plausible explanation for these cases than to assume that human personality (whatever it is) admits of reincarnation? Opponents of reincarnation must provide an equally plausible or better alternative explanation for the data if they are to undermine effectively the claim that the best available explanation for these sorts of cases is reincarnation. Let us now examine the alternative explanations and objections that have been raised by various sceptics.

The Sceptic's Response, Bypassing ESP

Bypassing, for the moment, any alternative explanation that would assume the legitimacy of extrasensory perception, or any other form of paranormal knowledge, there are four alternative theoretical explanations for such cases as we have just offered. The first seeks to explain the success of past memory claims by appeal to *cryptomnesia,* the second by appeal to *genetic memory,* the third by appeal to *linguistic possibility* (i.e., seeking to undermine the allegedly strongest cases—those that involve speaking in unlearned languages—by claiming that the amount of fluency involved in such cases does not require an explanation in terms of anything paranormal), and the fourth by appeal to *paramnesia.*

We will examine briefly these four alternative theoretical explanations and then discuss several objections based on the view that such cases always involve sloppiness, fraud, hoax, or incredible stupidity.

Cryptomnesia?

In a recent essay entitled "Are Past-life Regressions Evidence of Reincarnation?" Melvin Harris argues that all reincarnation–type cases in which people are regressed and describe details of past lives are actually fascinating instances of cryptomnesia.[27] In his view, we can explain so-called memories of past lives by saying that in all such cases the information the subjects convey about past events has been acquired quite normally from such sources as parents or newspapers, lectures, radio, TV, books, and so forth. Shortly after acquiring the information, the subjects forget it; and when, under regression, they later remember what they normally learned, they have forgotten the origin of the information. Because they have forgotten its origin, they naturally identify the information as the product of memories of those events.

By way of reply to this objection, however, we should note that Harris and others tend to generalize from one or two cases to all cases in which regression is used. Moreover, anyone who reads Stevenson's work will readily see that he includes no cases that could be explained by appeal to cryptomnesia. Indeed, in all the richer cases the subjects testify to past events that nobody could have known about except the subject. Bishen Chand, for example, remembered where the father of Laxmi Narain had hidden gold in the house. Nobody else knew where the gold was. From whom could he have originally learned this, then? Also, how did Bishen learn to play the drums skilfully? Nobody taught him. Similarly, who could have taught Lydia Johnson eighteenth-century Swedish, or Gretchen a regional nonstandard German? Indeed, one of the criteria for a rich case—a criterion Stevenson explicitly states from the beginning[28]—is that we not be able to explain it by appeal to cryptomnesia; and in every case, he offers reasons why cryptomnesia does not work as an alternative explanation. In every rich case, there are facts the subject has testified to that are subsequently confirmed but that nobody alive could have known. And this frustrates the appeal to cryptomnesia.

Genetic Memory?

The second alternative explanation asserts that we need only suppose everybody is born with a certain genetic memory—that, just as we inherit the genetic physical traits of our ancestors, so too the memories of our ancestors are coded in our genes. Then, so the argument goes, under certain circumstances the inhibitors of these traits are relaxed, and the memories of our ancestors emerge. When these memories emerge, they are experienced by the subject as though they were the subject's own memories. In this alternative explanation, we are asked to believe that Bishen Chand Kapoor, for example, inherited Laxmi Narain's memory (even his memory of how to play the drums and speak Urdu) and mistakenly identified these memories as his own. Similarly, Lydia Johnson inherited the memory of Jacob Jensen, and this extends to her remembering how to speak Jensen's language. In both cases, the subjects obviously mistakenly believed that what they were remembering were events in their own respective lives. In fact, however, they were remembering events in the lives of others who had passed those memories on to their ancestors in and through the gene pool. Is this explanation any more forceful than that based on cryptomnesia?

Not really. If appeal to the phenomenon of genetic memory were the proper explanation for Bishen's knowledge of Laxmi Narain's life, then we would expect Bishen to be in Laxmi Narain's genetic line—though clearly he was not. This point was emphasized by Stevenson,[29] and it seems to be the most important factor in many xenoglossy cases that suggest reincarnation. That is, no genetic connection is discernible between the subject and the alleged ancestor whose language the subject can speak. In the case of Lydia Johnson and Jacob Jensen, tracing the genetic line is pretty much out of the question. But as the explanation of genetic memory does not apply in many of the richer cases described above, it seems that the appeal in general will not work. In some of the strongest cases, we know for certain that no genetic line connects the subject to the allegedly reincarnated person.

Besides, as Stevenson has also noted, this explanation will not work in those cases where the subjects describe in rich detail the manner of their own death: "A parent could only transmit genetically to his or her offspring memories of events that had happened to the parent *before* that child's conception. It follows, therefore, that the memory of a person's mode of death could never be inherited."[30] This seems to be the most conclusive reason for rejecting the argument that past-life memories are simply inherited from one's ancestors through natural genetic mechanisms. It does not explain the more interesting cases.

Finally, what also undermines the sceptic's appeal to genetic memory is the fact that, while some purely genetic traits (such as the genetic diseases Huntington's chorea, hemophilia, and PKU) are nondispositional, other genetic traits are *dispositional*. That is, we inherit the disposition—more or less—to certain traits. Quite clearly, the emergence of the actual trait requires some input from the environment. The acquisition of a skill such as speaking a language cannot be explained in terms of an inherited trait, because contemporary genetics tells us to view the ability to speak a language as a function of an inherited ability *plus* an additional component supplied by the environment. And this holds equally well for the ability to play an instrument.

A Linguistic Possibility?

The linguistic objection consists in urging that a closer look at the regression cases in which subjects are alleged to speak an unlearned language appropriate to a particular past life would reveal that the subjects are so lacking in fluency that we cannot really say they know the language they are said to speak without having learned. Sarah Thomason offers this objection in her article "Past Tongues Remembered."[31] Thomason's claim is that, if we scrutinize the Gretchen case, we will see that of 172 possible responses made by Gretchen in German to questions asked in German, *only 28* answers are appropriate, and that we surely do not need a paranormal explanation of her knowledge of so few German phrases. Even a limited exposure to German books, or to World War II movies, could explain whatever fluency is present.[32]

To this objection, we can give three basic replies. First, Thomason illegitimately generalizes from one case. Second, the objection overlooks the force of the fact that we would all say a man knows German if, when asked questions in German, he responded appropriately to 28 of them. It still needs to be explained how somebody who has never been taught German can successfully understand the language enough to respond successfully to unrehearsed questions 28 times. Third, we cannot plausibly explain the latter by appeal to World War II movies or casual glances at German books, because one would need to know what was being said in such movies or books. Besides, this latter explanation would never work in the Lydia Johnson qua Jensen case where the subject is responsively fluent in eighteenth-century Swedish. We cannot explain Jensen's limited but appropriate responses in eighteenth-century Swedish by appeal to casual contact with books, movies, or people speaking Swedish. Moreover, there are other cases (for example, the Sharada case in Stevenson's *Unlearned Language*)[33] in which there can be no doubt whatsoever that the subject is very fluent in speaking the unlearned language.

There are many other deficiencies involved in Thomason's analysis (such as the criteria employed for what counts as an appropriate answer), but these three replies suffice to make the point. Let us turn to other explanations and objections and to the general charge of hoax and fraud.

Paramnesia?

The fourth alternative theoretical explanation is the appeal to paramnesia. This objection asserts that the so-called favorable evidence for reincarnation can be easily explained and dismissed by taking certain cultural facts into consideration. In this view, the young child makes a few statements that, in a culture strongly disposed to belief in reincarnation, the gullible parents interpret as memories of a past life. They then proceed to encourage the child to make more statements, and frequently ask leading questions. From the material they so derive from the child, they identify a deceased person whose life fits, more or less, the statements. The parents then rush to the family of the deceased to relate what the child has said. The latter family, still grief stricken over the deceased member, accepts uncritically the statements as corresponding to the life of that member. The child is asked more questions, and is frequently asked to identify family members, with patently obvious cues and leading questions. The families exchange information about the child's memories. Thereafter, informants on both sides credit the child with more detailed memories than she or he had. There is no conscious fraud or hoax involved in all this; it is simply the result of cultural conditioning combined with sloppy methodology. The fact that most of the evidence garnered in most cases has come from spontaneous past-life memories, the contents of which are typically conveyed to researchers by members of the families involved—and that little of it has been induced by investigators in direct interviews with the subjects—makes this a particularly forceful objection. In fact, some critics regard it as the most decisive refutation of the allegedly most compelling cases.

Stevenson, for example, takes paramnesia quite seriously. In *Children Who Remember Previous Lives* he grants that this objection certainly does apply in a certain number of cases—those wherein the families involved have contact before the researchers can take testimony from the subject (if possible) and the family members.[34] And Stevenson has published reports on cases wherein this objection turns out to be the decisive reason why the cases cannot be taken seriously.[35] For this reason also, some interesting cases that occurred long ago—cases such as the Shanti Devi case—and in which the families apparently contacted each other before independent researchers were summoned cannot be regarded as clearly verified. Even so, Stevenson has argued persuasively that paramnesia breaks down as an alternative explanation for more than a few cases. Among other reasons, it certainly would not apply in those more than 20 rich cases in which someone made a written record of what the child said before there was any verification of his or her statements.[36] Nor would such an explanation fit the more interesting xenoglossy cases described above. More on this later.

Sloppy Methodology?

Apart from paramnesia, but related to it, is a general method-ological objection one sometimes hears. According to this objec-tion, we must be sceptical about all these so-called cases for reincarnation primarily because investigators typically show up on the scene quite some time after the child begins to make the memory claims, and they depend on the parents' or relatives' memories and interpretations of what the child in fact said and did (because the child often does not respond to the investigator or has forgotten what the parents and relatives are claiming the child remembered). Then too, altogether too often these richer cases require the services of a language translator, which intro-duces an even deeper possibility for misunderstanding just what the principals are asserting. Given these possible sources of error, so the objection goes, there is just too much room for honest but serious mistake in describing and verifying the salient features of the so-called richer cases. Until we can minimize this inherent potential for error associated with the methodology, it is unwise and very unscientific to accept the case descriptions at face value, as indicative of what actually transpired. There is just too much room for honest error. Even if we can eliminate all possibility of fraud and deception in the richer cases, the data are just too problematic to warrant serious consideration as evidence.

To this general objection, there are at least two persuasive replies we might give. The first is that the same objection applies to most historical knowledge and eyewitness testimony to past events. Thus, in itself the objection is not enough to discount the data—not until one can positively show that the testimony is in fact mistaken. The second reply is that the richer cases are rich precisely because the probability of this sort of error is made negligible: often no translation is involved; the time gap between the origination of the case and the investigation is not significant; and the number and variety of independent witnesses provide a check for the accuracy of crucial testimony. One need only look closely at the recent cases described above to see that this objection is implausible, given the actual detail of the cases and the careful way in which they were investigated.

A Recent Critique of Stevenson's Case Studies

Ignoring the above alternative theoretical explanations seeking to undermine Stevenson's argument, Paul Edwards in a recent extended essay has compiled a number of his own and others' objections.[37] If Stevenson's case studies are evidence for reincarnation, Edwards says, then they must also be evidence for certain "collateral assumptions" that are just too incredible for a rational person to take seriously.

> What these objections enable us to see is that somebody who opts for reincarnation is committed to a host of collateral assumptions, the most important of which I will now enumerate. When a human being dies he continues to exist not on earth but in a region we know not where as a pure disembodied mind or else as an astral or some other kind of "non-physical" body; although deprived of his brain he retains memories of life on earth as well as some of his characteristic skills and traits; after a period varying from a few months to hundreds of years this pure mind or "non-physical" body, which lacks not only a brain but also any physical sense organs, picks out a suitable woman on earth as its mother in the next incarnation, invades this woman's womb at the moment of conception of a new embryo, and unites with it to form a full-fledged human being; although the person who died may have been an adult and indeed quite old, when he is reborn he begins a new life with the intellectual and emotional attitudes of a baby; finally, many of the people born in this way did not previously live on earth, but (depending on which version of reincarnation one subscribes to) in other planes or on other planets from which they migrate (invisibly of course), most of them preferring to enter the womb of a mother in a poor and overpopulated country where their life is likely to be wretched. The collateral assumptions listed so far are implied by *practically all forms* of reincarnationism, but in

Stevenson's case there is the additional implication that the memories and skills that the entity took over from the person who died and that are transmitted to the new regular body appear there for a relatively short time during childhood to disappear forever after. *If Stevenson's reports are evidence for reincarnation they must also be evidence for the collateral assumptions just mentioned. These assumptions are surely fantastic if not indeed pure nonsense; and, even in the absence of a demonstration of specific flaws, a rational person will conclude either that Stevenson's reports are seriously defective or that his alleged facts can be explained without bringing in reincarnation. An acceptance of the collateral assumptions would amount, to borrow a phrase from Kierkegaard, to the "crucifixion" of our understanding.*[38]

Prior to examining Stevenson's argument, Edwards had asserted in this essay that we have no known evidence of consciousness existing independently of brains, and that the very idea of an astral body (which sees without eyes, hears without ears, and thinks without a brain) capable of existing in the temporal interval between reincarnated lives is absolutely incredible.[39]

Before proceeding to the other contentions in Edwards's essay, a general point is in order about this sweeping objection. The passage just quoted, and Edwards's prior assertions, have the disturbing ring of a dogmatic materialism committed to showing that, owing to the incredible nature of the reincarnationist thesis, the cases offered by Stevenson *must* be instances of fraud, or hoax, or cultural fabrication, or delusional imagining on the part of Stevenson himself. From a logical point of view, if Stevenson's main cases are flawed in any of the ways just suggested, then certainly the case for reincarnation (and whatever is strictly implied by it) fails. But—as noted at the beginning of this chapter—we cannot, without begging the question against the case studies, argue that we *know* consciousness cannot exist without a brain. We know nothing of the sort. Indeed, in the absence of our being able to document that the case studies are flawed in one of the ways just suggested, what the cases do show is that human personality (whatever it is) survives death and, by implication, human consciousness can exist (along with propositional memories and nonpropositional skills) independently of brains, flourish for a period without a body as we know it, and reincarnate. So, the charge that all this is just too incredible for any rational person to believe is a blatant bit of question begging, unworthy of a reasoned response.

Moreover, the argument for reincarnation implies nothing specific about the nature of an "astral body," where it goes during the period between incarnations, how the astral body reincarnates, why it reincarnates, how frequently it reincarnates, whether everybody reincarnates, and what the point of it all is. As a matter of fact, given the cases involved, one need never mention the expression *astral body*. The argument implies only that some core elements of human personality occasionally survive bodily corruption (and hence cannot be identified with the physical body) and reincarnate.

The Objections of Edwards et al.

Edwards then proceeds to summarize detailed objections to Stevenson's argument and, in so doing, paraphrases various charges made by other thinkers, as follows:

1. Stevenson generally dismisses the possibility of fraud on the part of children, parents, and other interested parties in these cases on the flimsiest of grounds when, in actuality, motives for fraud are only too evident. For example, Ian Wilson has pointed out that several of the children remember belonging to a higher caste in their previous lives and seem to be motivated by a wish for better living conditions.[40]
2. Stevenson tells us little about the parents, who are usually vital informants. "In many cases, too, there was or there easily could have been contact between the parents and the persons connected with the 'previous personality' about whose life the child had accurate recollections."[41]
3. In only seven of the cases were the child's statements about a previous life recorded prior to the attempt at verification; and in those seven cases, the child lived "within the geographical or social circumference of the previous personality."[42] This raises the question of "sensory cues," by which is meant "normal sources of information."[43] Edwards ascribes this ob-

jection to William Roll and notes that Roll "charitably assumes" that Stevenson's investigations have ruled out such normal channels.[44]

4. Stevenson is incredibly naive, and the cases he offers have no evidential value. According to C. T. K. Chari, the cases are all cultural artifacts and culturally manufactured because most of them occur where people already believe in reincarnation.[45]

This last objection leads Edwards to ask why, if Stevenson's cases were not cultural artifacts, we have not had any such cases in Western society. For Edwards, the answer lies in the fact that we have higher critical standards in the West and do not have a host of witnesses with an ardent belief in reincarnation—witnesses who are only too willing to manufacture past-life proofs. And if anybody did produce such proofs here, we would have an abundance of thoughtful sceptics to challenge them. Besides, children in America just do not report such stories.[46]

The question is whether any of these objections are worthy of rational acceptance. So let us take a closer look at them.

Reply to the Objections of Edwards et al.

As for objection 1—that Stevenson dismisses too easily the possibility of fraud on the part of the various parties involved in these cases—anybody who actually reads Stevenson's *Twenty Cases Suggestive of Reincarnation* and the other works mentioned and quoted above cannot help but be impressed with the seriousness of Stevenson's effort to detect fraud in each of the major cases. For example, in both the case of Swarnlata and the case of Bishen Chand, he straightforwardly raises the question of fraud. In the Bishen Chand case, it is of course possible that the two families conspired and tutored little Bishen Chand. But, for Stevenson, a fraud of this sort would need to involve a number of people in both families as well as strangers (Laxmi Narain's classmates), and the likelihood of such a fraud's being detected subsequently is pretty high. More importantly, neither Bishen Chand nor either of the two families had anything to gain financially from a fraud, because both families were poor. Further, both families were embarrassed by the notoriety and wished it had not occurred. In fact, because of the public ridicule involved, Bishen Chand's family did everything possible to keep the case from going public. And neither family believed in reincarnation as a matter of religious or philosophical commitment before Bishen Chand started telling his story. Also, Bishen Chand's accomplished drum playing could have been taught to him secretly by his father; but surely this is precisely the sort of thing that is very difficult to do without somebody's knowing about it.

Similarly, in the Swarnlata case, Stevenson considers—as noted in our earlier discussion of the case—the possibility that Swarnlata was tutored by somebody and that her knowledge of past events was acquired through natural means. These are Stevenson's own words:

> As already mentioned, there is a slight possibility that Swarnlata and the Mishras may have known some few facts unconsciously absorbed about the Pathak family in Katni. The Pathak family of Katni (with members and a branch of their business in Jabalpur) was well known in the area and public items of information about them could easily have been picked up. There is no evidence that Swarnlata or her family did acquire any such knowledge, but we cannot exclude this possibility. The strength of paranormal explanations then seems to rest on (a) Swarnlata's knowledge of details of the family and the house which would not be in the public domain, e.g., the fact that Biya had gold fillings in her front teeth, a detail even Biya's brothers had forgotten; (b) her recognitions of members of the Pathak and Pandey families; and (c) her knowledge of the former (as opposed to the present) appearances of places and people. If we count her witnessed recognitions of people alone (not places), these amount to twenty in number. If we believe the witnesses who have been carefully questioned, most of these recognitions occurred in such a way that Swarnlata was obliged to give a name or state a relationship between Biya and the person in question. It was not a question of "Am I your son?" but of "Tell me who I am." And on several occasions serious attempts were made to mislead her or deny that she gave the correct answers. And her recognitions usually came quickly. In judging various possibilities, we may consider first that of a rather widespread conspiracy among all the witnesses, especially the Mishras, Pathaks, and Pandeys. But

a family of prominence, with extensive business interests such as
the Pathaks have, is not going to participate in a hoax to which a
large number of false witnesses would have to subscribe, any one of
whom might later defect. If a hoax has occurred in this case, it
must have come from the Chhatarpur side. Nothing I learned about
the character of Sri M. L. Mishra among people who knew him in
Chhatarpur gave grounds for any suspicion whatever that he had
perpetrated a hoax. According to his own statement, he doubted
for a long time the authenticity or veridicality of his daughter's
statements, and he made no move to verify them for more than six
years. When Sri Banerjee visited the area of the case in 1959, he
indicated a wish to observe personally any recognitions of the
Pathak family on the part of Swarnlata. He was therefore chagrined
when the two families got together without notifying him so he
could be present. In a letter to me of August 6, 1962, Sri Mishra
stated that he did not want Sri Banerjee present because he feared
Swarnlata would not accomplish the recognitions and that this
would publicly embarrass him. We can suppose that if he had
contemplated some gain to himself from fraud, he would have
wished to involve independent witnesses to lend support and fame
to the case.[47]

These are not the words of a person indifferent to the possibility
of fraud or hoax or a natural source of the knowledge Swarnlata
demonstrated. Clearly, the suggestion that Stevenson is not sen-
sitive to the possibility of fraud or hoax, or even to natural
alternative explanations, is not supported by a close examination
of the case studies he offers.

As for Wilson's explicit claim that fraud is suggested by the fact
that many of the children who remember previous lives remember
richer lives—thus indicating that their stories are motivated by the
desire to escape current poverty—there is also the fact that memories of such earlier more opulent lives do *not* occur in well over
one-third of the richer cases. Besides, as noted above, even if some
children were so motivated, this would not explain how their
memories can be so verifiably accurate when there had been no
prior contact between the families before the investigation was
conducted. Also, anybody who reads Stevenson's specific reply to
this objection, in his *Children Who Remember Previous Lives,* will
find it to be very convincing.[48]

Certainly, there is some possibility of fraud in every case. And in terms of degree of evidential support, no two cases are precisely alike. Therefore, the question ought to be whether there is—in each case—a real likelihood of fraud or hoax. Short of subjecting everybody to polygraph examinations (which a good sceptic would not take seriously anyway), what else could one do, that Stevenson has not done, to detect a possible fraud or hoax? As for those who think that fraud *must* be involved in each of these cases, let them establish it (rather than the theoretical possibility of it) in at least a sufficient number of the richer cases to warrant the inference that it is therefore in some way likely in the remaining cases also. Until then, we have only the *suspicion* of fraud; no reasonable sceptic will be able to detect actual fraud in any of the richer cases investigated by Stevenson. After actually examining the cases, the unbiased reader may well come to view the charge of fraud as a peculiar throwback to the dogmatic attitude that stood behind the refusal of astronomers and philosophers to look through Galileo's telescope. If the opponents of reincarnation refuse to acknowledge any and all evidence for the thesis (because it is just too incredible for any reasonable person to believe), then their opposition to reincarnation is purely dogmatic. Later on we will say more about the possibility of fraud and hoax, in order to put it in proper perspective.

Objection 2 is similar to objection 1 and is offered by the same critic, Ian Wilson. Here again, however, to charge that there is a real possibility of fraud or error because Stevenson does not tell us more about the parents involved seems quite arbitrary. Indeed, as long as one establishes that these people have no known motive or inclination for any fraud, and that all who know them generally regard them as truthful and honorable, what else exactly does one need to know about them? In any event, no amount of fraud and collusion on their part, even for reasons of sheer entertainment, will account for the memory claims about past events that nobody alive could have known about, or for the nonpropositional skills (such as speaking in an unlearned language or playing an instrument without having been taught), evident in the richer cases.

With regard to objection 3—that in only seven of the cases Stevenson examines does he or someone else actually record in writing the first interview before investigating the claims, and according to which William Roll (the author of the objection) only "charitably assumes" that in those seven cases Stevenson shows the charge of fraud to be unsubstantiated—there are three replies. First, if the above passage from Stevenson on the possibility of fraud in the Swarnlata case is typical of his general concern for examining the possibility of fraud (and any unbiased reader will see that it is), then it is ostensibly irresponsible to state that in the seven taped cases Roll "charitably assumes that Stevenson has eliminated the possibility of fraud."[49] Second, although, from a logical point of view, seven nonfraudulent cases will be quite sufficient to make the case for reincarnation, there are in fact considerably more cases.[50] The total number of cases with written records before verification stands presently at 24. And while this represents only 1 percent of the cases now on file, it is certainly more than seven.[51] Third, Edwards urges that because the aforementioned seven cases involved a child who lived, as Roll says, "within the geographical or social circumference of the previous personality" there is some possibility that the information the child had could have been normally conveyed. Here again, however, that possibility has not been substantiated in any of the Stevenson cases described in this chapter; and Stevenson's reasons for thinking that it will never be seem quite substantial. Besides, to repeat, the supposition of this sort of collusion would still not explain how the child knows facts that neither side could know (such as where Laxmi Narain's father hid money), or how the child could have appropriate unlearned skills. Regrettably, Edwards never even alludes to these aspects of Stevenson's cases, and hence he very much understates the force of Stevenson's argument. Edwards also completely overlooks the force of both the Lydia Johnson qua Jensen and the D.J. qua Gretchen cases.

Finally, with regard to objection 4 and C. T. K. Chari's claim to the effect that these cases are culturally fabricated because they occur only where people already believe in reincarnation, our reply is again threefold. First, although the earlier cases Stevenson investigated were frequently in cultures that have incorporated a belief in reincarnation, many of the richer cases involved families who did not believe in reincarnation. Second, even if these cases always did involve people who had an antecedent belief in reincarnation, one simply cannot *fabricate* the data necessary to confirm a hypothesis originally accepted for religious reasons. (How does one fabricate, for example, Bishen Chand's ability to recognize, without prompting, eight persons and places known to Laxmi Narain; or how does one fabricate a subject's being able to speak in an unlearned foreign language or play an instrument unlearned?) Third, as of 1990, there are literally hundreds of alleged reincarnation cases, varying in their degree of richness, currently under investigation and documented in Great Britain and the United States.[52] The cases of Mrs. Smith, Lydia Johnson, and Gretchen are clear demonstrations of the falsity of objection 4. Naturally, if one never found any reincarnation cases except in cultures where the belief in reincarnation is strong, then one might have *some* reason for being suspicious. But as the body of data comprised of cases similar to those we have discussed in this chapter grows, the grounds for such suspicion dissolves.

In sum, for those who do not accept the phenomena of ESP, the only plausible alternative explanation that would not dogmatically beg the question against the evidence presented in Stevenson's cases is that *all* the cases are instances of fraud, or hoax, or delusion, or simple error based on cultural factors or sloppy methodology. But, as we have just shown, the charge of hoax or fraud or delusion or simple error has not been substantiated in any of the above-described cases that Stevenson has offered as evidence.

Incidentally, we will need to be very careful *not* to reject all the described cases if one of them turns out to be an instance of fraud, or if some alternative that does not appeal to reincarnation becomes very persuasive as a way of explaining some particular case. Detecting one fraudulent case, or coming up with one plausible alternative explanation for some particular case with logical features different from a number of others, would in no way imply that the other cases reported as instances of reincarnation are fraudulent or admit of some purely natural explanation. The truth of the matter is that, given the logical differences among cases, what may count as a persuasive alternative explanation for one case may in no way whatsoever impugn the strength of other cases.

For example, suppose somebody were to show that the Lydia Johnson qua Jensen case and the D.J. qua Gretchen case are not really instances of people speaking responsively and fluently in an unlearned language. That in itself would be totally irrelevant to the strength of such cases as the Bishen Chand case, in which the best explanation of the data is reincarnation even though the subjects do not in any way speak a language other than the one they usually speak. In fact, the thesis of reincarnation becomes stronger as the logical differences between the various cases becomes more obvious. The confirmation becomes more robust because supported by logically different bodies of data and clearly diversified types of evidence. More on this shortly.

The Sceptic's Response, Based on ESP

There are some sceptics who offer a variety of alternative theoretical explanations that, unlike the above objections, are willing to grant legitimacy to forms of ESP, including clairvoyance and telepathy. These sceptics see the extraordinary knowledge, skills, and recognition associated with alleged cases of reincarnation as actually deriving from the paranormal powers of the mind, some of which are—they argue—of a nature and magnitude as yet recognized.

Clairvoyance plus Subconscious Impersonation?

The first of these ESP alternatives consists in appealing to clairvoyance plus subconscious impersonation. Under this explanation, in the Swarnlata case, for example, the sceptic may make these three claims:

1. Swarnlata is *unknowingly clairvoyant;* that is, although she does not know it, Swarnlata has paranormal knowledge of certain past events (and the persons in them) without having lived them, and without anybody having told her what happened.
2. Swarnlata, for some reason or other, *subconsciously identifies*

with a particular person (Biya) who lived in the past—a person whose life and beliefs Swarnlata clairvoyantly understands.

3. Swarnlata *subconsciously impersonates* or *dramatizes* that person (Biya) because Swarnlata sincerely but mistakenly believes that she is in fact that person.

Notice the force of this explanation. In the first claim, the sceptic appeals to a phenomenon—clairvoyance or ESP—that is generally established, and that would account for the subject's paranormal knowledge of past events.[53] In the second claim, the sceptic appeals to a psychiatric phenomenon that is also well known: the disorder of "multiple personality," or "alternating personality," or "secondary personality."[54] This is said to account for the subject's claim *to be* the reincarnation of a previously known person. It also accounts for the fact that the subject typically views his or her knowledge of the past as memories. And it further accounts for the fact that subjects usually (although Swarnlata was an exception in this regard) tend to forget their earlier lives as they get older. Finally, in the third claim, the sceptic accounts for the success the subjects usually have in convincing others (especially the deceased person's living family members) that they are indeed the reincarnated very familiar deceased persons. This first sceptical ESP explanation for alleged cases of reincarnation is offered by C. T. K. Chari (among others), who says,

> I am of the considered opinion that all these studies remain quite inconclusive; with the available data of psi [i.e., psychic] research, we cannot rule out some combination of the counterhypotheses of hidden and disguised memories acquired in a normal fashion, extrasensorially selective tapping of the memories of others, and a psychometric or psychoscopic ESP achieving a strong empathic identification with deceased persons and an apparent "resuscitation of memories" not belonging to the subjects in their normal lives. I have examined the counterhypotheses singly and jointly and conclude that a combination of them is not only feasible but actually illustrated by the empirical data of survival research.[55]

In spite of the sweet plausibility of this explanation, however, there is much that is wrong with it. As N. Hintze and J. G. Pratt have pointed out, the children with memories of an earlier life do not, as a rule, show any signs of being clairvoyant in any other respect.[56] Furthermore, if their "memories" are instances of clairvoyance, what would account for its being exhibited in such a specialized, narrow way? As far as we know, clairvoyance is typically a *general* ability—meaning not that people can be clairvoyant at any time under any circumstances, but rather that people who are clairvoyant are not specifically clairvoyant with respect to *one* past event or to a series of past events in *one* person's family. They tend to show their clairvoyant trait at different times to varying degrees under differing circumstances. Furthermore, information acquired clairvoyantly (or telepathically) is typically episodic (rather than systematically connected) and not experienced as something remembered.

In addition, as Hintze and Pratt also note, even if we were to explain the content of the alleged memories by appeal to some highly specialized form of disguised clairvoyance (or telepathy), these children—children such as Swarnlata—would need to be credited with "super-psi" (or "super-ESP") in order to acquire such a large number of correct details about the life, relatives, and circumstances of the dead person. *Super-psi* refers to psychic powers that are beyond the typical, that is, those of a kind and/or magnitude speculated to exist but not yet described scientifically, because their limits are unknown. Clairvoyance (or telepathy) of this special kind does not occur often, if ever; and according to Hintze and Pratt, it has never yet been empirically confirmed in children under five years of age.[57]

In *Children Who Remember Previous Lives,* Ian Stevenson reinforces these answers to the clairvoyance-plus-subconscious-impersonation claims.

During the first years of my research on these cases, I took extrasensory perception more seriously as a plausible explanation for them than I do now. I still consider it an important possibility, but I no longer give it the weight that I formerly did.

I have two main reasons for this change of opinion. First, the children subjects hardly ever show, or have credited to them by their families, any evidence of extrasensory perception apart from the memories of a previous life. I have asked hundreds of parents about such capacities in their children. Most of them have denied that the child in question had any; a few have said that their child had occasionally demonstrated some form of extrasensory perception, but the evidence they provided was usually scanty. I cannot understand how a child could acquire by extrasensory perception the considerable stores of information so many of these subjects show about a deceased person without demonstrating—if not often, at least from time to time—similar paranormal powers in other contexts.

In addition, as I said more than once already, a case nearly always includes more than the verbal statements that the child makes about the previous life. For one to several years, and sometimes much longer, most of the subjects show behavior that is unusual for their families, but that matches what we could learn, or reasonably infer about the behavior of the previous personality.

Many of the subjects respond with strong emotion and in appropriate ways to stimuli related to the previous personality. For example, Ismail Altinkilic clapped with joy when he learned that the murderers of the man whose life he remembered had—after particularly lengthy legal proceedings—been judicially hanged. I mentioned earlier that other subjects, for example, Imad Elawar and Sukla Gupta, were brought to tears by the mere mention of some untoward event in the life of a person of whom the previous personalities in their cases had been fond. The child shows a syndrome of behaviors that in the more developed instances amounts to a facsimile of the previous personality's character. . . . We have no grounds for thinking that processes of paranormal cognition can produce, in effect, an entire personality transposed to another person. Experimental parapsychology certainly offers no evidence for extrasensory perception of the kind required; and other types of spontaneous cases only rarely offer parallels.

Leaving aside the question of the incommunicability by paranormal processes of a complex group of behavioral responses, the subject's imitation of another person requires a strong motive on his part. In most cases, however, we cannot find any such motive. The unusual behavior of the subject, as I have shown, frequently embroils him in conflict with his family without bringing him any concomitant benefits. Nor can I find in most of the subjects' parents any reason why they should wish to impose a different personality on their child, assuming they had somehow obtained the necessary information—whether normally or by extrasensory perception.[58]

Incidentally, we should not assume that either Stevenson or Hintze or Pratt (or anybody else for that matter) is claiming that ESP cannot exist in highly specialized ways in children who show no previous abilities in clairvoyance or telepathy. It is just that appealing to this sort of ESP to account for the cases at hand is arbitrary because, while its existence is certainly logically possible, we have no empirical evidence that telepathy or clairvoyance of the sort necessary for this alternative explanation exists in children under age five. If we could point to some cases—other than these memory cases—in which children have been demonstrated to have highly specialized or focused and unerring clairvoyance or telepathy, then this alternative explanation would not look so ad hoc. Further, our saying as much should not be viewed as imposing arbitrary limits on ESP; rather, we are simply requiring of the explanation that it appeal to some particular form of ESP whose existence has been empirically verified. In short, the fact that nobody has established the limits of ESP by no means implies that we can appeal to the unconfirmed existence of forms of ESP (or super-psi) when offering alternatives to an explanation that rests on only those features of the case for whose existence we have empirical evidence.

Therefore, what seems problematic about the first claim made under this sceptical explanation is that it requires of the subjects a highly restricted form of ESP not generally encountered or confirmed (either inside or outside the lab) in cases of successful telepathy or clairvoyance. Besides, even if such narrowly restricted forms of clairvoyance existed, the very best of clairvoyants make a predictable number of mistakes—whereas Swarnlata and Bishen Chand, for example, made virtually no mistakes in their memory claims. As one critic of this sceptical position has noted, the frequency of error associated with the memory claims of Swarnlata and Bishen Chand is just too low to fit with our general understanding of clairvoyance.[59] Hence the evidence strongly suggests that clairvoyance or telepathy is out of the question as a way of explaining how subjects such as these acquired knowledge of the past events they so accurately described.

When we turn to the other claims of this alternative explanation, things get no better. Apart from the fact that there is no known evidence of children ever mistakenly identifying themselves with other people whom they have never met,[60] the argument that these children successfully impersonate deceased people whom they mistakenly identify with is ad hoc in the extreme. After all, can anybody honestly believe that Swarnlata, an eight-year-old child, was so good at impersonating Biya that nobody in Biya's family (brothers, sisters, father, mother, and husband) could detect it as a clever bit of impersonation? It seem very unlikely that she could have duped the whole family. Of course, some will suggest that the family members were all duped because they all believed in reincarnation. But in this case as in other similar cases, although the family members did believe in reincarnation, they expressed scepticism about anyone's ever having past-life memories.

Also, we cannot forget that some parts of a person's character defy successful impersonation over a long period of time. A look, for example, or a way of walking, or a peculiar sense of humor, or the way one laughs—these are all sufficiently personal that it would take only the most competent of impersonators to imitate or dramatize them. Can we plausibly attribute such an ability to Swarnlata (and others), when she never showed a general ability to imitate anybody else successfully? In short, if this sceptical explanation were credible, we would expect to find in subjects like Swarnlata and Bishen Chand a *general* ability to imitate successfully the difficult traits of other personalities as well. But this is not what we find. The sceptic's explanation requires the existence of a very specialized ability—the ability of eight-year-old children (and even younger ones) to impersonate flawlessly the most personal traits of only one person, this person being someone they have never met. Apart from making the sceptic's explanation come out right, there is no reason to think that such a specialized ability exists. Certainly it has never been shown to exist either in the lab or outside. So, even if we accept the general phenomenon of clairvoyance and add to it the typical indications of multiple personality, this alternative explanation seems very unconvincing.

Clairvoyant Xenoglossy and Clairvoyant Skills?

The argument for reincarnation becomes even stronger when we consider the cases involving xenoglossy. What is important about the Lydia Johnson case, the Gretchen case, and other similar cases in which the subjects show an ability to converse in a foreign language demonstrably not learned in this life is that the sceptic cannot begin to explain such an ability by appealing to ESP. Knowing *how* to do something (like knowing how to speak a foreign language) is quite different from knowing *that* something or other is so. Knowing that something or other happened in the past might be explainable in terms of ESP, but knowing how to speak a foreign language (or a different dialect) is not. When we try to explain the acquisition of such skills by appeal to clairvoyance or telepathy, we are distorting the nature of clairvoyance as it is presently understood. And we do this solely to account for these cases when in fact, outside such cases, clairvoyance or telepathy has no history of ever being associated with acquired skills, such as speaking a language or playing an instrument. Only if we could plausibly argue that *knowing how to do* something or other actually reduces to some form of *knowing that* something or other is so could this alternative explanation work for alleged cases of reincarnation.

Some authors have suggested, however, that there is evidence extending the concept of clairvoyance to the phenomenon of acquired skills. This would be an instance of super-psi. They sometimes refer to experiments, touted in various tabloids or written for mass appeal by journalists of the popular press, in which the subjects were hypnotized and then told that they were distinguished artists (such as Renoir or Gauguin) or mathematicians (such as Boole or DeMorgan). Then these subjects were sent off to paint or to do mathematics. In each case, we are told, the subjects had little or no previous skill in either painting or mathematics. The results of these experiments are sometimes reported in the popular press as remarkable in that the first subjects began to paint just like the distinguished artist they were told to be. And the second subjects were reported to have advanced remarkably in mathematics. The Soviets, who are alleged to have conducted such experiments, refer to them as cases of instant or artificial reincarnation.

However, these reported experiments are not independently documented or verified outside the popular press. From a critical point of view, they are worthless. Moreover, even if such alleged cases did occur, it is extremely important to note that the skills reported did not extend to responsive xenoglossy. Nor did the skills in question include being able to play a musical instrument without previous instruction. Remember that in the case of Bishen Chand, however—in addition to his having a rich set of memory claims independently verified in various ways—Bishen Chand (like Laxmi Narain before him) could also play the drums skilfully. But Bishen had not been taught how to play the drums, nor had he ever been exposed to them. And Bishen Chand's skill at playing the drums cannot be explained by appeal to ESP, for the very same reason that we cannot explain responsive xenoglossy by appeal to ESP. We may not know the limits of psi, but we have no justification for extending it arbitrarily to such items of nonpropositional knowledge in order to make up an explanation for them. There is simply no public evidence of ESP extending to these forms of nonpropositional knowledge. Thus, we cannot explain Lydia Johnson's ability to speak eighteenth-century Swedish, say, by appeal to ESP.

Importantly enough, however, these considerations suggest what *would* count as splendid evidence for falsifying the reincarnation hypothesis. It is this: if a person could be hypnotized and succeed, under hypnotic suggestion, to play an instrument he or she has not been taught to play, or to speak in a dialect not learned, or to respond in a foreign language that he or she has never heard before, then the sceptic would have good grounds for discounting responsive xenoglossy and unlearned musical ability as distinctive evidence for the belief in reincarnation. Presently, we do not have this sort of evidence. If we ever do, we will have to extend our notion of clairvoyance (or ESP) to include acquired skills—skills such as playing an instrument and speaking a foreign language. But until that time (should it ever come), responsive xenoglossy as well as the ability to play an instrument without having been taught it cannot be explained without our assuming reincarnation or some form of possession (see the next section) as a fact. And the need to appeal to reincarnation is especially strong when the language or musical skill involved is known to be the language or the musical skill of the person the subject claims to have been in a past life.

Incidentally, as suggested in examining the reasons offered by Hintze and Pratt and Stevenson for rejecting the clairvoyance-plus-subconscious-interpretation argument, and in light of the reasons just given for rejecting clairvoyance (or telepathy) in cases of responsive xenoglossy and acquired skills, some people think that such a rejection rests on the erroneous assumption that there are not any forms of psi (such as super-psi) of precisely the sort needed to account for the memory claims and behaviors in the above-described cases. Along with Jule Eisenbud[61] and others, Stephen Braude, for example, has for some time argued in various places that any attempt to argue for survival by appeal to the principle that we have no way of accounting for certain forms of paranormal knowledge or behaviors in terms of ESP or PK (psychokinesis) are actually given over to the totally unjustifiable assumption that certain forms of ESP or PK cannot exist simply because we do not have laboratory empirical evidence for them.[62] As Braude sees it, altogether too frequently in the past we have erred in concluding that some item of paranormal knowledge could not be a form of ESP; and survival evidence loses its power, he says, as soon as we admit that we are unjustified in assuming the nonexistence of certain forms of super-psi (such forms as would accommodate very refined and accurate forms of clairvoyance and telepathy, extending to forms of nonpropositional knowledge). In his view, both abstract and empirical considerations suggest that psi functioning in human beings may be considerably more extensive and uncontrollable than its laboratory manifestations would make it appear.[63]

More specifically, for Braude (and for Eisenbud, as noted above)—apart from the fact that appeal to super-psi may provide certain explanatory virtues (systematicity, plausibility or simplicity, and fecundity) not provided by alternative explanations for such items as precognition—his more abstract reason for taking seriously "the possibility" of super-psi consists in claiming that given our present state of ignorance concerning the nature of psi, we must (at the very least) entertain the possibility of extensive psi. . . . In fact . . . the only way we could ever be entitled to insist that psi effects have inherrent limits would be on the basis of a thoroughly developed and well-supported full scale psi theory, one that embraces the *totality* of available evidence for psi (not just laboratory evidence), and explains how or why psi functions both in and out of the lab. But at present, no decent theory forbids large-scale or super-psi (most simply ignore it), and certainly no scientific theory renders any form of psi improbable.[64]

Braude goes on to assert that arguments dismissive of super-psi as an explanation of so-called survival evidence are severely defective. On this point, he engages the following three standing objections to the existence of super-psi: (1) there is no evidence for the existence of super-psi; (2) there is evidence against super-psi; and (3) the super-psi hypothesis is not falsifiable. In response to the first of these objections, Braude claims that it assumes we would know super-psi if we saw it, and that this assumption is clearly indefensible because there need be no observable difference between a heart attack or a plane crash caused normally and one caused by PK. (The only difference may be in their *unobservable* causal histories.) He claims further that those who assert the first objection are also guilty of the more general methodological error of offering only theory-dependent arguments, that is, of using arguments and data that presuppose the denial of super-psi. In response to the second objection, Braude argues—as against Roger Anderson who asserted that we have solid and obvious evidence for the limits of PK[65]—that such an objection assumes unjustifiably that the best known forms of psi determine what forms psi would take in different circumstances or even in circumstances where no one is on the lookout for psi. Braude also twits Anderson for the unwarranted assumption that the best available evidence is for psychic phenomena a long way from super-psi, on the grounds that we must not forget that large-scale psi *might* occur surreptitiously in less contrived or ritualized human contexts.[66] Finally, in response to the third objection, Braude admits that the existence of super-psi is not falsifiable, but says that nonfalsifiability is theoretically uninteresting and certainly does not undermine the super-psi hypothesis.

> Even if hypothesis H is non-falsifiable, there may still be other grounds for deciding between H and rival hypotheses—for example, higher level pragmatic considerations concerning theoretic systematicity, explanatory fecundity, and conceptual cost. Besides, the non-falsifiability of an hypothesis may simply reflect the intractable nature of the phenomenon in question, rather than a theoretical deficiency, or the fact that the phenomenon does not exist.[67]

By way of reply to Braude's defense of the super-psi hypothesis as a possible way of explaining the facts in the above-described cases suggestive of reincarnation, a few brief comments seem in order. First of all, it is certainly possible—logically possible—that super-psi exists and that it functions in ways distinct from our current understanding of what the limits of ESP and PK may be. Also, nobody should place any a priori limits on what forms psi may take in the future. That said, however, it seems reasonable to point out that, before one can appeal legitimately to super-psi as an alternative way of explaining anything, one should have some empirical evidence that in fact super-psi exists. This evidence is not provided simply by noting that it is possible—logically possible—that such super-psi exists. Pratt and Stevenson and the others who reject super-psi explanations do so, presumably, because they think the burden of proof should be on the proponents of super-psi to provide evidence for its existence if appeal to it is to serve as an alternative explanation for an existing body of data. As we have just seen, however, Braude (and presumably Eisenbud also) admits that the existence of super-psi is neither confirmable (because we cannot empirically distinguish it from normal physical causes) nor falsifiable. Insisting that super-psi be empirically confirmed to exist before it may be used to explain anything seems less an instance of assuming erroneously that there are a priori limits to psi than simply just that: a request for some evidence of the causes cited in offering an explanation. Jones could hardly be the robber of the Rabun Gap Bank if we have no good reason to think that Jones ever existed.

Further, Braude's admission that the hypothesis of super-psi is not falsifiable may be more damaging than it at first appears. After all, if nothing could count for the nonexistence of super-psi, there is good reason to think that the hypothesis may be empirically meaningless—confirmability and falsifiability being necessary conditions for the empirical significance of any hypothesis about the physical world. If we do not know what to accept for the falsity of the hypothesis, then anything and everything could count as a positive confirming instance of the hypothesis; and this makes the hypothesis meaningless. Appealing to so-called higher-order criteria (such as explanatory fecundity, simplicity, and systematicity) for theory selection seems pointless if the meaning of the hypothesis cannot be clearly specified in terms of the evidence that would need to be present for justifiably accepting or rejecting the hypothesis.

For these reasons, then, we need to have some independent empirical evidence (which is not to say, necessarily, laboratory evidence) for the existence of super-psi in other contexts before we can appeal to it as a way of explaining those features of our alleged cases of reincarnation that do not fit into established (confirmed) views about the limits of psi. It is possible that some day we may come to accept ESP as extending to the phenomenon of nonpropositional knowing (i.e., knowing how to do something or other). But until that occurs, it is purely gratuitous and very implausible to suggest that we might appeal successfully to ESP in order to explain the acquisition of unlearned skills such as playing instruments or speaking in an unlearned language.

Possession?

One of the most interesting and plausible of the alternative explanations based on ESP asserts that in each of the rich cases we need not believe that the subject is reincarnated, but should rather see the subject as being possessed by a disembodied spirit with memories of its own past life, a spirit who takes over the personality of the subject. According to this alternative explanation, possession is as plausible an explanation of the data in these cases as is reincarnation.

Well, the most immediate reply to this alternative explanation is that in cases of possession, as they have been documented, the subject seldom says, "I remember having lived as so and so at such and such a time." An allegedly possessed subject seldom, for example, identifies himself or herself as a person who once lived in the past as Napoleon but who now lives as Joe Smith, Mary Jones, or whoever. In other words, in typical cases of possession (as we shall see in Chapter 3), the subject claims to *be* Napoleon, or Caesar Augustus, or Mozart—in the present time. They are not cases in which the subject claims to remember having lived as Napoleon, or Caesar Augustus, or Mozart in some past life. In cases of possession, a person's current well-established personality is simply replaced by a new personality who makes no claims about remembering having lived a past life as so and so. He or she *is* so and so! Thus, because a crucial clinical feature that is present in typical possession cases is often absent in the spontaneous uninduced cases (such as Bishen Chand and Swarnlata) of the reincarnation type, it is difficult to see how the latter can be an instance of the former.

To be sure, the possession alternative seems to be considerably more plausible in reincarnation-type cases wherein the subject is regressed and the subject does not explicitly claim to remember having lived a past life as so and so. For example, if we do not regard the Lydia Johnson qua Jensen and the D.J. qua Gretchen cases as clear instances in which past-life memories are hypnotically induced (a plausible option), it is difficult to distinguish them from possession-type cases. And if we had only such cases, it would certainly seem that the possession hypothesis made as much sense as the reincarnation hypothesis. Fortunately, however, cases such as the Bishen Chand and the Swarnlata cases are, in the crucial ways just mentioned, remarkably different from possession-type cases wherein typically there seems to be a clear displacement of a previously well defined personality.[68]

But certainly a great deal more does need to be said about this possession hypothesis precisely because it seems the most plausible of alternative explanations for those who accept the phenomenon of possession. Of course, resolving this particular dispute provides no comfort whatsoever for those materialists who deny that there is any form of personal existence independent of the body.

Stevenson, for one, has given other reasons (besides past-life content) for discouraging the possession hypothesis as a way of explaining the richer cases. Most notably, possession would not explain the presence of particular body scars—or birthmarks— corresponding to fatal wounds received by the former personality the subject claims to remember having been.[69] Stevenson lists the presence of such birthmarks as part of an ideal case, as we shall see later in the chapter. Such scars establish a causal connection between the subject and the earlier body, thereby supporting reincarnation rather than possession. But we need not elaborate on Stevenson's reasoning at this point. We will return to this discussion in some detail in Chapter 3 after considering more closely the phenomenon of ostensible possession. There we will examine further why possession is not a plausible alternative for explaining the data in the richer cases of the reincarnation type.

Two Final Sceptical Responses

In the interest of completeness, we must acknowledge two other basic objections to the thesis of reincarnation. The first is that the hypothesis is not scientifically established, because the evidence is not repeatable under controlled conditions. The second is that belief in reincarnation requires belief in the existence of many more persons than there are bodies. This latter is sometimes referred to as the population objection. Neither objection is very telling, as we shall now see.

The Repeatability Objection

There are sceptics who say that the reincarnation thesis is not empirically or scientifically established, because the data are not repeatable; this objection is unacceptable for two reasons. First, the thesis is empirically verified each and every time a nonfraudulent case like the case of Bishen Chand emerges. The fact that we cannot produce the cases at will is no more evidence against reincarnation than our inability to produce new dinosaur bones at will counts against the empirical nature or even the verification of our belief in the past existence of dinosaurs. Indeed, belief in the past existence of dinosaurs is empirically verifiable and verified as the best available explanation of the cause for the data that consist in certain footprints and skeletal remains. Similarly, belief in the past existence of Julius Caesar is simply the best available explanation for certain historical data. Doubtless, it is possible (however remotely) that there were no dinosaurs, that the data were all fabricated by someone interested in deception. It is also possible that the man Julius Caesar never existed, that an imposter killed him at an early age and falsified certain records. But in the absence of solid evidence that the possibility of error in these instances is any more than a mere possibility, we do not have any grounds for questioning our belief in the existence of dinosaurs or Julius Caesar. What makes these two beliefs empirical or scientific is not that we can produce at will the data to be explained, but rather that we know what it will take to falsify or verify the hypotheses.

Similarly, we know what it would take to verify or to falsify the belief in reincarnation. More cases like that of Bishen Chand, for example, will continue to verify the hypothesis (assuming that no reasonable grounds are found for suspecting fraud or hoax); and actual evidence of fraud or hoax in cases like the Bishen Chand case will falsify the hypothesis. We tend not to question our belief in the past existence of dinosaurs and certain historical figures until we have more than the mere possibility of error—or, in other words, until we have falsifying evidence. But, even though the logic of the situation is precisely the same with respect to reincarnation, we tend to be very sceptical about belief in reincarnation as an empirically confirmed belief. The difference, of course, lies in the fact that belief in reincarnation commits us to the present existence of an object that is not in principle observable by the methods of direct observation currently available in natural science, whereas belief in the past existence of dinosaurs or Julius Caesar does not so commit us. Nevertheless, since this is the reason for the difference, we all need to be reminded that belief in the existence of the theoretical components of quarks accounts for certain data, but nobody can in principle observe such entities by current methods of observation. Belief in such entities is just the best available explanation for some body of observed data that we cannot account for in any other way.

Second, it is simply not true to the facts of the best available studies to say that the reincarnation hypothesis is not an empirically established thesis for the reason that the evidence is not repeatable. The evidence *is* repeatable (and testable), although it is certainly not reproducible at will. As a matter of fact, an appropriate testing procedure consists in following these five steps:

1. examining and taping a large number of subjects (and their families) who are reported as having past-life memories;
2. before any contact occurs between the subject's family and the family of the alleged past-life subject, finding among these subjects those who have a very rich set of memory claims of the sort present in cases like the Bishen Chand case;
3. verifying independently the memory claims;
4. among those who have such verified memory claims, finding those who manifest certain unlearned skills (such as speaking in an unlearned language) appropriate to the life they claim to have lived earlier; and
5. excluding the reasonable possibility of fraud, hoax, and a natural explanation of the subject's memories and skills.

If we follow this procedure in earnest, and if after a long time no new cases similar to the Bishen Chand case occur, then we might be justified in thinking that there must be something fraudulent or amiss with the cases examined thus far. So, in a very clear sense the hypothesis is testable because quite falsifiable. We will return to the question of repeatability in Chapter 6.

The Population Objection

The population objection consists in noting that the human population of the world has increased dramatically from 8000 B.C., when the population was roughly 5 million, to the present 5 billion—and that, if current trends continue, the world population will be 10 billion by the year 2016. From this it is supposed to follow that the thesis of reincarnation is false. But why exactly? The evidence for reincarnation does not entail that there is a set number of persons that reincarnate. Nor does it entail that new persons are not created, just as it does not entail that the process goes on forever. So why exactly would an increase in population be a reason for thinking that reincarnation could not be true? Certainly, there is nothing logically impossible here. Is it, then, that the thesis of reincarnation requires that at any given time there be more persons than there are reincarnated persons? Well, if it did, so what? This is not a reason for thinking reincarnation false, but could, rather, be seen as an implication of the thesis itself. The data for reincarnation per se do not preclude special creation, the creation of new souls with new bodies. Nor do the data entail it, or require it. There is no factual evidence that explains the increase in the number of reincarnated persons. But reincarnationists do not need to explain as much *because the evidence for reincarnation would establish the thesis no matter what the explanation may be for the increase in the number of reincarnated persons*.

In sum, taking the population objection seriously requires making certain assumptions about the number of persons there are, the duration of the process of reincarnation, and the uncreated (i.e., newly uncreated) and limited number of persons. None of these assumptions are necessary, or implied by the data for reincarnation. The most that can be said is that, if reincarnation is true, then the number of reincarnated persons has probably increased along with the population—unless, of course, not everybody reincarnates and new persons are often created. Indeed, the population objection is totally irrelevant to the question of the truth of reincarnation.

Stevenson's Own Reservations: The Ideal Case

As is evident in the title of his book *Twenty Cases Suggestive of Reincarnation,* Ian Stevenson is reluctant to say that the cases he examines prove the point. On the contrary, Stevenson believes the argument for reincarnation would be won only by finding an *ideal case,* that is, one that meets the following conditions:

1. It is rich in verified memory claims not accountable in terms of clairvoyance, ESP (telepathy), or cryptomnesia.[70]
2. It is attended by the presence of a complicated skill (such as speaking a foreign language or playing an instrument) that demonstrably could not have been learned by the subject in his or her present life.
3. It is attended by appropriate birthmarks corresponding to wounds received in the earlier life remembered by the subject, and the occurrence of the wounds in the previous life is independently verified.
4. It is a case wherein the memory claims are not very much diminished with age, nor do they need to be induced under hypnotic trance or regression.
5. It is a case in which the subject's identification with a past personality is recognized by the subject as continuous with his or her present personality rather than as substitutive of the present personality, and the identification is maintained over a long period of time—preferably into adulthood.[71]
6. It is a case wherein the subject's identification with the past personality cannot be explained by the influence of parents or other persons.[72]
7. It is a case wherein the subject, as a result of his or her identification with a past personality, manifests predictable emotional responses to specific events and persons remembered in the past life.
8. It is a case wherein the subject is recognized as the past person reincarnated, and accepted over a long period of time, by many extant family members or friends (who have nothing to gain by the recognition and acceptance) of the past personality.[73]

Some of the cases described in this chapter combine many but not all of these conditions. The case of Swarnlata, for example, is a very rich case, but it lacks conditions 2 and 3. And while the case of Bishen Chand is also very rich, it clearly lacks condition 3. Indeed, in no one case have all the conditions Stevenson lists appeared. For this reason, Stevenson refrains from urging that reincarnation has been conclusively established.

Certainly, on the principle that extraordinary claims require extraordinary evidence, we *should* be somewhat cautious in our assessments of the strength of the evidence offered here for reincarnation. Even so, it seems excessively cautious to think that the belief in reincarnation is not established by the rich cases described in this chapter, and that we ought to await the appearance of the ideal case. Admittedly, one might want more evidence. As long as there are imaginable ways to strengthen the evidence, seeking more evidence is a desirable project. And, of course, the question of how much evidence is enough tends to be relative to both the kind of claim made and the degree of initial plausibility associated with the claim. But is it *necessary* to satisfy all the conditions of the ideal case offered by Stevenson before we are strongly justified in believing that the argument has been won in favor of reincarnation? Stevenson certainly seems to suggest as much; but I submit that, in so doing, he is actually understating the force of the existing evidence. At the moment, without denying that the ideal case would be nice to have, we seem quite justified in urging something stronger than does Stevenson. Let me explain.

Why, precisely, would we need any more evidence for belief in reincarnation than that provided by a nonfraudulent case in which the subject has a rich set of memory claims, some of which refer to past facts that are items of public knowledge and some of which are verified as facts that only the subject could have known if the subject had indeed lived a past life as the person the subject claims to have been? On this point, we should keep in mind the discussion on human personality offered by Alfred J. Ayer in his book *The Problem of Knowledge*.[74] Ayer there argues that it would be sufficient for the truth of the belief that the man beside you is Julius Caesar reincarnated if that man had all the memories that one would ordinarily expect of Julius Caesar, and if he had some verified memories that appealed to facts that were not in any way items of public information.[75]

At the time, incidentally, Ayer was not attempting to prove the truth of reincarnation. He was simply arguing that human personality need not be identified in any way with the body rather than with the collection of one's memories. What is important for us about his discussion, however, is that it literally stipulates the conditions sufficient to establish that the man beside you is Julius Caesar reincarnated. But those conditions have certainly been satisfied in many of the cases described in this chapter—especially the Bishen Chand case, the Swarnlata case, and the Mrs. Smith case. If these cases are not demonstrable instances of hoax, fraud, or purely natural phenomena, why do we not accept them as compelling evidence for reincarnation—as Ayer's argument allows us to do? Why add any more conditions having to do with the presence of body scars, or the manifestation of unlearned skills such as speaking a foreign language or playing an instrument? We would need to add to Ayer's conditions only if we had discovered that Ayer's conditions were not sufficient. But have we? Apart from the possession hypothesis (which, as we shall see in Chapter 3, may be quite relevant to determining the necessity of body scars as a condition for proving reincarnation), have we come across a reasonably plausible alternative explanation showing that the presence of private but verifiable past-life memories is not sufficient for establishing the validity of reincarnation? Given all the alternative explanations offered above (and bypassing the possession hypothesis, for the moment), it seems clear that nobody has yet *shown* either that Ayer's general requirements for human personality are unacceptable or that the cases described in this chapter are not legitimate instances of those conditions and thus evidence of reincarnation. We seem to have here one of those problems wherein people readily agree on what it would take to establish something they very much do not want to believe—and then when, contrary to anyone's expectations, the evidence actually emerges strongly supportive of the belief, they return (for no persuasive reason) to add more conditions to what it would take to establish what they very much do not want to accept. And they continue doing so until it is virtually impossible that any such evidence should ever emerge.

At any rate, the point is that, in the absence of plausible alternative explanations that do not require reincarnation, it will be sufficient for the truth of reincarnation that the memory conditions laid out by Ayer, and clearly instanced in a number of the cases described in this chapter, be satisfied. Thus, the knowledge that reincarnation occurs is simply the product of the best available explanation for the existence of such memory claims as indicated above. Until somebody comes up with the appropriate alternative explanation, the evidence for reincarnation appears to be quite strong.

Moreover, while satisfying Ayer's memory conditions would be sufficient for justifying belief in reincarnation, it really is not necessary. As we have seen, the Lydia Johnson qua Jensen and the D.J. qua Gretchen cases do not satisfy the memory conditions (or the body-scars condition) just noted. But, apart from possession (for which, again, see Chapter 3), there is no minimally plausible alternative explanation to that of reincarnation that fits anywhere near as well. So it appears that the idealized conditions offered by Stevenson as necessary for conclusively establishing reincarnation contain a number of separately sufficient conditions, not all of which are uniquely necessary. This is to say that Stevenson may have underestimated the force of his own research (which plausibly confirms the thesis of reincarnation) by requiring for a conclusive proof a set of conditions that go past the point of strong rational justification. If the ideal case should happen to emerge, it would certainly put the thesis of reincarnation into a special category as one of the most robustly and richly confirmed beliefs in empirical inquiry. And if that occurs, well and good. But if it does not, the evidence presented here still establishes reincarnation in terms of at least two separate sets of conditions, each of which is separately sufficient.

Indeed, it seems unreasonable to accept any belief other than reincarnation to explain the cases described in this chapter. This conclusion is much stronger than Stevenson's. His conclusion is that *it is not unreasonable to believe in reincarnation* in order to explain his best cases. While that result certainly is an incontrovertible and revolutionary finding in itself, the proper conclusion should be that *it is unreasonable to reject belief in reincarnation.* And the strength of this latter conclusion follows from our preceding analysis of the sceptic's alternative proposals and their demonstrable failure.

Two Remaining Questions of Interest

Finally, two interesting questions remain. First, is reincarnation a universal phenomenon, or is it that only *some* people reincarnate? Second, assuming the truth of universal reincarnation, what is the cash value of the belief? In other words, apart from rendering the traditional mind–body question obsolete and perhaps orienting our philosophical ventures more in the direction of ethics, would belief in reincarnation have any personal value or significance?

Does Everybody Reincarnate?

With regard to the first question, the cases examined in this chapter show that the subjects in those cases reincarnated, but they do not show that everyone reincarnates. Is it possible that only a few people reincarnate, namely, only those who remember their past lives, or who can be induced to remember their past lives? Certainly, this is possible. As a matter of fact, strictly speaking, the evidence cited in this chapter establishes the reincarnation of only those subjects cited in those cases. However, it is very tempting to believe that, if anybody reincarnates, then everybody does. This is because among the subjects examined in these cases nothing indicates that they are, in terms of moral or intellectual superiority, different from the rest of us. And if everybody reincarnates, then the interesting point seems to be that some people are able to remember their past lives and some are not.[76] However, believing that *everybody* reincarnates is only a conjecture and is not strictly supported by the evidence for reincarnation.

What Real Difference Does It Make?

The answer to the second question bears on something we just noted. As long as one cannot remember anything of any past life, belief in reincarnation may not have personal significance beyond satisfying one's curiosity in understanding the nature of human personality and the falsity of traditional materialism. However, that in itself would be no small achievement.

Moreover, lest anyone be tempted to think that belief in reincarnation will carry with it a genuine capacity for self-understanding as a result of employing regression techniques to "get in touch" with one's past lives, a word of warning is in order. Even though there are cases in which regression has produced important results for verifying reincarnation (the Lydia Johnson case, among others), the vast majority of so-called past-life regressions are worthless as such. Stevenson recently commented that anybody who knows anything at all about hypnotism would regard the buying of hypnotic regression to establish contact with one's earlier lives as more like buying a pig in a poke than like viewing one's past lives.[77] At any given time in Brooklyn alone, no fewer than ten different people will claim—as the result of hypnotic regression— to be the reincarnation of Cleopatra, or Napoleon, or Socrates. This is not to say that we will never come up with any verified and verifiable past-life memories under hypnotic regression; rather, it is to say that the neighborhood is full of snake-oil artists selling the promise of past-life revelations, when in fact verifiable past-life memories have by and large occurred spontaneously in children under age three who typically suffer complete amnesia about such past-life events after the age of nine. So, if hypnotic regression were a reliable technique for putting people in contact with their verifiable past lives, then the belief in reincarnation might hold out the hope of coming to a deeper understanding of one's personality as a result of past-life events. But because it is *not* a reliable technique for that purpose, a justifiable belief in reincarnation may actually have no practical value as far as providing us with useful information about our own past lives and their effect on our current personality.

A Brief History of Reincarnation in the West

Much of the world has always believed in reincarnation. Even in the West, reincarnation was widely accepted until the middle of the sixth century A.D. The ancient Pythagoreans, along with later

Greek philosophers like Plato, believed in reincarnation. While it was an item of religious belief for the Pythagoreans, it was an item of philosophical belief for Plato. For Plato, belief in reincarnation followed from belief in innate knowledge (knowledge one has without learning it in this life); and innate knowledge was simply implied by the fact that we have some knowledge we could not have acquired by reliance on our sensory organs. But Plato's justification for belief in reincarnation was thus dependent on his claims that, first, we do have knowledge that is absolutely certain and, second, we cannot have such knowledge and it be the product of inferences based on sensory input. As might be expected, the history of philosophy challenged Plato on both claims; and so the *philosophical* foundation for the belief in reincarnation was undermined by heavy discussion on the nature and limits of human knowledge. This discussion continued into the sixteenth century, when the whole of modern philosophy in the West split into two camps: one believing in the doctrine of innate ideas (and thus, by implication, in some form of reincarnation); and the other accounting for the whole of human knowledge simply by appealing to the power of the human mind to organize the data of sense experience into a coherent picture of the world. The latter alternative was adopted by the philosophers Locke, Berkeley, and Hume; the former was adopted by Descartes, Leibniz, and Spinoza.

In more recent times, the ongoing debate between behavioristic psychology and innatist psychology suggests that the philosophical debate on the nature of human knowledge endures. By implication, the debate on reincarnation also endures. But in all the history of philosophy we find no evidence offered for innatism or reincarnation that is in any way similar to the remarkable evidence uncovered and examined by Ian Stevenson. This fact is important because it is, I submit, with this kind of empirical evidence that the debate is resolved in favor of innatism and the doctrine of reincarnation.

One reason that reincarnation is only *now* being established as a valid belief is that the cases that establish it would never have been taken seriously in the past, and thus would never have been examined with the seriousness so evident in, say, Stevenson's research. Why were such cases never taken seriously in the past? Here we can only speculate. However, the strength of organized Christianity—with its cultural rejection of reincarnation—certainly contributed. Moreover, in the absence of knowing what would count as a method for *showing* its truth, any person's claim to be reincarnated could only be viewed as evidence of insanity or witchcraft. In view of the doctrinal control exercised by Christianity in the West, belief in reincarnation never got much of a foothold after the Second Council of Constantinople in A.D. 553. No doubt, the strength of early Christianity's repudiation of the doctrine certainly had much to do with the tendency to view claims of reincarnation as instances of insanity.

Interestingly, however, a strong argument can be made to the effect that early Christianity never really condemned belief in reincarnation and further that, when reincarnation is properly understood, Christians still have very good reasons to believe in it. Let us turn to this argument now and so take a closer look at what some consider both good theological as well as moral grounds for believing in reincarnation.

Christianity and Reincarnation: MacGregor's Argument

Generally, the Christian community does not endorse belief in reincarnation. Indeed, the Christian community typically shuns the belief. Many lay Christians and Church leaders even regard reincarnation as incompatible with Christian doctrine and tradition. Lately, however, a growing number of Christian theologians has called for a serious reconsideration of the doctrine of reincarnation. One such theologian is Geddes MacGregor. In *Reincarnation in Christianity: A New Vision of the Role of Rebirth in Christian Thought,* MacGregor argues not only that reincarnation is compatible with Christianity, but also that Christians *ought* to believe in it.[78] We will examine MacGregor's argument and then offer some independent reasons why Christianity will sooner or later need to accept reincarnation as a part of Christian teaching that had long been overlooked for a number of understandable but unacceptable reasons.

MacGregor's argument is composed of three parts, primarily. First, there is strong scriptural evidence to support the view that Jesus taught reincarnation. Second, Christian resistance to reincarnation is based on the false belief that the Church condemned reincarnation per se at the Second Council of Constantinople in A.D. 553. And third, the doctrine of reincarnation is philosophically compelling in that it satisfies our deepest instinct for justice.

Scriptural Evidence

There are basically four New Testament texts that Geddes MacGregor (and others) cite in favor of reincarnation. The first is from the gospel of John, and it concerns the man born blind whom Jesus cured:

> As Jesus passed by, he saw a man blind from birth. And his disciples asked him, "Rabbi, who has sinned, this man or his parents, that he was born blind?"[79]

Commentators have noted that the disciples apparently thought there were only two possible explanations for the blindness: either the man preexisted his body and was being punished for sin in that earlier existence, or the parents sinned and the punishment was passed on to the offspring. Jesus responded that the man was blind so that the "works of God could be made manifest in him."[80] It is what Jesus does not say here that is important. Jesus does not deny the doctrine of reincarnation that his disciples apparently accept. One would expect Jesus to deny the doctrine here if it were something he was opposed to. In fact, he does not deny it. Of course, Jesus does not answer the question he was asked, either; but the significance of the text lies in its implication that Jesus and his disciples accepted reincarnation.

The second text—also from John—is stronger in that it reveals that Jesus actually taught reincarnation:

> Jesus answered him, "I assure you, most solemnly I tell you, that unless a person is born again, he will not enter the kingdom of God." Nicodemus said to him, "How can a man be born again

when he is old? Can he enter his mother's womb again and be born?" Jesus answered, "I assure you, most solemnly I tell you, unless a man be born of water and the spirit, he cannot ever enter the kingdom of God. What is born of the flesh is flesh—of the physical is the physical; and what is born of the spirit is spirit. Marvel not—do not be surprised, astonished—at my telling you, you must be born again."[81]

The interesting question is why this text has always been interpreted as a call to baptism, and never regarded as literal support for belief in reincarnation. After all, Jesus quite clearly says it is the spirit or soul that must be born again, and not the body—which gives us the dualistic situation in which reincarnation occurs.

The third text is from Matthew, and it is the one in which Jesus asks his disciples who people think he is:

Now when Jesus came into the district of Caesari Phillipi, he asked his disciples, "Who do men say the Son of Man is?" And they said, "Some say John the Baptist, others say Elijah, and others Jeremiah or one of the prophets."[82]

Clearly, the disciples are saying that some people believe Jesus is the reincarnation of John the Baptist, Elijah, Jeremiah, or one of the prophets. But Jesus does not correct them and insist that the doctrine of reincarnation is false; rather, he makes the point that he existed before all the prophets.

Finally, also in Matthew, Jesus' disciples ask him how he can be the Messiah when Elijah has not yet returned. They are referring to the Old Testament prophesy made by Malachi to the effect that God will send Elijah back before the arrival of the Messiah. In this text, Jesus asserts that Elijah *has* returned in the person of John the Baptist:

As they went away, Jesus began to speak to the crowd concerning John. . . . "This is he of whom it is written, 'Behold I send my messenger before thy face, who shall prepare thy way before thee.' Truly I say to you, among those born of woman there has arisen no one greater than John the Baptist. . . . And if you are willing to accept it, he is Elijah who is to come. He who has ears to hear, let him hear.[83]

Thus there are a number of pointed texts in which Jesus not only does not object to the doctrine of reincarnation (when there is ample opportunity to do so), but also asserts the doctrine of reincarnation. Moreover, it also seems very clear from these texts that his disciples saw in reincarnation nothing at all incompatible with the teachings of Jesus. Nor are there any texts in the New Testament that explicitly or implicitly deny the doctrine of reincarnation. So, on the basis of scriptural evidence alone, why is reincarnation not a permissible, or even a mandated, belief for Christians? Alluding to these texts, MacGregor (and others) make a strong case for the doctrine's place in Christianity.

Tradition: Origen and the Early Church

Independent of the argument from scripture, it appears that up until A.D. 553 there was a strong commitment on the part of some Christians and some of the early Church Fathers to some form of reincarnation. Most notable of these advocates among the early Church Fathers were Justin Martyr and Origen. Origen is generally regarded as the most learned and the most original thinker of the early Christian Fathers; and even though all but a few of his written works were subsequently condemned and destroyed, his teachings had a commanding and long-standing effect on the early Christian community. Saint Gregory of Nyssa called Origen "The Prince of Christian Learning in the third century," and the *Encyclopaedia Britannica* claims that Origen was "the most prominent of the Church Fathers with the possible exception of Augustine." However much devoted to scriptural authority, Origen was also a Platonist of the sort that flourished for more than 400 years in Alexandria, where Origen was born and received his early Christian education.

Origen was born about A.D. 185 in Egypt, probably at Alexandria, and is said to have studied as a young man with Clement of Alexandria, who is also thought to have believed in reincarnation. Alexandria was the center of Neoplatonism, which included Plato's belief in reincarnation. When Clement fled the persecution of the Christians shortly after A.D. 202, he was succeeded by Origen as head of the catechetical school of Alexandria. Origen's father had been martyred during the persecution of A.D. 202 and Origen himself sought martyrdom, much to his mother's consternation. MacGregor notes that Origen's ascension to head of the catechetical school in Alexandria at such a young age is evidence of his renowned genius.[84] As a testament to his equally renowned self-discipline, incidentally, there is a much recounted (and often denied) story[85] to the effect that Origen emasculated himself in a literal acceptance of the gospel injunction.[86] At any rate, after a full life of teaching and writing, Origen was imprisoned by Decius in A.D. 250 during a state-inspired persecution of the Christians; he was tortured, and died a few years later.

Origen's teachings were very popular; but, for reasons we shall examine shortly, they became the object of considerable hostility on the part of other theologians for the next 200 years. Then, on May 5, 553, the Byzantine emperor Justinian the Great called a council of the whole Church, a convocation known as the Second Council of Constantinople or the Fifth Ecumenical Council of the Church. It is certainly worthy of mention here that—owing to the political machinations of Justinian (who controlled the council)—Pope Vigilius refused to attend. The decrees of the council are not clear, and (as MacGregor and others have noted) the actual extent to which Origen's teachings were condemned is quite unclear. Reincarnation per se was never condemned. Rather what *was* condemned—one of 14 doctrinal positions thusly rejected—was the doctrine of the preexistence of the soul and universal salvation. Whether belief in reincarnation was thereby implicitly condemned we shall discuss shortly. One of the major decrees of the council that, by implication, is supposed to have outlawed belief in reincarnation is the following:

> If anyone assert the fabulous preexistence of souls, and shall assert the monstrous restoration which follows from it: let him be anathema.[87]

This is sometimes regarded as a direct response to Origen's teaching on reincarnation, and especially to *De Principiis,* Origen's only remaining principal work in systematic theology (the rest having been destroyed after Origen's works were officially condemned in A.D. 400 by Theophilus, patriarch of Alexandria, in a council called at that city). Origen writes,

> Every soul . . . comes into this world strengthened by the victories or weakened by the defeats of its previous life. Its place in this world as a vessel appointed to honor or dishonor is determined by its previous merits or demerits. Its work in this world determines its place in the world which is to follow this.[88]

At any rate, after the Second Council of Constantinople, the Christian Church and the Christian community believed that reincarnation had been condemned by the Church in A.D. 553; and reincarnation came to be regarded as the doctrine of pagans inspired by Plato and the Gnostics, the latter being a heretical Mideast Christian sect flourishing in the deserts during and shortly after the time of Jesus. Later both the Council of Lyons in 1274 and the Council of Florence in 1439 simply assumed that belief in reincarnation had long ago been outlawed by the Church. But it is far from certain that this assumption was correct.

Although both Origen and Augustine were Platonists, Origen—unlike the later Augustine—believed firmly along with Plato that the human eternal soul preexists the perishable body as we know it, is cast into the perishable body, and transmigrates through different bodies until it has overcome the darkness of bodily existence and returns to God. Thus, in one of the very few remaining letters written by Origen (and quoted by Saint Jerome, who knew Origen personally and attacked him for believing in the transmigration of souls), he says,

> If it can be shown that an incorporeal and reasonable being has life independently of the body and that it is worse off in the body than out of it; then beyond a doubt bodies are only of secondary importance and arise from time to time to meet the varying conditions of reasonable creatures. Those who require bodies are clothed with them, and contrariwise, when fallen souls have lifted themselves up to better things their bodies are once more annihilated. They are thus ever vanishing and ever appearing.[89]

And elsewhere, in *Contra Celsum,* Origen writes,

> We do not talk about the resurrection, as Celsus imagines, because
> we have misunderstood the doctrine of reincarnation, but because
> we know that when the soul, which in its own nature is incorporeal
> and invisible, is in any material place, it requires a body suitable to
> the nature of that environment. In the first place, it bears this body
> after it has put off the former body which was necessary at first but
> which is now superfluous in its second state. In the second place, it
> puts a body on top of that which it possessed formerly, because it
> needs a better garment for the purer, ethereal, and heavenly regions.
> When it came to be born in this world, it put off the afterbirth,
> which was useful for its formation in the womb of the mother so
> long as it was within it; and underneath that it put on what was
> necessary for one that was about live on earth.[90]

And in the *De Principiis,* he clearly asserts the doctrine on the
preexistence of souls, as well as their need to transmigrate through
various bodily existences to achieve spiritual perfection:

> Whole nations of souls are stored away somewhere in a realm of
> their own, with an existence comparable to our bodily life, but in
> consequence of the fineness and mobility of their nature they are
> carried round with the whirl of the universe. . . . There the
> representations of evil and of virtue are set before them; and so long
> as a soul continues to abide in the good it has no experience of
> union with the body. . . . But by some inclination toward evil these
> souls lose their wings and come into bodies, first of men; then
> through their association with the irrational passions, after the
> allotted span of human life they are changed into beasts; from
> which they sink to the level of insensate nature. Thus, that which is
> by nature fine and mobile, namely the soul, first becomes heavy
> and weighted down, and because of its wickedness comes to dwell
> in a human body; after that, when the faculty of reason is extin-
> guished, it lives the life of an irrational animal, and finally even the
> gracious gift of sensation is withdrawn and it changes into the
> insensate life of a plant. From this condition it again rises through
> the same stages and is restored to its heavenly place.[91]

Interestingly enough, while Origen never denied the preexistence
of souls that take on different bodies relative to the merits or

demerits they freely achieved prior to entering human bodies, he did subsequently deny that he had ever adopted—rather than discussed seriously—the possibility of transmigration into bodies of thoughtless brutes or insensate plants.[92] Saint Jerome, and others who knew Origen well, ultimately rejected and attacked both views while ascribing them to Origen. As it is, however, in none of his extant works do we get a very clear endorsement of the view that the human soul transmigrates regularly into new human bodies in this world. For this reason, some commentators do not see Origen as adopting the concept of reincarnation in which some current human being lived as a human being in an earlier life with another human body. L. Chadwick, for example, claims that this concept of reincarnation is fatalistic, and that for this reason Origen explicitly rejected it.[93] And Jean Cardinal Daniélou agrees on that point, but nevertheless charges Origen with being corrupted by the Platonist theory of metempsychosis insofar as his views clearly imply that the soul has many existences before and after being in the body.[94] Other scholars, however, claim that in his extant writings Origen never denies the past-life-as-human view—a view most Neoplatonists from Alexandria accepted as a matter of fact.[95] All, in any case, generally agree that Origen was committed to the preexistence of souls that enter human bodies typically as a punishment for freely chosen sins committed in their disembodied state,[96] and that through a series of transmigrations all souls ultimately return to God purified.

But why exactly did the Church reject belief in reincarnation if, as we have shown, there is no scriptural justification for doing so and if, as we have also shown, many early Christians and Jesus himself certainly seemed to take the doctrine of reincarnation for granted? Scholars vary in their attempts to answer this question.

Some say it is simply a matter of what was required by Justinian in order to achieve political control over his empire. Most, however, say the rejection occurred for the good doctrinal reason that reincarnation carried with it a heavy dose of fatalism inconsistent with the freedom of choice necessary for belief in sin, merit, reward, and punishment. In the above-cited texts, Origen does not hesitate to assert that, to some degree, what happens in one's earlier lives determines what can happen in the present life. This suggested quite strongly to Saint Jerome and others that a good deal of what happens to us by way of our moral failures and successes need not be regarded as the product of free choice in this life. Most people who believed in reincarnation also believed in fatalism of a certain sort. In short, it was the doctrine of reincarnation insofar as it carried with it the belief in *karma* and its subsequent fatalism that caused the problem in the early Church.

But is this true of Origen? Did Origen's apparent belief in reincarnation carry with it a denial of freedom of choice? This is the important question; and it looks as though we will never know, because the few fragments of his work that escaped the flames were translated by friends (especially Rufinus) anxious not to have Origen viewed as a heretic, and there are serious questions about the validity of these translations.[97] As a matter of fact, for this reason there is still serious historical debate on whether Origen in fact taught any form of reincarnation rather than simply some form of the preexistence of souls, the latter not strictly entailing the former.

Nevertheless, if reincarnation could be divorced from a doctrine of fatalism that is inconsistent with freedom of choice, this form of reincarnation would not be objectionable for the philosophical reasons that reincarnation came to be rejected later in the Church. Presumably, those segments of Christianity that came after Luther, and that were happy to accept theological determinism as part of Christian doctrine, would not have any strong reason for rejecting reincarnation. Indeed, it is a mystery why those sects that deny freedom of choice are not open to belief in reincarnation as part of Christianity.

Prior to Luther, however, the Manichees and the Albigensians were roundly condemned by the Church partly because they believed in reincarnation, and because that belief carried with it the view that what a person does in one life has a determining effect on what happens in the next life. Such a view is akin to reincarnation with a heavy dose of karma because it asserts that one's freedom of choice is very much constrained by what one achieved or failed to achieve in one's earlier life or lives.

The question for us, however, is whether reincarnation, by definition, carries with it any particular view relating to freedom of choice or whether that aspect is something added to the doctrine and easily misunderstood as essential. Certainly, we may view the evidence offered by Stevenson and others as supporting belief in reincarnation, but yet need not make any statement at all on whether and to what degree anything that transpires in one's life undermines freedom of choice in the next. Moreover, there is no obvious reason to deny that, even if what one does in the life at hand determines in some way the capacities and talents one has in a subsequent life, it does not follow that one's freedom of choice is constrained thereby, although it may well mean that one will have different choices. We will return to this point shortly.

Philosophical Reasons

Apart from providing scriptural justification for belief in reincarnation, and apart from showing that the Church never in fact officially condemned belief in reincarnation, MacGregor argues the point that belief in reincarnation offers the best explanation for a world in which there is much undeserved suffering and misfortune. Without belief in reincarnation, the suffering of innocent persons seems to be arbitrary and unworthy of an all-good God Who wills that all people be saved and come to God. As MacGregor says,

> Reincarnationism takes care of the problem of moral injustice. To the age-old question of Job (why do the wicked prosper and the righteous suffer?) the reincarnationist has a ready answer: we are seeing, in this life, only a fragment of a long story. If you come in at the chapter in which the villain beats the hero to a pulp, of course you will ask the old question. You may even put down the book at that point and join forces with those who call life absurd, seeing no justice in the universe. That is because you are too impatient to go on to hear the rest of the story, which will unfold a much richer pattern in which the punishment of the wicked and the vindication of the righteous will be brought to light. Death is but the end of a chapter; it is not, as the nihilists suppose, the end of the story.[98]

For the reincarnationist who is a Christian, then, there is an answer to Job's question, and it is an answer consistent with the goodness of God and the doctrine of universal salvation. This last point, as we saw above, seems to have been part of the reason why Origen adopted reincarnation. And while it would have been nice if the Book of Job did not leave the question hanging, it certainly seems that many theologians are finding themselves empathetic to the doctrine primarily because, when properly understood, it provides for a degree of moral justice in the world—a degree of justice not obviously present, and fitting for an all-good God. In 1957 Dr. Leslie Weatherhead, a former president of the Methodist Conference of Great Britain, gave a lecture entitled "The Case for Reincarnation," in which he said,

> The intelligent Christian asks not only that life should be just, but that it should make sense. Does the idea of reincarnation help here? . . . If I failed to pass those examinations in life which can only be taken while I dwell in a physical body, shall I not have to come back and take them again?[99]

An Examination of MacGregor's Argument

The first part of MacGregor's argument—namely, that the New Testament has a number of persuasive texts supporting belief in reincarnation—is indeed convincing. Certainly, there are no texts in the New Testament that explicitly or implicitly reject belief in reincarnation. Also, with the possible exception of one, the texts cited above indicate that not only did Jesus and his disciples accept reincarnation without question, but also Jesus actually appeals to it when he asserts quite explicitly that John the Baptist is the reincarnation of Elijah. The one text cited above that admits of some possible difficulty is the one in which Jesus responds to Nicodemus and urges that, unless a person is born again, he will not enter the kingdom of heaven. The problem with this text is that it is somewhat ambiguous. Some have taken it to indicate that, unless one is baptized with water and thereby "spiritually" reborn, one will not enter the kingdom of heaven. Interestingly enough, however, the text supports a literal endorsement of rein- carnation equally well because it asserts that one's spirit (soul) must be reborn, and—since we obviously cannot do this by reentering the womb with our current bodies—there would seem to be no other way to get literally reborn except by the mechanism of reincarnation. Why is this not a more compelling understanding of the text? Moreover, if we add this text to the others cited above, the belief that Jesus was asserting the literal doctrine of reincarnation gains even more credibility. So, not only are there no texts in the New Testament prohibiting belief in reincarnation, there are a number that strongly support it as a core teaching of Jesus and his disciples. What still needs to be explained, however, is why there are not more frequent and explicit references to reincarnation in the Acts of the Apostles and in the letters of Saint Paul and Saint Timothy.

The second part of MacGregor's argument for reincarnation as an essentially Christian belief is that Origen and others (such as Justin Martyr) explicitly taught it and, even though Christendom after A.D. 553 rejected all forms of reincarnation, the truth of the matter is that the Church never *explicitly* condemned it. Moreover, to those who insist that reincarnation was *implicitly* condemned when the Second Council of Constantinople in A.D. 553 explicitly condemned the doctrine on the preexistence of souls, MacGregor (as well as some other Christian theologians) point out that the Council of 553 should not be accepted as a valid council of the Church. It was not called by the pope; and the condemnations issued in it were, primarily, politically inspired and hence more a reflection of what Justinian needed (while holding Pope Vigilius captive) to maintain political harmony. And even if the council's condemnations were valid, the question remains whether Origen's particular view on the nature of reincarnation was implicitly condemned, or whether what was condemned was a belief in reincarnation that undermined freedom of choice—a particular form of reincarnation we need not suppose that either Origen or Jesus and his disciples actually accepted and taught. In other words, even if the Church did in fact condemn reincarnation, the condemnation would extend only to those forms of reincarnation that are inconsistent with freedom of choice (and perhaps universal salvation), and hence not to those forms of reincarnation that do not suppose a denial of freedom of choice. What can we say about this part of MacGregor's argument?

To begin with, the fact that Justinian convened a Church council in A.D. 553 to resolve, in part, the differences between the Origenists and the anti-Origenists certainly seems to suggest quite strongly that there was a vigorous tradition beginning within the early Christian community that endorsed some form of reincarnation. The real reasons that precipitated the condemnation of 553, and even the reasons actually given at the council, are by no means clear and will need to be established by historians. Such an investigation may even bring to light that Origen did not teach reincarnation as we currently understand it. The best and most charitable conjecture at this point seems to be that sometime just after Origen there began to emerge the notion that reincarnation per se implied a heavy dose of karma and hence, by implication, a heavy dose of fatalism. Since fatalism denies freedom of choice, it is inconsistent with the concept of sin, just as it is inconsistent with rewards and punishments justly deserved. Because the early Christians believed in freedom of choice, rewards and punishments, and a set of commandments that one was morally obliged (under pain of eternal damnation) to follow, they could not accept reincarnation because they saw it as implying fatalism of a pernicious sort. Accordingly, if this is the basic reason for the implicit condemnation of reincarnation in A.D. 553 (and I submit that this could be the only sensible one), then, if the condemnation is to have any validity at all, it can only be valid to the extent that it implicitly condemns the form of belief in reincarnation that is inconsistent with freedom of choice. On this point MacGregor's thesis is well taken: even if we were to accept the Council of 553 as validly and implictly condemning belief in reincarnation, there would be no reason for thinking that the Church condemned all forms of reincarnation rather than all forms that imply a denial of freedom of choice.

Accordingly, given scripture and tradition, Christians who accept the validity of the condemnation of A.D. 553 are still at liberty to believe in any form of reincarnation that does not entail a repudiation of freedom of choice. Presumably, all those Christians who, after Luther, believe in divine predestination and thus do not require of Christianity a strong belief in freedom of choice will have no difficulty in accepting reincarnation even if it entails a heavy dose of fatalism. Therefore—however one looks at the issue—Christians everywhere are still at liberty to believe in reincarnation if reincarnation in its most defensible form neither requires nor repudiates freedom of choice. I hasten to add, of course, that the evidence Stevenson and others have uncovered in favor of reincarnation neither requires nor rejects belief in freedom of choice. It is consistent with either, whatever the truth of the matter turns out to be.

Whether Origen in fact taught a fatalistic form of reincarnation is difficult to say because, as mentioned earlier, most of his work was condemned and destroyed; and what *is* extant has been suspect because the earliest translators expressly changed what Origen wrote in order to protect him from the charge of heresy.[100] Even so, MacGregor notes that Cardinal Daniélou, in his famous work on Origen, says the whole of the Origenistic system depends on two principles: the love of God, and human freedom. Daniélou even claims that, for Origen, souls remain eternally free, and that the freedom they enjoy entails the possibility of further falls.[101] So, as a historical point, there is some reason for thinking that Origen's teaching may have been misunderstood and consequently not rejected by the condemnation for what it really asserted, rather than for a doctrine that would constrain freedom of choice.

Finally, the last part of MacGregor's argument is that belief in reincarnation is philosophically compelling because it satisfies our deepest need for justice. Indeed, as we said earlier, without belief in reincarnation we have difficulty explaining why there is so much undeserved suffering and so much undeserved good fortune, why the wicked often prosper and the righteous so often suffer. Certainly, anybody can see that some people are born into circumstances strongly disposing them to undeserved suffering and undeserved pain. How can an all-good and all-just God allow something like this to happen? Perhaps we are indeed only seeing one chapter in the book of their life, so to speak. And if each life has a certain moral lesson, then it is to be expected that we too will need to learn the moral lesson that comes with suffering undeserved pain and shame, or the moral lesson that comes with exercising power over other people, or the moral lesson that is learned from dying painfully and young, and so on.

Of course, why a Being Who is all good and simultaneously all powerful would need to revert to a painful method for teaching moral truths is a deeper problem that MacGregor does not confront.

In any case, belief in reincarnation does have the decided advantage of lending credibility to the doctrine of universal salvation—the view that God wills that everybody be saved. It does this in a way that supports freedom of choice, by allowing that the lessons one learns in each life are in important ways the product of free choice, and that in time—sooner or later—we will learn whatever lessons we need to learn in order to return to God permanently.

In the end, the Christian must believe in a God Who is all good and all loving, a God Who wills that everybody achieve eternal beatitude and rest in the presence of God. In the absence of believing in some form of reincarnation wherein, as a result of various moral lessons learned in and through different incarnations, we escape the wheel of rebirth and return to the presence of God, it is hard to justify the belief that there is an all-good, all-loving God Who wills that everybody be saved. This then is the sort of reasoning MacGregor and others have in mind when they urge that belief in reincarnation allows us to explain the presence of undeserved suffering and apparent wickedness in a world created by an all-good and all-loving God. Incidentally, this sort of reasoning was also behind Origen's appeal to reincarnation; and in virtue of it, he argued that even the fallen angels, including Lucifer himself, will ultimately be saved by God.[102]

The last part of MacGregor's argument, then, certainly seems attractive as a way of answering Job's question. In fact, no doubt many a Christian will find belief in the core components of Christianity acceptable only if it carries with it the doctrine of universal salvation and something like the mechanism of reincarnation as the way in which such salvation is achieved. Belief in some form of reincarnation would make it considerably easier to accept the idea of an all-good, all-just God Who wills that everybody be saved. Along with MacGregor and others, I too think this constitutes a persuasive reason (in addition to the reasons based on scripture and tradition) for any Christian to believe in reincarnation.

Reincarnation and the Future of Christianity

If, as we saw earlier, the evidence Ian Stevenson uncovers for reincarnation is neither philosophical nor theological but rather purely empirical, and if the belief in reincarnation turns out to be as empirically well established as the belief in the past existence of dinosaurs, then the Christian community will need to adjust its attitude toward reincarnation. Otherwise, Christianity has the makings of the Galileo fiasco all over again.

No doubt, the Christian community has been primarily responsible for the unpopularity of the belief in reincarnation in the West. And as long as that belief appeared to be the object of either philosophical or theological speculation and reasoning, the Church could resist it with equanimity. But what is surprising is the thoroughly empirical force of the evidence that has emerged recently and continues to emerge primarily as a result of Stevenson's research. If, as we have urged, there are sound scriptural, traditional, and philosophical reasons for Christians to endorse the belief in reincarnation, and even stronger reasons to think that there is nothing inconsistent with believing in the core doctrines of Christianity and simultaneously believing in some form of reincarnation, then there should be little further resistance on the part of Christians to the belief in reincarnation.

Admittedly, the Christian community will need to acknowledge that, since the Council of 553, Christianity has not endorsed reincarnation for various historical reasons that seemed sound at the time. But the truth of the matter is that we can no longer view them as sound reasons for rejecting all forms of the belief in reincarnation, rather than those forms explicitly in conflict with the Church's core doctrines.

In the end—any way we view it—Christians are at liberty to accept reincarnation to the extent that its definition does not extend beyond the evidence for its nature, the evidence painstakingly uncovered recently and continuing to be uncovered by people such as Ian Stevenson.

Conclusion: The Emergence of Scientific Evidence for Reincarnation

With the sophistication of science, the advent of regression therapy, and the general perception of the difference between insanity and moral (or philosophical) distinctiveness in human thought and behavior, a new willingness to consider alleged cases of reincarnation under the empirical methods of science has recently brought forward a body of evidence that establishes the validity of the belief in reincarnation. What is impressive about the cases compiled by Stevenson and others is that, taken seriously, their tendency to establish the doctrine of reincarnation outstrips philosophical biases and theological dogmas. By way of implication, they also tend to render obsolete several long-standing philosophical disputes.

Indeed, one of the most notable consequences of these findings is that, if we accept them as compelling evidence for reincarnation, we resolve all the disputes that raged heretofore around the mind–body question (that question being whether there are separate minds as traditionally understood or whether an adequate explanation of human nature can be had simply by appeal to physical matter and the laws of physics). Further, this suggests that the future of philosophical discussion should be oriented more toward questions of ethics or toward what the larger implications of personal survival after death may be.

This is not to say, however, that in the interest of predicting and controlling human behavior there may not continue to be long-standing disputes on what shape the future of psychology and psychiatry should take. As a matter of fact, we may still (and doubtless will) argue over just *what* it is that survives death and is so essential to human personality. But it is to say that where the doctrine of reincarnation is established, the nature, tone, and direction of philosophical speculation on the nature of human personhood will need to take a dramatic turn into different paths. Different sets of questions will become more pressing. How long, how frequently, and to what end does the process of reincarnation occur? What will count as a method of resolving disputes among the conflicting answers to these questions? Will we need to accept the fact that in these matters the human mind is radically incapable of providing clear answers and that, as a result, there will always be more questions asked in this life than we can ever answer—even if we endure in a scientific spirit forever? Whether this last question can ever be answered is, of course, also an important question.

Unscientific Postscript: The Problem of Personal Identity

With the help of A. J. Ayer, we saw earlier that if a man claimed to be Julius Caesar reincarnated, we would be free to accept that claim if the man had all the memories we would ordinarily expect of Julius Caesar, along with some memories that only Julius Caesar could have. Of course, these memory claims would need to be verified. Moreover, if the man conveyed this information in fairly fluent Caesarian Latin or played well an instrument we know Caesar played, and if we could also establish that the man had never learned Latin or how to play the instrument, we would have commanding evidence for reincarnation. On the other hand, refusal to accept this man's verified memory claims and acquired skills (unlearned in this life) as strong evidence for reincarnation would constitute a dogmatic refusal to accept any and all evidence for reincarnation.

Interestingly enough—and something we might have discussed earlier when we introduced Ayer's thought experiment—some people have argued that, while personal identity is basically a matter of having a certain set of systematically coherent memories, personal discarnate survival (and, by implication, reincarnation) is quite impossible because bodily continuity is necessary for having a memory. According to this view—a view proposed by Terence Penelum for one[103]—it makes no sense whatever to suggest that memory, or a systematic set of personal memories, could survive bodily corruption.

Penelhum's argument begins by asserting that a person can remember something only if his or her memory claim is true. He then says why no account of disembodied identity can be given.

> This requires that we should be able to distinguish between those occasions when what someone thinks he remembers actually happened to him, and those occasions when they did not. This we cannot do in terms of the recollections themselves. There has to be some independent way of determining that the person who did or experienced what Smith believes he remembers doing or experiencing was, or was not, Smith himself. And this, it seems, has to be his physical presence at the occasion in question.[104]

There are at least two basic rejoinders to this argument. First, we can surely infer from the nature of the recollections themselves that the person was there, because there may be no other way to account for his or her knowing what in fact took place when there is no public record of that event and when nobody except somebody who was there could possibly know about it. For example, if Jones claims to remember having hidden his pocket knife in a certain location, and if we can ascertain that nobody knows where the pocket knife is and that there is no public or private record of the event, then we are certainly at liberty, upon finding the knife where Smith says it is, to conclude that Smith remembers where the knife was hidden—even if the knife is determined to have been hidden many years before Smith, as we know him, was born. Similarly, there are memories that only Napoleon could have had; and if somebody claims to remember those things that only Napoleon could remember, the belief in reincarnation explains how he could have this information and experience it as a memory or a recollection.

Second, Penelhum's argument is as smooth an example of question begging as we are ever likely to see. After all—granting that in order to determine whether a man, say, remembers (rather than falsely claims to remember) something or other, we must establish that he was present at the events remembered—who is to say that, when determining whether "he" was at the event professedly remembered, the personal pronoun *he* must refer to his present body rather than to one he previously occupied? Is this not precisely the question at issue? Is this not, for example, precisely what the data from cases suggestive of reincarnation question? Is not the reincarnationist who bases her or his belief on the sort of data provided by Stevenson trying to find an explanation for the apparently baffling fact that some people seem to remember events they could not possibly have been present to so long as we construe personal identity in terms of bodily continuity? If the only response we can offer is that they do not in fact remember what they claim to remember because it is impossible that one could remember anything before one was born into one's present life, then the reincarnationist wants to know precisely why we should adopt an a priori interpretation of memory that would make reincarnation (as well as discarnate survival generally) conceptually impossible when in all other respects the hypothesis of reincarnation fits an important body of data not otherwise capable of explanation.

The reincarnationist, then, is recommending that we not too quickly assume an interpretation of the definition of memory that makes both reincarnation and discarnate survival conceptually impossible, rather than look at the data and see whether it might make sense to understand the definition of memory in a way that is at least neutral to the question of survival and reincarnation. Openness to the empirical data allows us to infer that memory may or may not be tied to bodily continuity. And it may also lead us to believe that indeed so-and-so must have been present at the physical event he claims to remember (because there is no other way to explain the accuracy and richness of what he claims to remember), but obviously he could not have been there in his current body. Why should we not regard the belief in reincarnation as the best available interpretation of the empirical facts in the richer cases offered by Stevenson and, as such, a forceful repudiation of precisely that interpretation of memory in which one can only remember those events one witnesses during one's current lifetime as a biological organism. In the end, then, our second reason for rejecting Penelhum's argument is that it begs the question against survival in general and against reincarnation in particular.

Our own interest in the problems of personal identity that the doctrine of reincarnation engenders is directed toward demonstrating how fertile a field for psychological and philosophical study has been opened up by the evidence offered in the richer cases. But to return to Ayer's man who says he is Julius Caesar reincarnated, we noted earlier that the evidence provided by this hypothetical situation seems equally consistent with simple possession; and often the same evidence that would count for one seems to count just as strongly for the other. This should not be so surprising, because possession is a form of reincarnation. However, we saw that, in the richest cases of the reincarnation type, the subject does not typically and persistently claim to be Julius Caesar, for example, but only to remember having lived as

Julius Caesar, and now has some of the memories that only Julius Caesar could have. Even so, there are quite frequently cases in which the children insist on identifying themselves fully with the previous personality and even rebuke others for not recognizing them as the former personality, forgetting that they are in a new small body. So, in order actually for the sort of evidence noted in Ayer's hypothetical situation to count for reincarnation, it can only be in those cases where the subject at least sometimes claims to remember having lived as Julius Caesar in a previous life. But at this point, some very perplexing philosophical questions emerge, and it is by no means clear just how to answer them. Some philosophers think these questions need to be answered before we can justifiably feel confident that all the material amassed in the above-described case studies do count for justifying the belief in reincarnation. What are some of these questions?

To begin with, what about the man who claims to remember having lived as Julius Caesar? Do we say that the man making the claim *is* Julius Caesar? Well, if the person had all *and only* the memories of Julius Caesar (as is alleged to occur in some cases of possession), that would certainly follow. But in the Bishen Chand case (and other such richer cases of the reincarnation type), the subject seems to have an identity and memories that Laxmi Narain could not have had—unless the subject simply *is* Laxmi Narain continuing his life in a new body and acquiring new beliefs and memories while in this new body. If so, we would expect the subjects in such cases to identify themselves accordingly. We would expect them to say something such as "I am Laxmi Narain, here to continue my former existence." And certainly such locutions do often occur. Sometimes we hear subjects say, "I used to live in such and such a place, and I did such and such." But we also hear other expressions—expressions that seem to imply the subject is not Laxmi Narain, for instance, but remembers having lived as Laxmi Narain without now being Laxmi Narain. So, is it Laxmi Narain remembering that he lived an earlier life and is now continuing that life with additional memories derived from his life in a new body designated by the name *Bishen Chand?* Or is it another person, Bishen Chand, part of whose personality contains the personality of the former Laxmi Narain? Would Bishen

Chand's memories of this life, in other words, be simply Laxmi Narain continuing in a new body (which has picked up a new name) and adding more memories to the memories of Laxmi Narain? It seems very natural to describe the phenomenon in this way. But might it not also be that Bishen Chand is a distinctly different person who has subsumed as part of his own identity the person Laxmi Narain was? It seems equally natural to describe the phenomenon this way. But it cannot be both.

In the end, for any number of reasons we may need to decide which way to describe it, and it is unclear that this can be decided by appeal to the facts in the cases studied. Even if we ask the people in these cases how they would describe it, it is very possible that their answers would be philosophically loaded or the product of some antecedent bias. But perhaps we ourselves can use a philosophical approach to determine which way to describe it.

Suppose for the sake of discussion that the second way of describing the phenomenon is correct, that is, the person Laxmi Narain was exists simply as a subset of the personality of Bishen Chand or is subsumed into the identity of Bishen Chand. Is there any separate person to be identified with the name *Bishen Chand?* Is Bishen Chand one person rather than the collection of two persons? Is the person Bishen Chand simply the composite of both the person Laxmi Narain and whatever other person is to be identified with the memories that are not the memories of Laxmi Narain? If only to have an adequate theory of human personality, it seems important to answer this question. But how is the question to be answered? It is difficult to say. All we can discern at this point is that the problem per se seems to emerge as a result of taking the second description.

Suppose, on the other hand, that for the sake of discussion the first way of describing the phenomenon is correct, that is, Bishen Chand is actually Laxmi Narain continuing on in a new body and adding more memories and dispositions to his existing personality. Given this first description, when we ask Bishen Chand "Who are you?" and he responds "Bishen Chand," what has he told us? Has he told us who he is? Certainly not, because we want to know who the person Bishen Chand really is. The name *Bishen Chand* simply designates a body that some person occupies—a person evolving through various reincarnations and therefore in transit, as it were. Moreover, we will not know who Bishen Chand really is until we get beyond asking "And who is he?" or "And who is she?" When we get back to the original person who began the reincarnation process, however, we now have a problem. Is that person really the person Bishen Chand is? Hardly. The person Bishen Chand now is cannot be identified with the person who started the process. The memories Bishen Chand has now are dramatically different from the memories of the original person. But if this is so, can we ever identify who anybody is?

Even though these problems have less to do with the strength of the evidence for reincarnation than they have to do with the logic of identity, special sorts of problems will emerge depending on just what we mean when we say, "So-and-so is the reincarnation of so-and-so." The evidence supports one of the above descriptions, and not both. But one of them may be more philosophically acceptable on the grounds that accepting one of the descriptions leads either to a peculiar kind of absurdity (such as "nobody knows who anybody is") or a theory of human personality that could not in fact be true (because we cannot say what a person is).

There are other questions, besides. Consider the following. If you reincarnate, will you be the same person in your next body as you now are? In a sense yes, and in a sense no. If you have essentially the same traits and memories in the next body, yes; if you add dramatically to those traits and memories because of being in that body, no. But if the latter occurs, will the person you now are disappear? Yes, in the same way that something may evolve into something it now very much is not. One's personality would not so much disappear from the earth as it would evolve into something very unlike what it formerly was. But this is not to suggest that people do not survive death as persons; for we often become persons very much different from the persons we were. Still, something essential to us must remain throughout the process. However, it is difficult to say what this something is.

But of course (and here is the rub), if it is hard to say what this something is, how can we be so sure what we should take as evidence that the man before us (or the lady beside us) is the reincarnation of Julius Caesar? Intuitively we do not seem to have any problem with this, because most philosophers agree at least on memory as a criterion of personal identity. That is why the reincarnation hypothesis is so persuasive as a way of explaining the rich cases described in this chapter. But a number of philosophical questions about identity remain, and even though we may not be able to say precisely what human personality is, our core intuitions about what counts for identifying distinct personalities are sufficient to sustain the belief that human personality in some important measure survives and sometimes, in some way and to some degree, reincarnates. Whether the reincarnated person is just the former person with a new body, or whether the reincarnated person is in some way a distinct personality that has subsumed into itself the former person without losing its own identity, or whether the reincarnated person is a composite in the way indicated above—this is arguably all academic because, however we decide, it will be on the basis that reincarnation does in some interesting way occur.

Notes

1. Ian Stevenson, *Twenty Cases Suggestive of Reincarnation,* 2nd ed. (Charlottesville: University Press of Virginia, 1974).

2. For the original details on this case, see Ian Stevenson, "The Case of Bishen Chand Kapoor," in *Cases of the Reincarnation Type,* vol. 1: *Ten Cases in India* (Charlottesville: University Press of Virginia, 1975), pp. 176ff.

3. Ibid., p. 177.

4. Ibid., p. 178.

5. Arthur Guirdham, *The Cathars and Reincarnation* (London: Neville Spearman, 1970).

6. Ibid., p. 108.

7. Ibid., p. 10.

8. Ibid., pp. 73–84.

9. Ibid., pp. 107ff.

10. Ibid., pp. 125ff.

11. Ibid., pp. 94–95.

12. Ibid., p. 89.

13. Arthur Guirdham, "Reincarnation and the Practice of Medicine," lecture delivered at the College of Psychic Science, London, March 1969, unpublished. See also Guirdham, *Cathars,* pp. 92ff.

14. Ian Stevenson, *Xenoglossy* (Charlottesville: University Press of Virginia, 1974).

15. Ian Stevenson, *Unlearned Language* (Charlottesville: University Press of Virginia, 1984), ch. 1. Incidentally, we will not discuss here the Sharada case, the second case discussed in *Unlearned Language*. The Sharada case is different in that the communicating spirit was not induced by hypnosis, stayed for long periods of time, and spoke Bengali with incontrovertible fluency.

16. Stevenson, *Xenoglossy*.

17. Stevenson, *Unlearned Language,* ch. 1.

18. Ibid., appendix.

19. Incidentally, Stevenson in ibid., p. 33, claims that Gretchen introduced no fewer than 237 words, 120 of them spoken in ten sessions before anybody spoke German to her; and on p. 37, he offers a list of well-formed German phrases and expressions spoken before anybody spoke German to her.

20. Ibid., p. 11.

21. Ibid., p. 15.

22. The Shanti Devi case is originally described in L. D. Gupta, N. R. Sharma, and T. C. Mathur, *An Inquiry into the Case of Shanti Devi* (Delhi, India: International Aryan League, 1936). See also S. C. Bose, *A Case of Reincarnation* (Ligate, Satsang, S.P., 1952). For other references on this case, see Stevenson, *Twenty Cases,* p. 17, n. 6. Incidentally, although Jane Singer, "The Return of a Woman Who Died in Childbirth," in Martin Ebon, ed., *Reincarnation in the Twentieth Century* (New York: Signet Books, 1969), pp. 42–48, describes the Shanti Devi case as one in which the subject exhibits an ability to speak a foreign dialect not learned in the subject's current life, Ian Stevenson claims, in correspondence with the author, that Shanti Devi's alleged capacity to speak in an unlearned foreign dialect is not verified and, for that reason, should not be regarded as a feature of the case. The point is well taken and constitutes another reason why we will not use it later on as a verified case for critical discussion.

23. See note 15 above.

24. For details on the Swarnlata case, see Stevenson, *Twenty Cases,* pp. 78ff.

25. Stevenson, *Xenoglossy,* p. 14.

26. Stevenson, *Twenty Cases,* pp. 80–83.

27. Melvin Harris, "Are Past-life Regressions Evidence of Reincarnation?" *Free Inquiry* (Fall 1986).

28. Stevenson, *Twenty Cases,* p. 80.

29. Ibid., p. 342.

30. Ian Stevenson, *Cases of the Reincarnation Type,* vol. 3: *Twelve Cases in Lebanon* (Charlottesville: University Press of Virginia, 1980), p. 359n.

31. Sarah Thomason, "Past Tongues Remembered," *Skeptical Inquirer* 11, no. 4 (Summer 1987).

32. For a fuller statement of Thomason's argument, my reply, and her subsequent answer to my reply, see the *Skeptical Inquirer* 12, no. 3 (Spring 1988).

33. See note 15 above.

34. Ian Stevenson, *Children Who Remember Previous Lives* (Charlottesville: University Press of Virginia, 1987), pp. 150–53.

35. Ian Stevenson, *Cases of the Reincarnation Type,* vol. 1: *Ten Cases in India* (Charlottesville: University Press of Virginia, 1975).

36. Stevenson, *Children,* pp. 150–53.

37. Paul Edwards, "Reincarnation," *Free Inquiry* (June 1987), pp. 24–48.

38. Ibid., p. 26; emphasis added.

39. Ibid., p. 28.

40. Ibid., p. 27, citing Ian Wilson, *Mind Out of Time* (London: Victor Gollancz, 1981), pp. 58–60.

41. Ibid.

42. Edwards, "Reincarnation," p. 27, citing William Roll, "The Changing Perspectives on Life after Death," in S. Krippner, ed., *Advances in Parapsychological Research,* vol. 3 (Metuchen, N.J.: Scarecrow Press, 1982).

43. Edwards, "Reincarnation," p. 28, citing Roll, "Changing Perspectives," p. 199.

44. Edwards, "Reincarnation," p. 27.

45. Edwards, "Reincarnation," p. 27, citing C. T. K. Chari, "Reincarnation Research: Method and Interpretation," in Martin Ebon, ed., *The Signet Handbook of Parapsychology* (New York: New American Library, 1978), p. 319.

46. Edwards, "Reincarnation," p. 28.

47. Stevenson, *Twenty Cases,* pp. 80–81.

48. Stevenson, *Children,* pp. 215–16.

49. Edwards, "Reincarnation," p. 27.

50. See Stevenson's *Xenoglossy, Children,* and *Unlearned Language.*

51. Stevenson, *Children,* pp. 215–16.

52. An estimate of the number of similar cases as well as other pertinent information is contained in N. Hintze and J. G. Pratt's *The Psychic Realm: What Can You Believe?* (New York: Random House, 1975). In the chapter "Memories of Another Life," p. 251, which touches on Stevenson's research, Hintze and Pratt report that "as of July 1974 the

files on reincarnation cases in the University of Virginia, Division of Parapsychology, contained a total of 1339 distinct instances of persons claiming such memories that had been reported directly to the investigator or to his associates in the field." In 1990 the most recent census revealed—according to Stevenson, in correspondence with the author—about 2,400 cases in the files. And although it is true that most of these cases come from the East where belief in reincarnation is strong, some of the cases come from the United States. In the West, there is a strong tendency to ignore and suppress statements from children about the time previous to birth. Even so, the number of cases in the United States, Australia, England, and Western Europe is growing. For a discussion on recent American cases, see Ian Stevenson, "American Children Who Claim to Remember Previous Lives," *Journal of Nervous and Mental Disease* 171, no. 12 (1983), pp. 742–49.

Moreover, Stevenson's results have been independently replicated in India by an independent researcher using Stevenson's current methodology in new cases. On this latter point, see Antonia Mills, "A Replication Study: Three Cases of Children in Northern India Who Are Said to Remember a Previous Life," *Journal of Scientific Exploration* 3, no. 2 (1989), pp. 133–84. Mills is also in the process of replicating Stevenson's results in a population of North American Indians living in British Columbia, Canada.

53. See, for example, Stephen Braude, *ESP and Psychokinesis* (Philadelphia: Temple University Press, 1979); and Hintze and Pratt, *Psychic Realm*.

54. See S. I. Franz, *Persons One and Three: A Study in Multiple Personalities* (New York: McGraw-Hill, 1933); M. H. Congdon, J. Hain, and I. Stevenson, "A Case of Multiple Personality," *Journal of Nervous and Mental Disease* 132 (1961), pp. 497–504; and C. H. Thigpen and H. M. Cleckley, *The Three Faces of Eve* (New York: McGraw-Hill, 1957).

55. Chari, "Reincarnation Research," p. 315. See also C. T. K. Chari, "Regression 'Beyond Birth,' " *Tomorrow* 6 (1958), and "Buried Memories in Survivalist Research," *International Journal of Parapsychology* 4 (1962). The same objection is offered by Martin Ebon, *Reincarnation in the Twentieth Century* (New York: Signet, 1969), p. 7; and by Louisa Rhine, "Review of Ian Stevenson, *Twenty Cases Suggestive of Reincarnation,*" *Journal of Parapsychology* 30, no. 4 (December 1966), pp. 263–72.

56. Hintze and Pratt, *Psychic Realm,* p. 243.

57. Ibid., p. 5.

58. Stevenson, *Children,* pp. 154–56.

59. Hintze and Pratt, *Psychic Realm,* p. 5.

60. Stevenson, *Twenty Cases,* pp. 343–44.

61. Jule Eisenbud, *Parapsychology and the Unconscious* (Berkeley, Calif.: North Atlantic Books, 1983), ch. 14.

62. See Stephen Braude, *Limits,* pp. 27–28.

63. Stephen Braude, "Evaluating the Super-psi Hypothesis," in George Zollschan, John Schumaker, and Greg Walsh, eds., *Exploring the Paranormal: Perspectives on Belief and Experience* (Dorset, England: Prism Press, 1989), p. 25.

64. Stephen Braude, *The Limits of Influence* (London: Routledge and Kegan Paul, 1986), pp. 27–28.

65. Rodger Anderson, as cited in ibid., p. 28.

66. Braude, *Limits,* p. 33.

67. Ibid., p. 35.

68. See Stevenson, *Twenty Cases,* pp. 91–105 and 149–71.

69. Ian Stevenson, *Birthmarks and Birth Defects: A Contribution to Their Etiology* (New York: Paragon House Publishers, 1992).

70. The justification for this idealizing condition lay in the fact that its satisfaction would diminish the force of the objection that the subject subconsciously identifies and impersonates the deceased person's traits clairvoyantly grasped, as discussed earlier in this chapter. For further discussion on the rationale behind this condition, see Stevenson, *Twenty Cases,* pp. 169ff and 359–60.

71. See Stevenson, *Twenty Cases,* pp. 145ff. Here again, this idealizing condition has for its purpose to distinguish between the psychiatric phenomenon identified with multiple personality or alternating personality and cases of reincarnation in which the subject claims to be an extension of the previous personality, as discussed earlier in this chapter.

72. See Stevenson, *Twenty Cases,* pp. 366–72.

73. See ibid., pp. 145ff.

74. A. J. Ayer, *The Problem of Knowledge* (Baltimore: Penguin Books, 1962), ch. 5.

75. Ibid., pp. 194ff.

76. In Robert Almeder, *Beyond Death* (Springfield, Ill.: Charles C Thomas, 1987), I erred in suggesting that we could test for the *universality* of reincarnation by taking a random number of people who are capable of being regressed in trance—people who do not, in their ordinary state of mind, claim to have had an earlier life—and then seeing whether they could, under trance, come up with memory claims of past lives, claims independently verified and not the product of telepathy or clairvoyance. I noted that, presumably, those living their first life would not have such memories under regression. Given such an experiment, we would expect

some subjects (how many cannot be said) to have no memories of a past life—unless these reincarnations go on forever, and it is hard to say what will count scientifically for showing that they do. So, failure to come up with rich cases under such a procedure would not falsify the hypothesis, but the development of more rich cases under this experimental procedure would certainly add confirmatory value to the existing hypothesis. The only problem is that, if under this hypothesis we failed to get any rich independently confirmed cases, we would need to regard the hypothesis as falsified—because if the hypothesis of reincarnation were true, we would expect the occurrence of a certain number of such cases under this experimental procedure if it were conducted sufficiently frequently under the proper conditions.

Ian Stevenson has noted, in correspondence with the author, that this proposed test is not sound because it falsely presupposes that the method of hypnotic regression is a reasonably reliable technique for inducing independently verifiable past-life memories. If Stevenson is right, then certainly a failure to come up with rich independently verified cases under the above experimental procedure over a long period of time would *not* disconfirm the hypothesis. His advice is to continue looking for the cases in which the subjects come up with past-life memories spontaneously, because those are the cases that have proven to be the richest in terms of independently verified evidence. Ostensibly, Stevenson's point is that while hypnotic regression as a methodology may very infrequently produce some independently verifiable past-life memories, it is unreliable as a general methodology because, in any given case, failure to come up with the rich past-life memories is quite consistent with the hypothesis being true. In light of this sensible rejoinder, I now abandon that earlier suggestion for demonstrating the universality of reincarnation.

77. Stevenson, *Children,* pp. 213–15.

78. Geddes MacGregor, *Reincarnation in Christianity: A New Vision of the Role of Rebirth in Christian Thought* (New York: Barnes and Noble, 1978).

79. John 9:1–2.

80. John 9:3.

81. John 3:3–7.

82. Matthew 16:13–14. This text is also found at Mark 8:27–28 and at Luke 9:18–19.

83. Matthew 11:7–15.

84. MacGregor, *Reincarnation in Christianity,* p. 49.

85. Ibid.

86. See Matthew 19:12.

87. As cited at MacGregor, *Reincarnation in Christianity*, p. 64. See also Joseph Head and S. L. Cranston, *Reincarnation, the Phoenix Fire Mystery* (New York: Crown, 1977), pp. 144–48, 156–60.

88. Origen, *De Principiis,* trans. H. DeLubac (New York: Harper and Row, 1966), p. 134.

89. Ibid., p. 325, n. 1.

90. Origen, *Contra Celsum,* trans. L. Chadwick (Cambridge, England: Cambridge University Press, 1965), bk. 7, sec. 32, at p. 420.

91. Origen, *De Principiis,* p. 72.

92. Origen, *Contra Celsum,* bk. 3, sec. 75, at p. 179.

93. L. Chadwick, *Early Christian Thought and the Classical Tradition* (New York: Oxford University Press, 1966), p. 82.

94. Jean Cardinal Daniélou, *Origen,* trans. W. Mitchell (New York: Sheed and Ward, 1965), pp. 249ff and 288ff.

95. See J. W. Tregg, *Origen* (Atlanta, Ga.: John Knox Press, 1949), p. 67.

96. Origen, *De Principiis,* bk. 2, ch. 9, at p. 134, and bk. 4, ch. 3, at p. 303, see esp. n. 3.

97. Ibid., preface by DeLubac.

98. MacGregor, *Reincarnation in Christianity*, p. 5.

99. Leslie Weatherhead, "The Case for Reincarnation," in *The Christian Agnostic* (London: Hodder and Stoughton, 1965), p. 26.

100. MacGregor, *Reincarnation in Christianity*, p. 58.

101. Ibid., p. 52.

102. Ibid., pp. 53ff.

103. Terence Penelhum, *Survival and Disembodied Existence* (New York: Humanities Press, 1970). See also Sidney Shoemaker, "Persons and Their Past," *American Philosophical Quarterly* (October 1970).

104. Penelhum, *Survival,* p. 56.

2

Apparitions of the Dead

Some people believe that the best evidence for post-mortem personal survival appears in certain case studies involving apparitions of the dead. They say that disembodied persons survive biological death because people sometimes "see" them. Doubtless, some people have what we may call "apparitional experiences of the dead," but whether in these experiences people see disembodied persons or whether even what they see is evidence for believing that there are postmortem disembodied persons is by no means clear. For most of us, such claims are perplexing. After all, how could a disembodied person appear to someone so that the person appears precisely like the deceased before death? Indeed, if being such a disembodied personality means not having a body, how could such a personality appear as though it were in possession of its original body? Frequently people claim that apparitions of the dead appear so real that they are misidentified and mistaken for the original person by a viewer who does not know that the person in question is dead. Is this possible? If so, is there any evidence for its occurrence? May we explain these frequently reported "apparitions of the dead" without having to believe in some form of personal survival after death? Might they not all be very interesting but nonetheless hallucinatory experiences of a special sort? In this chapter we will examine and assess some of the best available evidence bearing on apparitions of the dead. The conclusion this chapter offers is that, while we can easily dismiss the vast majority of such experiences under the rubric of hallucination, or delusion, or hoax, or fraud, nevertheless

97

there are a number of cases that we cannot so dismiss. These cases constitute plausible evidence for some form of postmortem personal survival even though people having these apparitional experiences may not be seeing what they think they see.

Collective and Iterative Apparitions of the Dead

For the sake of discussion, let us define *ghost* as *a disembodied spirit identifiable as the postmortem surviving personality of a deceased human.* This is a popular definition. Later we shall examine and reject this definition for one offered by F. W. H. Myers in his 1903 classic *Human Personality and Its Survival of Bodily Death.*[1] But for now, we need not enter into the reasons why the popular definition is not quite correct. The basic question is whether, on the basis of direct and immediate apparitional experiences, we can certify that there are ghosts as popularly defined, that is, whether there are postmortem surviving persons or person-parts.

Presumably, if only one man testifies to seeing a ghost on one occasion only, then we have no compelling reason to accept this man's testimony as good evidence for the existence of the disembodied person that the man saw. We may well grant, for the sake of discussion, that he indeed had an apparitional experience. Of itself, however, his apparitional experience does not require of us that we believe such entities exist just because he believes they do on the basis of his experience. Given the extraordinary nature of his claim, it seems more likely that his experience is in some sense delusional or hallucinatory. The very idea that one could see directly a disembodied person seems to be a contradiction in terms.

Suppose, however, that a number of people, gathered for some specific purpose, *all* claim to have had quite unexpectedly the same apparitional experience of a deceased person; and suppose also that this phenomenon occurred only once. We call this a "group apparition" or a "collective apparition." Should we accept their testimony that they saw a postmortem and surviving personality and that therefore such entities exist?

There is always some real possibility of an undetectable hoax or fraud when the testimony is of an event that occurs only once. For the sake of argument, however, just suppose that we are able to discount the possibility of intentional deceit on the part of those testifying to the apparition. Should we then accept the testimony as evidence for the existence of a disembodied postmortem person? Not really. While collective testimony from honest and thoughtful persons may be seldom mistaken, still there is some evidence that such mistakes do occur. In the past, for example, a large number of people have testified to the one-time appearance of UFOs when in fact we subsequently came to explain the testimony in terms of an honest but mistaken belief based on unusual but natural atmospheric conditions distorting natural light from various astral bodies. Similarly, there is ample evidence that a number of people have mistakenly believed—on what they all testified to as seeing with their very own eyes—that oases exist in certain parts of the Sahara Desert. Thus, an equally plausible explanation for a collective sighting of a disembodied deceased person on one occasion is that the group had a collective but mistaken belief that what they saw was a ghost. Here again, given the extraordinary nature of the claim, it seems more plausible to suppose some sort of perceptual error, or visual hallucination, or illusion of some sort.

Also, for all we know, some collective desire unknown even to the members of the group may well have caused the experience of "seeing" a postmortem disembodied person on this one occasion, when in fact there is no such thing as a postmortem disembodied person. Although a collective mistake in belief of this sort may be rare, the sceptic will still remind us that it is more probable to suppose that the people who "see" disembodied deceased persons are mistaken in what they claim to see than it is to suppose that such entities exist. We have a noncontroversially rich history of people "seeing" things that are not there; but we have no noncontroversial history of ghost sightings, or of veridical apparitional experiences of postmortem disembodied persons even when they are collectively experienced on one occasion. For these reasons it seems wiser to believe that those people who report collectively seeing a ghost on one occasion are for some reason or other simply mistaken in their belief that such an entity exists. The vast

majority of apparitions of the dead are either the product of claims
made by individuals whose apparitional experiences are not shared
with anybody else or the product of claims made by a group
whose collective apparitional experience occurs on one occasion
only. In either case we need not accept such testimony as establishing that anything—much less a disembodied deceased person—
exists causally independently of the mind.

But are there any cases that we cannot so readily dismiss? What
about the testimony of different groups of people on different
occasions under different circumstances over an extended period
of time, all testifying to the same apparitional experience? In other
words, what about *collective and iterative* apparitional experiences
of the dead? Were such testimony to occur as evidence for belief
in the existence of disembodied postmortem persons, would the
same possibility of error exist warranting an explanation in terms
of hallucination, or delusion, or fraud, or hoax, or simple perceptual mistake? Presumably not, and that is the reason why the
logical features of the following cases warrant serious consideration as offering plausible evidence for belief in some form of
postmortem personal survival. After looking at these cases as they
have been reported, we will examine them as evidence for personal
survival.

The Butler Case

Consider the case noted by C. J. Ducasse in *A Critical Examination of the Belief in Life after Death*—a case that Ducasse thinks
provides striking evidence for life after death.[2] The original account was written in 1826 by the Reverend Abraham Cummings,
a graduate of Brown University and a Baptist minister in Maine,
in a pamphlet entitled *Immortality Proved by Testimony of Sense*.[3]

The apparitions were of the deceased Mrs. George Butler and
occurred in a village near Machiasport, Maine. The "specter" of
Mrs. Butler appeared *a number of times over a period of several months*.
She was seen on different occasions by groups of people number-
ing as many as 40 persons, and appeared both indoors and
outdoors.[4] She presented extended discourses and moved freely

among the gathered people. She also accurately predicted both births and deaths, and conveyed intimate and allegedly very private details of the lives of those in the group.[5] For example, she accurately predicted that the new Mrs. Butler would have one child and shortly thereafter die. She also provided one man with the information—unknown to him and everybody else in the group at the time—that his father in a distant town had recently died.[6] Given the time factor involved, Cummings argues that nobody in town could have had normal knowledge of that death. Moreover, Reverend Cummings was astute enough to obtain at the time more than 30 sworn affidavits from some of the 100 or more persons who had heard and/or seen the specter under different circumstances in the company of others.[7] These affidavits are reproduced in the pamphlet.[8] He also examined the testimony very closely and rejected the possibility of fraud or hoax.[9]

Furthermore, on one occasion Captain Butler (Mrs. Butler's living husband) placed his hand "upon" the apparition, and his hand passed through as if its body were made of light. Six or seven persons witnessed this event and made it part of their sworn testimony.[10]

Assuming the absence of fraud or hoax, and assuming that other similar cases exist in which we can equally assume the absence of fraud or hoax (both assumptions we shall establish later), what can be said about this case?

To begin with, the frequency of the apparition, the changing circumstances in which it appeared, and the large and varying numbers of persons involved in testifying to each instance of the apparition suggest that the likelihood of a collective perceptual error on each occasion is remarkably low. Certainly we cannot dismiss this case as readily as we would a report of an apparition by one person or a group of persons on only one occasion. Here, any appeal to delusion or hallucination seems much more difficult to argue, and not very convincing. Certainly the probability of such a mistake on each occasion is remarkably lower than it is in the case of a group sighting on only one occasion. As a matter of fact, the probability of a large group of people being mistaken in their perceptual beliefs about what they have seen when they testify to seeing the same thing repeatedly under different circumstances (both indoors and outdoors) over an extended period of time (many months) in which the membership of the group changes frequently is zero. I know of no case in which a collective mistaken belief of precisely this sort has ever been established.

Also, inasmuch as the specter accurately predicted both births and deaths, and conveyed to the group information (some very private) that nobody in the group could plausibly have known at the time, we cannot easily dismiss as mistaken the information the group obtained in the apparitional experience. If the people in this case were seeing and hearing something other than the postmortem surviving personality of Mrs. Butler (but mistakenly believed that they were seeing as much), what indeed could they have been seeing that is not evidence of personal survival?

It is fashionable to say that they must have been seeing things that were not really there, or seeing things that were really there but not the things they thought they saw. Such a response is predicated on the assumption that they did not see what they say they saw—and what exactly is the evidence that they could not have seen what they say they saw?

We will consider specific sceptical responses to the Butler case in a later section of this chapter. However, it is important to see here that the Butler case is not an isolated instance of its kind. In more recent times we have a case much like it in which the specter appeared to a number of different people under different circumstances over a long period of time. Moreover, as in the Butler case, this specter made certain predictions that were subsequently borne out. Let us consider this case: the "Ghost of Flight 401."

The Ghost of Flight 401

In the dead of night on December 28, 1972, Eastern Airlines Flight 401 plunged into the Florida Everglades, killing 101 passengers and crew. Two months later the alleged ghosts of its pilot and its second officer began to appear on sister ships carrying or using parts salvaged from the original crash. The pilot's name was Captain Robert Loft; the second officer's was Don Repo. According to John Fuller (the principal investigator of the case), testimony regarding the apparition of the two ghosts grew to alarming proportions. Most of the sightings occurred in the galley of Eastern plane 318, which—like a few other L-1011s—was using some of the salvaged parts of the L-1011 that crashed in the Everglades.[11]

One incident occurred on plane 318 as it prepared to depart Newark, New Jersey, for Miami, Florida. The second officer had completed his preflight walk-around check. The captain and the first officer were in the cockpit. The food for in-flight meals had been delivered to the plane, and everything was set for takeoff.

In the first-class section, the senior stewardess was making the usual head count, and her count was off by one passenger too many. An Eastern captain in uniform was in one of the seats. She inferred that he was "deadheading" (going back) to Miami, where the flight originated; he was not on her list, thus accounting for the extra passenger. It was necessary, however, to confirm the count, and she advised the captain that he was not on her list. She asked if he would be riding in the jump seat back to Miami. The captain did not respond, looking straight ahead. She asked him again whether he was a first-class traveler in the jump seat. Still he did not answer and looked straight ahead. Perplexed, she brought the flight supervisor over to ask the same question, and she too received no response. The captain seemed normal in every respect except that he seemed to be in some sort of daze. His unresponsiveness worried the two attendants, and one of them went into the cockpit to tell the flight captain what was transpiring. The flight captain, too, was perplexed. He left the cockpit and went to the first-class compartment.

In reporting this incident, John Fuller notes that half-a-dozen regular first-class passengers were in the immediate vicinity of the silent deadheading captain, and all of them were curious about what was going on.[12] As the flight captain approached the seat, he was puzzled that there was no record of another Eastern captain's being listed as jump-seat occupant, and that this one apparently had no pass for the flight.

With the flight's two stewardesses and their supervisor beside him, the captain leaned down to address the other captain and, just as he did, he froze. "My God, it's Bob Loft," he said. The cabin was totally silent and then, as it is reported, the captain in the seat disappeared before the eyes of all.

The flight captain returned to the operations officer in the cockpit. After a bit of delay, the plane was totally searched. The missing captain could not be found. Plane 318 finally did take off for Miami, its passengers and crew still stunned.

When the three attendants on the flight later sought to examine the flight log (in which, by FAA regulation, every unusual incident had to be recorded), they found the page for that flight missing, even though the entire crew reported the incident. All the pages up to and including the incident had been removed, contrary to general practice. The captain's and the crew's comments were completely missing.[13] Thereafter, the plane 318 log book was removed after every flight—a practice not followed in any other planes at Eastern.

Captain Loft was later sighted again on the same plane, in the galley, simultaneously by two stewardesses and the captain. After this incident, however, the flight was canceled.[14]

Don Repo, Captain Loft's second officer, was seen even more frequently on plane 318. Indeed, whereas Loft's appearances stopped after a short while (seemingly restricted to the one flight that was canceled), the specter of Don Repo continued to be visible for at least two years after the crash. I shall recount here only a few of the more interesting incidents in which Repo appeared to a number of people. However, in no fewer than two dozen incidents by the end of 1973, various people reported seeing Repo. In general, he appeared in order to do little repairs for the stewardesses or to advise the flight crew of potential mechanical problems. He was a friendly and a helpful specter who was frequently reported to have had discussions with various people on the plane.

Then there was the incident involving a woman passenger in the first-class section of plane 318, scheduled for a New York to Miami flight. The plane was at the ramp, and the head count had not yet been taken by the flight attendant in the first-class section. The woman passenger was seated next to an Eastern flight officer, in the uniform of a flight engineer.

Something about the officer worried the woman. He looked so

ghastly pale and ill; and when she said something to him, he would not respond. She asked him if he felt all right and if she should call the stewardess to help him. Still no response came from the sickly looking flight officer. The woman called the stewardess, who agreed that he seemed ill. The stewardess asked him if he needed any help. Other passengers also noticed him. Then, in front of the group—as before—the flight engineer disappeared. The woman became almost hysterical. Later she and the flight attendant picked out a picture of Repo as the officer who had been in the first-class seat.

In 1974 an Eastern captain allegedly told John Fuller that he had once been warned by a flight engineer riding in the jump seat of his L-1011 that there was going to be an electrical failure.[15] The captain ordered a recheck, which revealed a faulty circuit. Later, after a second look, the cockpit crew identified the intruding second officer sitting in the jump seat as Don Repo.

Finally, there is the Mexico City incident. In February 1974, plane 318 was readied for a flight to Mexico City. During the preparations, one of the flight attendants—working in the galley below—looked at the window of one of the ovens and clearly saw the face of Don Repo looking out at her. She ran to the elevator, went up a deck, and grabbed another flight attendant. Together they went down into the galley and approached the oven. The second flight attendant also saw the image. It was not a reflection. They called the flight deck and gave the story to the flight engineer. Immediately he came down. He also recognized Repo's face in the oven window; and as he gazed at Repo, Repo spoke audibly to the engineer and said, "Watch out for fire on this plane." Then he disappeared. Later that day the plane's third engine burst into flame on takeoff, and it returned to the ground on one engine.

Eastern Airlines' official position on the Ghost of Flight 401 (which principally refers to the sightings of Repo) is that it is gossip, and that nobody ever reported seeing any such ghosts. But the log book of plane 318 has never been made available. Sightings of the ghosts did finally stop—after all the salvaged parts were removed from plane 318.

Like the Butler case, this case involved various persons—sometimes in groups—under various circumstances and over a long period of time, who simultaneously had the same apparitional experience. And nobody had anything to gain by reporting such stories. As we shall see later, however, the Ghost of Flight 401 is a somewhat weaker case than the Butler case because, among other things, it involved fewer predictions.

Shortly, we shall examine some theories about apparitions and the strength of their reports, and then look at the sceptical response to the Butler case in particular. But first, let us review two others. Like the case of the Ghost of Flight 401, these are similar to the Butler case in that they involve the frequent sighting of the same apparition over a long period of time by different individuals under relevantly different circumstances. But unlike either the Butler case or the Ghost of Flight 401, these two cases do not involve diverse collective sightings and the acquisition of precognitive information from apparitions that allegedly speak with the living. I include these two cases here because they are strong ones, even though at first reading they may seem not so strong as the Butler case or the case of the Ghost of Flight 401. In the end, they may be even stronger, however, because of the more refutable methods used in examining the first two cases.

The Grey Lady and the Dying

In September 1956, Nurse E. L. was making her evening rounds in the ward of a large London hospital—a ward designated for treating malignant diseases. She was filling the water dispensers at each patient's bedside. The dispenser was empty at the bedside of a 75-year-old man who had been admitted with cancer of the lung and Paget's disease. As the nurse reached to fill the dispenser, the old man told her that there was no need to do so because he had already been given a glass of water. Nurse E. L.—wondering how that could be (as she knew no other nurses were dispensing water)—asked him who had given him the water.

He replied that the nice lady standing at the foot of the bed, and dressed in grey, gave him the water. Nurse E. L. could see no one else in the room. The man died a week later.

At the behest of Dr. Paul Turner, Nurse E. L. signed the account she wrote of this incident. In 1957 Dr. Paul Turner began investigating the long-standing legend to the effect that in this particular ward of the hospital a lady in grey frequently appeared in order to comfort dying patients. Invariably, the patients died a short while after her ministrations.

The nurses in this hospital had, at one time, worn grey; but in the 1920s the uniform was changed to an Oxford blue dress with white apron and collar.

In 1959 Dr. Turner published the results of his investigation in the *Journal of the Society for Psychical Research* under the title "The Grey Lady: A Study of Psychic Phenomenon in the Dying."[16] Here are some of the results in his report.

The woman in grey was generally said to be of a gentle disposition and middle-aged. Part of the legend was that she helped dying patients in various ways and made them comfortable. Although the identity of the apparition remains a mystery, some surmise that she was the ghost of a nun who fell down an elevator shaft at the turn of the century. Others thought that the ghost was an administrative nun who had been found dead in the hospital.[17]

Dr. Turner obtained six separate accounts of patient "encounters" with the grey lady from nurses willing to sign their names to the record.[18] Many other similar experiences were reliably conveyed by mouth; but since they were not written down, they did not form part of the record of the investigation. Here are some of the reported accounts.

Nurse J. F. K. signed a statement that in November 1956 she was bathing the back of a patient who, although ill with a malignant disease, was expected to recover. This patient asked the nurse whether she always worked with the other nurse. The question puzzled Nurse J. F. K., because she knew no other nurse was with her. When she asked him what he meant, the patient pointed at what he was seeing. There was nobody there. He also said that the "nurse" was dressed differently from the other nurses and that she frequently came to visit him. Shortly afterward he died.[19]

Nurse J. M. P., in another signed statement, related how in

December 1957 she was asked by a 37-year-old male patient dying of cancer, "Who is that lady warming her hands by the fire?" In fact, no one was by the fire. When the nurse asked him what he saw, he said, "That person in the grey uniform." He, too, died shortly thereafter.[20]

Nurse S. T. related that in February 1958 a woman suffering from a malignant disease told her that during the night a very kind lady dressed in grey gave her a cup of tea. A year later in the same ward, a patient—a young woman of 28 with myelomatosis—told Nurse R. A. C. that a kind lady was standing at the foot of her bed during the night. This patient died three to four weeks later.[21]

A number of years earlier than this last reported incident, a Sister E. F. was night nurse in the same ward. When she asked a dying patient if she could make her more comfortable, the woman replied that the other sister had already done so. No other sister was on duty at the time, nor had the night nurse attended to the patient recently. This patient died the following day. Sister E. F. signed her account of this incident.[22]

In reflecting on this case, Andrew MacKenzie grants that the patients who experienced "drinking tea" or "drinking water" may have been hallucinating that part of their experience.[23] But could each of them have been hallucinating the grey lady? Even if they were all being medicated in some way (and some of them were not medicated at all), we know of no drug that would allow a large number of people to hallucinate the same object described in the same way, even to the same color. Besides, these events took place in only this ward of the hospital. Such events were not reported in other hospitals treating people with the same diseases.

Might not the nurses be conspiring to create a wonderful hoax? Well, of course, that is possible. But it does not seem likely. With nothing to gain, why would all these nurses (including some nuns) lie? Then too, if they did lie, we would expect certain elements of their separate testimonies to be the same. As Andrew MacKenzie notes, if the nurses were hoaxing us, we would expect them to describe the actions of the grey lady in the same way. But significant differences occur in the descriptions, indicating that they were not in collusion in their accounts.[24]

Finally, might it not be possible that these sick people all learned about the legend of the grey lady and that this information helped to form the same hallucinatory object? Dr. Turner's response to this question is that, although the legend of the grey lady was widely known by the hospital staff, it was a secret guarded closely from the patients.[25]

Could the information reported by the patients have been telepathically and unwittingly conveyed to them by the nurses? Possibly—but is there any reason to think that likely? And if so, why would all those people who had the experience die? Nobody who survived from that ward reported seeing the grey lady. If the information had been telepathically conveyed, then we would expect some of the survivors to have had the experience also. But none did.

The grey lady was never seen collectively, and only sick people saw her. The possibility of hallucination in which the content of the apparition was telepathically conveyed cannot be ruled out. Some telepathic "leak" may have occurred from one or more nurses to only those who precognitively knew they were going to die. As we shall see, however, this same sort of objection cannot be used against the Butler case, or the case of the Ghost of Flight 401, because these two cases involved frequent collective sightings by relevantly diverse groups with little or no possibility of telepathic leakage. But more on this objection later.

The Cheltenham Ghost

The story of the Cheltenham ghost was first noted by F. W. H. Myers in the *Proceedings of the Society for Psychical Research* in 1892. Myers interviewed the involved individuals and took written testimony from firsthand witnesses. Later, a book by B. Abdy Collins entitled *The Cheltenham Ghost* examined the case.[26]

The Cheltenham ghost first appeared in 1882 to Rose Despard, who was then a 19-year-old medical student residing at Cheltenham, her family home. Rose heard someone at the door, but when she got there nobody was there. On returning along the passage, and while carrying a candle, she saw the figure of a tall lady dressed in black, standing at the head of the stairs. The figure began to descend the stairs but vanished when the candle burned itself out.

Captain F. W. Despard had moved his family into this house two months prior to this event. It had remained unoccupied for the previous six years, except for two short periods.

The appearance of the tall lady in black occurred most frequently between 1882 and 1886. Thereafter, the appearances gradually faded away. But during the active period, at least seven different persons saw the apparition, and numerous others heard strange noises that they attributed to the ghost. Statements were taken from the seven persons in support of Rose Despard's testimony. Rose Despard, who saw the figure many times, described the figure in her diary as

> a tall lady, dressed in black of a soft wollen material, judging from the slight sound in moving. This is all I noticed then; but on further occasions, when I was able to observe her more closely, I saw the upper part of the left side of the forehead, and a little of the hair above. Her left hand was nearly hidden by her sleeve and a fold of her dress. As she had it down a portion of a widow's cuff was visible on both wrists, so that the whole impression was that of a lady in widow's weeds. There was no cap on the head but a general effect of blackness suggests a bonnet with a long veil or hood.[27]

Rose's sister Edith saw the ghost several times, and described one of her encounters thus:

> The next time I saw the figure was one evening at about eight o'clock in July 1885, a fine evening and quite light. I was sitting alone in the drawing room singing when suddenly I felt a cold, icy shiver and I saw the figure bend over me, as if to turn the pages of my song. I called my sister who was then in another room, she came at once and said she could still see it in the room, though I could not.[28]

On August 12, 1884, the apparition was seen by two of the Despard sisters independently at 8 P.M., when it was still quite light.

On one occasion, during teatime, the charwoman followed the apparition around the house.

The visual apparition at Cheltenham never seems to have appeared to more than one person at the same time. But it was once seen by the four Despard sisters (Captain Despard never saw the apparition) in quick succession in four consecutive positions on its route from the drawing room to the orchard. Rose Despard gave this report of still another incident:

> Once while coming up the garden, I walked towards the orchard, when I saw the figure cross the orchard, go along the carriage drive in front of the house, and in at the open side door, I following. She crossed the drawing room, and took up her usual position behind the couch in the bow window. My father came in soon after, and I told him she was there. He could not see the figure, but went up to where I showed him she was. She then went swiftly round behind him, across the room, out of the door and along the hall, disappearing as usual near the garden door, we both following her.[29]

Some unanticipated evidence of the haunting came to light nearly 60 years later when a solicitor named George Goodings wrote to the Society for Psychical Research in 1944 to note that as a small boy he had lived at Cheltenham with an aunt and frequently played with one of the Despard children in the haunted house. He had a clear recollection of seeing the figure in the garden in bright sunlight, and also of joining hands around it in the drawing room when it then seemed to walk out between two people and disappear. He also said that he (apparently like others) was not alarmed by the figure.[30]

In a more recent examination of the case, MacKenzie claims that, in fact, as many as 17 people testified to seeing the ghost under different circumstances at different times both before and considerably long after the Despards left the house,[31] and that numerous sightings occurred as late as 1961.[32]

Who was the lady in black? Nobody knows for sure. Some surmised (i.e., those who credited it as a disembodied postmortem personality) that she was one Imogen Swinhoe, the second wife of Henry Swinhoe, a retired official. Imogen Swinhoe died four years before the haunting started. Although some people think the evidence for the Cheltenham ghost is good (but by no means perfect), others are quick to note that, after Rose Despard's first experience had become known to other members of the Despard family, ordinary suggestion might have induced hallucinations in them. (This point was raised by W. H. Salter in *Zoar*.)[33] Indeed, such inducement seems quite possible. However, it seems implausible to think that the power of suggestion can explain all the many appearances of an apparition seen frequently by 17 or more people over a period of years, in daylight as well as dark. It certainly would not account for the independent evidence offered by the solicitor. Moreover, according to Collins's account, there had been no previous communication between the first seven percipients.[34]

In 1885 Mrs. Henry Sidgwick examined the case in the *Proceedings of the Society for Psychical Research* and suggested that a real but illicit lodger might have been living in the house—known only to Mr. and Mrs. Despard, who kept the information from everybody else. But, as MacKenzie was quick to point out, this suggestion would not fit well with the testimony to the effect that the ghost went through the door; and it would not fit later testimony to the effect that the same ghost occupied the house before the Despards arrived on the scene.[35]

At any rate, before we focus on the sceptic's response to the strongest case, the Butler case, it will be very useful to examine in some detail different theories about collective and iterative apparitions of the dead. Thereafter our continuing discussion on the above cases will be more historically and philosophically informed.

Theories on Apparitions of the Dead

In examining material associated with so-called apparitions of the dead, we find that existing explanatory theories fall neatly into two groups depending on whether we view such apparitions as constructs of inner experience only or whether we take them to be localized extended entities of some sort. The first group offers an explanation in terms of some form of telepathy and is therefore subjectivist, while the second group is usually seen as offering an objectivist thesis. As Stephen Braude has observed in his discussion on the nature of apparitions, both groups assume a variety of forms, particularly with regard to *collective* and *iterative* apparitions, that is, with regard to apparitional experiences had by a number of people simultaneously and on different occasions.[36] It will be helpful to examine these forms and to determine which theory, if any, is most likely to explain the data. In assessing this material, it is difficult not to rely on Stephen Braude's excellent classification and discussion of the various proposals offered in the history of psychical research. Even so, in the end, as we shall see, one might well disagree with Braude's final position on what counts as the best available theory for explaining the data found in the above collective and iterative cases of apparitions of the dead.

Forms of the Telepathic Theory

Basically, the telepathic theory proposes that a mental state in an agent A produces a mental state in apparition-percipient B, and that the telepathically induced mental state of B manifests itself in the form of a hallucination. According to H. H. Price, this general theory seems initially plausible because telepathy is usually and reasonably considered a two-stage process.[37] First, the agent telepathically affects the percipient; second, the effect manifests itself somehow in the percipient. The second part of the process can presumably take different forms. As far as the topic of apparitions is concerned, a readily available option is that the telepathic effect manifests itself as a hallucination of an extended object. According to the telepathic theory, then, apparitions would simply be one of the many possible kinds of effects of telepathic interaction. If this explanation is correct, we would expect (as Price also suggested) apparitions to be a particularly realistic or vivid subset of the set of telepathically induced hallucinations.[38]

The objectivist theory, by comparison, proposes that an apparition is the perception of a real, localized, externalized entity—and not simply a subjective hallucinatory construct of the percipient, induced telepathically. As Braude has noted, early proponents of the objectivist theory maintained that the entity was nonphysical although it bore certain similarities to ordinary material objects. The theory initially required only that the apparition not have certain properties usually associated with the material object it resembles. For example, "apparitions—but not persons—are able to pass through walls and closed doors."[39] (If Braude is right, the early proponents of the theory never imagined that the apparition was in fact of the person who, because he no longer had a body, was now able to pass through doors, etc.) F. W. H. Myers[40] and G. N. M. Tyrrell[41] were among those early members of the Society for Psychical Research who argued that, if apparitions are objective localized entities, they are nevertheless sufficiently unlike physical objects to be classed as nonphysical. As itemized by Tyrrell, the basic points of dissimilarity between such apparitional objects and physical objects as we know them are the following:

1. Apparitional objects appear and disappear in locked rooms.
2. They vanish while being watched.
3. Sometimes they become transparent and fade away.
4. They are often seen or heard by only *some* of those who are present and in a position to perceive any physical object genuinely at that location.
5. They disappear into walls and closed doors and pass through physical objects in their path.
6. Hands may go through them, or people may walk through them without encountering resistance.
7. And finally, they leave behind no physical traces.[42]

C. D. Broad was quick to note, incidentally, that some physical objects in fact share a number of these properties. Gasses and rainbows, for example, have Tyrrell's above stated properties 2, 3, 4, 5, and 7; and electromagnetic fields have properties 1, 4, 5, 6, and 7.[43]

At any rate, telepathic explanations of collective and iterative apparitions have taken basically three forms, which Braude dubs the Shotgun Theory, the Infection Theory, and the Extravaganza Theory.[44]

The *Shotgun Theory* was originally proposed by Edmund Gur-

ney, says Braude, and C. D. Broad named it "Multiply Directed
Telepathic Initiation." According to this form, agent A telepathically influences percipients B_1 through B_n, each *independently*; and
each B thereafter responds to the telepathic stimulus by creating
an apparition.[45] As Braude points out, Gurney quickly recognized
certain problems with his original theory, and thereafter offered
an alternative. We will say what those problems are shortly. The
second form of the telepathic theory—Gurney's alternative proposal—is the *Infection Theory*. According to this second form, an
agent A telepathically influences primary percipient B_1; and while
B_1 (in response to the telepathic stimulus) creates his own apparent
sensory image for himself, he in turn acts as a telepathic agent,
causing others in his vicinity to have similar experiences. Finally,
the *Extravaganza Theory*, proposed originally by Tyrrell, appeals
to *dramatic appropriateness* as a way of explaining why apparitions
are experienced collectively. Under this theory,

> agent A telepathically affects primary percipient B, and then B, in
> creating his apparitional experience, does whatever is necessary to
> render it dramatically appropriate. And since B is sometimes in the
> company of other people, it would be appropriate for at least
> properly situated members of that group also to experience the
> apparition.[46]

The Extravaganza Theory seems to combine elements of both the
Shotgun Theory and the Infection Theory. Which form of the
telepathic theory, if any, is correct?

One basic problem with the Shotgun Theory (a problem noted
by Gurney himself) is that all hallucinations use the subject's
personal experience—experience consisting of the subject's own
supply of past experiences, images, and symbols. So there is no
reason to suppose that percipients would all see basically the same
thing, described in basically the same way. Also, because it has
been established that telepathy works at different time intervals
for different individuals—that there are different latency periods
between the time the stimulus initially occurs and the hallucinatory response (i.e., telepathic deferment)—it seems unlikely that
different people would hallucinate at the same time when affected

by the same telepathic stimulus. Finally, a third difficulty for the Shotgun Theory (a difficulty noted by both Gurney and Broad)[47] is that there is good reason to believe that A and B will interact telepathically only if there already exists a *rapport* of some kind between the two—for example, blood relationship, friendship, love—in which case we would not expect A to induce an apparition telepathically in B when, as sometimes happens both in collective and in individual cases, A and B are strangers.

As it turns out, Gurney was equally dissatisfied with the Infection Theory for the same reason that it also could not account for people not in rapport having the same hallucination. And Broad pointed out that the fact that the percipients are spatially closer (as occurs in the Infection Theory) still fails to explain how the experience of all the percipients should be simultaneous with or similar to each other.[48] Myers also raised another objection to the Infection Theory, namely, that if the theory were true, we would expect to find cases of nontelepathic hallucination (arising from purely intersubjective causes) spreading by telepathic infection to others in the vicinity. But, according to Myers, there are no such cases.[49] Gurney came to admit that ordinary hallucinations do not seem to spread by infection. In the end, Gurney developed a hybrid of the Shotgun and Infection theories;[50] but this hybrid answered the objections based on simultaneity and identity of experience no better than its parent theories had.

The Extravaganza Theory—the third telepathic theory and the one proposed by Tyrrell—is again, as Braude asserts, no more capable in the end of explaining the simultaneity and similarity of the percipients' experiences than were the Shotgun or the Infection theories before it.[51] Therefore, given the necessity of rapport between subjects, and also because every form of telepathic theory tends to be nonparsimonious as a theory, Braude rejects telepathy as a suitable way of explaining the collective and iterative apparitional experiences of the dead.[52] He then moves on to a discussion based on the objectivist theory of apparitions.

From our point of view in this book, however, the question is whether the general objectivist position supports the survival hypothesis or not. And it by no means follows from the fact that all the percipients in collective and iterative apparitions of the dead see something objective that what they see is a postmortem discarnate person or even something we can plausibly regard as the causal product of such a person. Let me explain.

The Super-PK Hypothesis

While Braude does not seek to confront directly the survival hypothesis in any detail, by implication he sets it aside because he adopts the view that what subjects see in collective and iterative apparitions of the dead we can plausibly regard as the product of psychokinesis (PK) or even super-PK (i.e., psychokinesis on a grand scale).[53] In effect, he sees no reason for not adopting the view that what is seen in such apparitions is simply the causal product of some creative mental act, in much the same way that the materializations in the celebrated D. D. Home case (or in others such as the Palladino case, involving allegedly legitimate physical mediumship) must be seen as the physical product of mental agency. In this view, what is seen may well be a quasi-physical object; but there would be no reason to think it had an existence causally independent of, and temporally prior to, the creative act of some human mind or minds. What exactly is his argument for this view?

To begin with, in the second chapter of *The Limits of Influence*, Braude establishes what is ostensibly the most compelling argument yet for the existence of psychokinesis on a grand scale. This he does with a very painstaking and thorough discussion of the D. D. Home and the Eusapia Palladino material. As a result of this conclusion, he argues plausibly that we cannot assert any longer that PK cannot exist on a grand scale for the reason that we have no evidence of its occurring in that way in the past. So far, so good.

At this point, however, the argument now goes forward to assert that, once we are open to the possibility of PK (or ESP) on a grand scale, we cannot justifiably rule against it as a plausible explanation of paranormal phenomena without thereby arbitrarily assuming in advance what the limits of PK (or ESP) are. Accordingly, since we cannot justifiably assume in advance what the limits of PK (or ESP) are, we cannot exclude appeal to PK or ESP as a legitimate explanation for paranormal phenomena. As Braude frequently asserts in various ways,

> I consider it a sound general policy to be wary of ruling out any explanations of apparitions on the grounds that it posits a psi performance of implausible magnitude. Disheartening as it may be, we simply have no decent idea what (if any) magnitude of phenomena is implausible or unlikely, once we have allowed psi to occur at all.[54]

Braude's general strategy, then, consists in asserting that, whenever people assert that an explanation of the paranormal in terms of super-PK or super-ESP is unacceptable, it is because they are implicitly (or explicitly) claiming that such explanations are implausible or unlikely since we have no evidence of PK or ESP existing with the appropriate magnitude or refinement necessary for the explanation. But, for Braude, this latter implicit (or explicit) claim *assumes unjustifiably* that PK or ESP has limits we can specify in advance of empirical investigation. "Just as we have no grounds at present for assuming that PK has any limits at all, the same is no doubt true with regard to the forms of ESP."[55]

For the very same reasons noted back in Chapter 1, this argument is problematic. First of all, we certainly can reject an argument favoring ESP or PK without assuming unjustifiably in advance that PK or ESP must exist in some limited fashion. After all, one might well admit that super-PK (or super-ESP) exists and yet still reject explanations in terms of it on the grounds that, while it is certainly *possible* that such phenomena exist in such magnitude, one needs some reason to think their existence likely in the appropriate magnitude necessary to explain the current data. The fact that it is possible that PK and ESP exist in an unlimited way does not imply that they are the cause of paranormal phenomena. In other words, it is simply a matter of asking the proponent of the super-PK (or super-ESP) explanation for some positive evidence to suppose that super-PK (or super-ESP) is actually at work in the case at hand. This is by no means the same as asserting, or implying, that PK (or ESP) cannot exist on some grand scale. And if the only response the proponent of the super-PK (or super-ESP) explanation can give us is that we have no reason for thinking PK or ESP is limited, then we can grant as much and still ask what positive evidence there is for thinking that an explanation in terms of super-PK (or super-ESP) is likely to be true. Second and relatedly, if we reject explanations appealing to super-PK (or super-ESP), doing so by no means implies that we can never appeal to super-ESP or super-PK for the reason that we have no evidence of their occurring in our history; it simply means that before endorsing such explanations we should minimally have some reason for thinking that super-PK (or super-ESP) is the most plausible causal explanation of the data to be explained. Third, why, precisely, does it follow from the fact that one might reject an explanation in terms of super-PK (or super-ESP) that one is *thereby assuming* that PK or ESP *cannot, or does not*, exist in such a magnitude because we have not yet seen either one of them in such magnitude outside these cases? It is difficult to see precisely how that follows. What *might* follow is that it is difficult to establish as plausible an explanation appealing to a particular causal factor B on the sole basis that it is possible B exists in a way that would explain the phenomenon at hand. This seems to be the difference between an explanation and a merely possible explanation. Fourth, if Braude's argument is acceptable, we would not seem to have any grounds ever for rejecting any explanation appealing to the paranormal even when there is no reason to think it likely rather than merely possible that super-PK (or super-ESP) is at work. Indeed, in spite of Braude's protestations to the contrary, the argument makes it impossible ever to come up with any evidence favoring an explanation that is contradictory to the super-ESP or super-PK explanation when we are dealing with the paranormal, since if we reject it for the non-PK or non-ESP hypothesis we must also be guilty of putting antecedent limits on how PK or ESP exists in the world.

Put somewhat differently, one could never oppose the super-ESP or super-PK explanation without unjustifiably assuming that there are limits to PK or ESP. And if this is so, does not the explanation of the paranormal in terms of super-PK or super-ESP become arbitrarily nonfalsifiable by appeal to any evidence (and not simply laboratory evidence) whatever? Can this follow from the alleged fact that we do not know what the limits of PK may be in any given setting? What empirical evidence would it take to show that the explanation of collective and iterative apparitions in terms of super-PK is false and that the survivalist hypothesis is true? And if we cannot say, what then is the difference between such an argument favoring super-PK (or super-ESP) and a bald dogmatic assertion that, no matter what the evidence, there will never be a solid explanation of the paranormal unless we appeal to super-PK or super-ESP? If the argument Braude offers is to avoid the charge of dogmatism, we will need to know what it would take to refute an explanation of the paranormal in terms of super-PK or super-ESP. Unfortunately, as we saw above, Braude also claims that the existence of super-ESP or super-PK as a cause at work in any paranormal phenomena is not falsifiable by appeal to any evidence. For these reasons, then, it seems fair to conclude that Braude's reasons for adopting the objectivist explanation in terms of super-PK are flawed. While it is certainly possible that super-PK is at work in collective and iterative apparitions of the dead, we need more positive evidence to warrant the conclusion that super-PK is in fact the cause of the phenomena.

Finally, in the light of these considerations, it also seems to make sense to note that, if—given everything we know about ESP or PK—we have yet to see an instance of it with properties a, b, and c, then appealing to ESP or PK to explain the presence of a, b, and c is to assert without benefit of proof just those items one would need to make the explanation work. Presumably, this principle was at work when we, and Braude, agreed that the telepathic theory does not account for collective and iterative apparitions of the dead because we generally do not encounter telepathy in a way that allows for the property of many people seeing the same thing at the same time. By implication, we define what telepathy is (or what anything is, for that matter) in terms of common properties observed in the past; when one talks of telepathy (or PK) in terms of properties not yet seen, the existence of those properties are conjectural and need to be shown to exist before one can appeal to telepathy (or ESP) to explain some phenomenon as an instance of telepathy (or ESP). As we shall see, this basic principle of inductive reasoning turns out to be an important principle that is often violated when it comes to explaining the paranormal. And it is surely a principle on which those favoring the survivalist interpretation of the above apparitional material will want to insist.

In sum, given all these considerations, it is easy to agree with Braude and others on the reasons why any form of the telepathic theory of apparitions will fail to explain the data comprising collective and iterative apparitions of the dead. But from this it by no means follows that, if we adopt (as presumably we must) an objectivist interpretation, we must thereby adopt an explanation in favor of super-PK. Braude's argument for thinking as much is nonpersuasive for all the reasons just noted. Under the circumstances, there would not seem to be any better explanation for the data than to assume that what people see in these apparitions are in fact real objects having an existence independently of the causal powers of any human mind. The only question is whether what is seen is a disincarnate personality or an objective entity created for some reason or other by a disincarnate personality and resembling an historical personage. Once we abandon the explanation in terms of human telepathy along with the explanation in terms of super-PK, the idea that what people are seeing in these experiences is a disincarnate person or some sort of a sense datum created by a disincarnate person does not seem implausible at all.

At any rate, let us now return to the Butler case and the specific objections made to regarding it as evidence for survival. Given the above discussion, we are now in a better position to assess the strength of various alternative explanations offered by the sceptic for thinking cases like it do not warrant or even permit belief in personal survival.

The Sceptic's Response to the Butler Case: The Dommeyer Critique

Perhaps the strongest sceptical response to the Butler case comes from Frederick Dommeyer who, for the sake of argument, does not dispute the facts of the case but goes on to offer an alternative explanation that does not require belief in disembodied persons.[56] Here, quoted in length, is what Dommeyer says:

What can one make of such a case? I believe it is possible to bring it under the ESP hypothesis. There are some features of the specter story that provide hints as to what may have actually occurred. First the specter delivered discourses "sometimes over an hour long."[57] By what means were these discourses delivered? Were there physical sound waves in the air that caused the persons present to hear the specter's words? It is not likely there were, when one considers that Captain Butler's hand passed through the specter's body as though it were light. It is not reasonable to suppose that such a spectral body had a voice box capable of producing physical sounds. If the "auditory sensations" experienced by the witnesses were not caused by the sound waves, there is left only one plausible hypothesis to account for the discourses they heard. That hypothesis is that they heard these discourses clairaudiently. There are many recorded cases of clairaudience.

In this Butler case, then, why cannot one explain what happened by positing the parapsychological events needed to explain it? The work of Tyrrell has already clearly established the occurrence of "collective apparitions," i.e., an apparition that is seen by a number of people together. Why should it be supposed any less possible that there are collective clairaudient experiences? Why can it not be supposed that some person present, when the Butler specter appeared and spoke, was the "sender" of both visual and auditory "hallucinations" and that some others there had the capacity to "receive" them? Let it be further assumed that the "sender" had the retrocognitive or clairvoyant powers needed to duplicate some knowledge the living Mrs. Butler had had; let it be further assumed that he had the precognitive powers needed for the predictions the specter made. Or, several persons may have jointly functioned as "sender-receivers."

No one has ever established that apparitions "seen" singly or collectively are causally tied to discarnate minds; there is no more reason for positing that collective "hearings" are. Dr. J. B. Rhine has pointed out that the occurrence of telepathy, clairvoyance, precognition, etc., are associated with the states of mind of senders and receivers; the attitudes, the motivations and enthusiasm of the subject are important, as are those of the sender. It is not impossible therefore that these groups of persons in the Butler case were, by nature or by conditions of the time, in states of mind that led to these very unusual ESP manifestations. Whatever the explanation of the Butler case, it would have to refer to unusual conditions because the circumstances to be explained are themselves most unusual.

If the above explanation, in its main outline, is not accepted, what alternatives remain? Certainly, the "specter" was not the physical Mrs. Butler. Neither do we know of any causal chain that would lead from her physical body as cause to the specter as effect. Even if we did, this would have nothing to do with survival. But could the discarnate mind of Mrs. Butler (assuming there is such a thing possible) to be the phantasm? This is not a reasonable suggestion: the phantasm was in space and time; it walked about among the witnesses, and minds do not do that kind of thing. Could the discarnate mind of Mrs. Butler have caused the phantasm to be seen and heard collectively? Though this is conceivable, it is hardly more than that. It seems like a simple and desirable explanation only until one looks more closely at the mechanism of such a causal feat. How could Mrs. Butler as discarnate mind communicate by physical voice to those who heard her discourse? As discarnate mind she would have no physical voice box. Her only means of communication would have been by telepathic or other ESP means. She would have had to "send" the visual and auditory "hallucinations" that were experienced. Also, since she made accurate predictions about deaths and births, Mrs. Butler's discarnate mind must have precognitive powers posited of it. Then, there is the matter of "reception"; the witnesses had to have the capacity to hear "clairaudiently," to "see" clairvoyantly, etc., what they reported seeing, hearing, etc. The survival interpretation, therefore, does not exclude the positing of ESP powers to the same magnitude as those involved in the nonsurvival ESP explanation; the former view includes those powers and, in addition, posits the existence of a discarnate mind. The nonsurvival ESP interpretation is therefore logically simpler and more probably true than the other hypothesis as an explanation of the Butler case.[58]

Dommeyer's explanation asks us to make two suppositions: (1) that one member of the group consistently induced the same auditory and visual hallucinations on repeated occasions in differing circumstances in different groups of people; and (2) that this same person was clairvoyant and communicated precognitive and postcognitive information to all the members of the group during the induced hallucinations. Thus, all who claimed to see the specter of Mrs. Butler were, on each occasion, having visual and auditory hallucinations; but the information they allegedly received from her was correct because it was conveyed to them telepathically by the clairvoyant, who was inducing the hallucinations in all of them. Dommeyer's critique is an instance of that form of the telepathic theory Braude dubbed the Shotgun Theory, and we can suppose that everything we have said earlier about the failure of such a theory applies with equal weight against Dommeyer's critique.

Furthermore, for Dommeyer, his "ESP explanation" is allegedly more plausible than the explanation that appeals to the existence of disembodied persons. And this for two reasons. First, it is just too implausible to think that a disembodied person could be seen, could speak, and could be heard. Second, because a disembodied person is not made up of matter (and thus could not speak), it would need to communicate telepathically, thus requiring what is distinctly implausible, namely, that all the witnesses were capable of telepathic communication.

Apart from the general criticism of the Shotgun Theory sketched above, what is initially questionable about Dommeyer's alternative explanation of the Butler case is his assertion that his explanation—the ESP explanation—is simpler and more plausible than the explanation that appeals to the existence of a postmortem disembodied person. It hardly seems simpler. As for its plausibility—well, never in the history of paranormal research (whether in the lab or outside) has there been any success in inducing simultaneously the same auditory and visual hallucinations in a large number of people (not always the same) on many separate occasions under differing circumstances, and then providing them with accurate information clairvoyantly obtained. This latter point, as we saw above, is what Myers and others pointed out when criticizing both the Shotgun Theory and the Infection Theory. Moreover, for all the reasons urged a few pages back, this latter criticism does not entail that we have arbitrarily placed limits on the ways in which, in Braude's terminology, "psi" can exist in the world.

In addition, Dommeyer's explanation would require that all the people who were party to the same hallucinations were to the same remarkable degree influenced by telepathy to secure the information from the telepathic clairvoyant inducing the hallucination in each member of the group. More importantly, a close examination of the various sworn statements in the Butler case shows that on a number of occasions the specter was seen by three or four people who were not present on any other occasions when the apparition was collectively viewed.[59] If that is so, then Dommeyer's alternative explanation would further require *a number* of distinct percipients endowed with the capacity to induce visual and auditory hallucinations of the same object in the other members of the group (sometimes well over 20 in number) and also to convey telepathically to the group detailed knowledge the percipient clairvoyantly acquired through precognition and retrocognition.

No doubt this ESP explanation is logically possible, but there is not one shred of empirical evidence (either within or outside the lab) to suggest that it is plausible in light of what we presently know about ESP. In short, Dommeyer's alternative explanation is wildly ad hoc.

Predictably, Dommeyer (as well as those who would agree with some form of the telepathic theory discussed above) might be tempted to respond that no evidence favors the explanation that appeals to the existence of an extended quasi-physical object; and so, the more plausible explanation is the one that would explain the phenomenon by appeal to less problematic physical forces (such as ESP and PK), even if it might seem factually implausible. If Dommeyer were to respond in this fashion, we could only reply by repeating all the reasons noted in the preceding section on the plausibility of the objectivist position sans the Braude explanation in terms of super-PK. If that is not enough (and it should be), we need only review the evidence on reincarnation in Chapter 1, as well as examine the evidence we will give in the next three chapters on ostensible possession, out-of-body experiences, and possession mediumship, respectively, to secure the case in favor of the objectivist position. But, of course, this belief would not carry with it as a necessary correlate that a disembodied postmortem person would be directly visible.

Ultimately, Dommeyer places emphasis on the plausibility of his ESP hypothesis as a result of his belief in the extreme implausibility of thinking that a postmortem disembodied person could be seen or could be the causal source of anything being heard or seen by a group of people. This consideration motivates not only Dommeyer's specific explanation of the Butler case, but also, presumably, the telepathic theory in general.

Admittedly if, like Dommeyer and others, we continue to construe a disembodied postmortem person in terms of a purely nonmaterial object, then there would be no way to explain how such a being could speak or be seen, or even be causally effective in the physical world. But in Chapter 6 we shall argue, along with Broad,[60] that a disembodied postmortem person—principally because it is a form of energy—must be construed as a spatially extended object having some properties in common with physical objects as we now know them. On that basis, one may suppose that disembodied persons could be causally effective and visible in the physical realm under certain circumstances.

These considerations lend some credibility to the claim one sometimes hears that everyone has an "astral body," that is, a second body made up of a rare physical-like component invisible to the naked eye except under certain circumstances, and that this second body contains those essential dispositions associated with the core personality of the deceased human. This second body endures after the death of the physical body and is a replica of it. Either that, or the astral body as described has the power to make itself appear as a replica of the physical body. In any event, the fact that the astral body is construed as having some physical-like properties essential to the core of human personality would account for its visibility in certain circumstances. In short, if some form of mind–body dualism is true, the mind will turn out to be something like an energized body that, when seen, is identical in appearance to the original body and survives its death. So construed, the mind would thus be able to be causally effective either by making itself appear like the physical body before death, or by making itself appear so as to be readily identified with the person who had a certain body. Or so it might seem.

On this last point, however, it is important to note also that—as F. W. H. Myers argued persuasively[61]—the discarnate or disembodied postmortem person may in fact be quite different from the way it appears in the manifestations to which people testify when they testify to seeing a deceased person. As Myers noted, believing in disembodied persons does not require us to believe—however popular the view may be—that *what* is seen is the deceased person or even something essential to the personality of the deceased person. On this item, Myers said,

> We have no warrant for the assumption that the phantom seen, even though it be somehow *caused* by the deceased person, *is* that deceased person, in any ordinary sense of the word. Instead of appealing to the crude analogy of the living friend who, when he has walked into the room, *is* in the room, we shall find for the ghost a much closer parallel in those hallucinatory figures or phantasms which living persons can sometimes project at a distance.
>
> But experience shows that when—as with these *postmortem* phantoms—the deceased person has gone well out of sight or reach there is a tendency, so to say, to *anthropomorphose* the apparition; to suppose that, as the deceased person is not provably anywhere else, he is probably here; and that the apparition is bound to behave accordingly. All such assumptions must be dismissed, and the phantom must be taken on its merits, as indicating merely a certain connection with the deceased, the precise nature of that connection being a part of the problem to be solved.[62]

For this reason, Myers recommends defining the term *ghost* as the "manifestation of persistent personal energy."[63] And in this view, evidence of such manifestation may well be evidence for personal survival after death even though it may not be evidence for thinking that *what* is seen is the surviving personality or some essential aspect of the surviving deceased personality.

In his 1953 book *Apparitions*, G. N. M. Tyrrell seems to have agreed with Myers's interpretation for much the same reasons, and Tyrrell ends up with the view that an apparition is "a percept created by a psychological manipulator of sense-data in order to express an idea, or, as I have put it, a percept created from 'above.' "[64]

Given the implausibility of any form of the telepathic theory to explain the best cases (cases like the Butler case), the value of the interpretation offered by Myers and Tyrrell is that it allows us to take apparitional experiences of this sort as evidence for survival without having to believe that *what* is seen in these experiences is a disembodied postmortem person rather than the appearance of a person prior to death. Of course, if people mistakenly believe that what they see in such apparitions is the deceased person, then this belief may well be hallucinatory insofar as they do not *see* the deceased person, but only the apparition of the deceased person caused by his or her "persistent personal energy." But such apparitions are not hallucinatory in the sense of being caused by the perceiving subject; they cannot be dismissed so readily as, say, a man's delusive belief that he (and only he) just saw a flying horse.[65]

So, for all these reasons, while we must adopt the objectivist thesis, we need not suppose that there are disembodied spirits (or even astral bodies) that are *directly* seen by people, and that the seeing of them is the evidence for their existence. From the fact that we saw frequently something that we all regard as a person indistinguishable from Julius Ceasar, it by no means follows that we saw Julius Ceasar. We can just as easily have evidence for disembodied existence if we regard what is seen in these experiences as something like a hologram that could only be caused by a persistent source of personal energy that could only be identified with the deceased Julius Ceasar.

Consequently, it makes sense to suggest that, while there may indeed be disembodied postmortem personalities, it by no means follows that anybody ever *sees* them directly or that the proper evidence for such a belief consists in people directly seeing ghosts or "disembodied postmortem personalities." By the same token, however, Myers and Tyrrell by no means establish that in the case of such apparitions one *never sees* some quasi-physical object that either is, or looks like, the surviving personality of a deceased person. It is still something of an open question as to what one in fact directly sees in these experiences. The value of the interpretation offered by Myers and then by Tyrrell is that it shows the implausibility of the explanation purely in terms of telepathy while at the same time showing how such apparitional experiences can support belief in survival without our having to say that what one directly perceives in these experiences is a disembodied deceased person. Anyway, let us return to summarize and dispatch Dommeyer's critique of the Butler case.

Dommeyer's reason for thinking that people were simply hallucinating in the Butler case is a result of his thinking that a disembodied postmortem person is more like nothing than it is like something. But as long as a disembodied postmortem person must be viewed as something like a body—a very special kind of body—we may suppose that it could cause auditory and visual sensations, although, to be sure, we cannot say *how* it could do this. Disembodied postmortem persons may not have voice boxes, but they may well produce auditory sensations without having voice boxes. Given the implausibility of the telepathic theory in general and of Dommeyer's ESP explanation in particular, the production of such auditory sensations may well have occurred in the Butler case.

Conclusion

In the end, we may not be able to say *how* a disembodied person can be causally effective in producing visual and auditory sensations that are plausibly taken as evidence for its existence. The crucial point, however, is not that we be able to explain *how* all this can happen, or even *why* it happens. We need only show good reasons for thinking *that* it happens. Here again, demonstrating *that* something happens is no substitute for showing *how* or *why* it happens. But failure to show *how* or *why* is quite consistent with showing *that* it happens.

Is the Butler case unique? Well, if it were, this would be sufficient reason to suspect that the case was fabricated—that it was a hoax of some sort, or the product of some sort of a mistake we may not be able now to detect. Fortunately, the fact that there are other cases very similar to the Butler case—such as the Ghost of Flight 401 and the other cases described above—is good reason to think that the Butler case is not a hoax of some sort or the product of some undetectable mistake.[66]

Even so, we must admit that there is a serious problem with the case of the Ghost of Flight 401. The problem is that, unlike in the Butler case, the testimony and evidence is not a matter of public record and carefully recorded testimony. Nor was the matter investigated by more than the one person cited (a journalist) and the data independently verified with careful methodology. This affords good grounds to question the data and raise the question of hoax. And even if it is not a hoax or the product of careless but honest methodology, we cannot at this moment regard it as a well-established case investigated by careful inquirers. In this regard we can only hope that Eastern Airlines will release the log of flights of plane 318, that some of the principals will come forward to be identified, and that the data will be reexamined.

Similarly, there are those who will argue—plausibly—that a close examination of the Butler case as it is depicted in the pamphlet written by Reverend Cummings raises important questions that were not asked at the time. Moreover, the Butler case took place so long ago that the principals cannot be directly examined on the matter. Was Reverend Cummings the right person to investigate and report on the case? Might he have been altogether too careless and naive? For these reasons—while it seems fair to say that nobody has successfully disputed the Butler case, or even the case of the Ghost of Flight 401—the evidence for personal survival based on these cases is certainly not so strong as would be necessary for inducing anything like robustly confirmed belief rather than plausible or likely belief. However, the other two cases discussed in this chapter do not suffer from this particular criticism.

Finally, in Chapter 6 we will examine and reject the so-called philosophical reasons why human personality cannot in any form or to any degree—that is, *by definition*—survive biological death.

The literature and research on hauntings continue to grow, and it would certainly be interesting to find more verified cases with the logical features of the four cases described above—especially the first two: the Butler case, and the Ghost of Flight 401. Until we do, though, the evidence presented here—while persuasive in some ways—will seem something less than ideal from the sceptic's point of view.

Notes

1. F. W. H. Myers, *Human Personality and Its Survival of Bodily Death*, abridged and ed. S. Smith (Hyde Park, N.Y.: University Books, 1961; originally published 1903).

2. C. J. Ducasse, *A Critical Examination of the Belief in Life after Death* (Springfield, Ill.: Charles C Thomas, 1961), pp. 21–22.

3. The Reverend Abraham Cummings's *Immortality Proved by Testimony of Sense* was originally published by J. C. Torrey, in Bath, Maine, in 1826. A copy is available in the New York Public Library as well as in the Library of the Division of Personality Studies in the Department of Behavioral Medicine at the University of Virginia School of Medicine in Charlottesville, Virginia. The case has been closely examined by Muriel Roll in her article "A Nineteenth-century Matchmaking Apparition: Comments on Abraham Cummings' 'Immortality Proved by Testimony of the Senses,' " *Journal of the American Society for Psychical Research* 63, no. 4 (October 1969), pp. 396–409.

4. Cummings, *Immortality Proved*, pp. 29ff.

5. Ibid., pp. 32–34.

6. Ibid., p. 33.

7. Ibid., pp. 70ff.

8. Ibid., pp. 22ff.

9. Ibid., p. 34.

10. Ibid., p. 30.

11. See John Fuller, *The Ghost of Flight 401* (New York: Berkeley Publishing, 1978).

12. Ibid., p. 138.

13. Ibid., p. 141.

14. Ibid., p. 150.

15. Ibid., p. 159.

16. See P. Turner, "The Grey Lady: A Study of Psychic Phenomenon in the Dying," *Journal of the Society for Psychical Research* 40 (1959), pp. 124–29. A notice of this case appears in Andrew MacKenzie's book *The Unexplained: Some Strange Cases in Psychical Research* (New York: Abelard Press, 1966), pp. 45ff.

17. Turner, "Grey Lady," p. 126.

18. Ibid., pp. 124–26.

19. Ibid., p. 125.

20. Ibid.

21. Ibid., p. 126.

22. Ibid.

23. MacKenzie, *The Unexplained*, p. 49.

24. Ibid.

25. Turner, "Grey Lady," p. 128.

26. F. W. H. Myers, "On Indications of Continued Terrene Knowledge on the Part of Phantoms of the Dead," *Proceedings of the Society for Psychical Research* 8 (1892), pp. 170–252; B. Abdy Collins, *The Chelten-*

ham Ghost (London: Psychic Press, 1948). The case of the Cheltenham ghost is also reviewed by MacKenzie in *The Unexplained*, pp. 51–63, and more recently updated and discussed as possibly the best case available in his *Hauntings and Apparitions* (London: Heinemann, 1982), pp. 40ff.

27. MacKenzie, *Hauntings*, p. 43.

28. Andrew MacKenzie, *The Unexplained*, paperback ed. (New York: Abelard Press, 1972), p. 59.

29. MacKenzie, *The Unexplained* (1966), p. 54.

30. MacKenzie, *Hauntings*, pp. 41ff.

31. Ibid., p. 40, citing Collins, *Cheltenham Ghost*.

32. MacKenzie, *Hauntings*, pp. 55ff.

33. W. H. Salter, *Zoar* (London: Sidgwick and Jackson, 1961).

34. As cited by MacKenzie, *Hauntings*, p. 41.

35. Mrs. Henry Sidgwick, writing in the *Proceedings of the Society for Psychical Research* (1885); and discussion in MacKenzie, *Hauntings*, pp. 53ff.

36. Stephen Braude, *The Limits of Influence* (London: Routledge and Kegan Paul, 1986), pp. 192ff.

37. H. H. Price, "Apparitions: Two Theories," *Journal of Parapsychology* 24 (1960), pp. 110–28.

38. Braude, *Limits*, p. 194.

39. Ibid.

40. Myers, *Human Personality and Its Survival*, p. 43.

41. G. N. M. Tyrrell, *Apparitions*, rev. ed. (London: Society for Psychical Research, 1973; originally published 1953), p. 59.

42. Ibid.; see also Braude, *Limits*, p. 195.

43. C. D. Broad, *Lectures on Psychical Research* (New York: Humanities Press, 1962), pp. 234ff.

44. Braude, *Limits*, p. 196.

45. Ibid., p. 198.

46. Ibid., p. 204.

47. Ibid., p. 199.

48. Ibid., p. 202.

49. Ibid., p. 203.

50. Ibid., p. 204.

51. Ibid.

52. Ibid., p. 208.

53. Ibid., p. 209.

54. Ibid., p. 196, see also chs. 1.2, 1.3, and 4.2.

55. Ibid., p. 196.

56. Frederick Dommeyer, "Body, Mind, and Death," *Pacific Forum* (1963).

57. Ducasse, *Critical Examination of the Belief*, p. 155.

58. Dommeyer, "Body, Mind, and Death," pp. 31–33.

59. Cummings, *Immortality Proved*, pp. 22ff.

60. See Broad, *Lectures*, esp. pp. 414–15 and 416.

61. Myers, *Human Personality and Its Survival*.

62. Ibid.—this excerpt is from the chapter "Phantasms of the Dead" as it is reprinted in Martin Ebon, ed., *The Signet Handbook of Parapsychology* (New York: Signet Books, 1978), pp. 275–77.

63. In Ebon, *Signet Handbook*, p. 276.

64. Tyrrell, *Apparitions*, p. 95.

65. Given Myers's and Tyrrell's view—see notes 61–64 above—there is a sense in which all so-called apparitions of the dead may well be "hallucinatory" insofar as they might be cases in which people do not really see what they think they see—namely, the surviving person—but rather something the surviving person causes, which is not really representative of what the surviving person is like. We may want to call such a hallucination a *veridical hallucination* because it would lead to a true belief based on a mistaken belief of what one is perceiving in these experiences. In this view, a nonveridical hallucination would be one in which, first, what one perceives is totally the product of fabricating consciousness and, second, the belief that there is something corresponding to it in the real world is false. If Myers is right, then there is a sense in which perceptual data for belief in personal survival may well be hallucinatory but may nonetheless be a legitimate source of belief in the personal survival.

On this item, see also Ian Stevenson, "Do We Need a New Word to Supplement 'Hallucination'?" *American Journal of Psychiatry* 140, no. 12 (December 1983), pp. 1609–11. Stevenson urges that we (psychiatrists?) not use the word *hallucination* to designate unshared sensory experiences because such experiences may well be quite veridical and not the product of causes associated solely with mental illness. The point is well taken. Certainly, we all have sensory experiences (associated with private knowledge) that are not shared and are obviously not the product of mental illness. What is interesting about the Butler case and the case of the Ghost of Flight 401, however, is that they are instances of shared sensory experience (not so in the cases of the grey lady and the Cheltenham ghost). This is why the first two cases discussed in this chapter are so very interesting and why we should be seeking more verified cases like them. Still, as Stevenson points out, the mere fact that no one says they have shared a testifier's perceptual experiences is no good reason for thinking that the testimony is either false or the product of mental disease.

Chapter Two

66. For two other case studies very similar to the Butler case, see "The Case of the Green Lady" and "The Case of the Ghostly Pilot" in Ernest Bennett's *Apparitions and Haunted Houses: A Survey of Evidence* (Ann Arbor, Mich.: Gryphon Books, 1971), pp. 29ff and 139ff. Although both cases report on apparitions that are frequently seen by many individuals collectively over a long period of time and that communicate precognitive knowledge, they are reported as legends and have no sworn eyewitness accounts to document their basic facts.

3

Possession

Possession (or ostensible possession) is usually defined as the alleged phenomenon in which a clearly established and well-recognized personality is totally replaced, often only temporarily, by another personality occupying the same physical body. This definition assumes that human personality is distinct from, and not identifiable with, the physical body. When the alleged phenomenon of possession occurs, the replacing personality manifests the essential characteristics (both cognitive and behavioral) associated with a person quite distinct from the original personality, and none of the individuating characteristics of the former person are manifest at all.

Back in Chapter 1 we examined briefly the possession hypothesis as a plausible alternative explanation for those cases offered principally by Ian Stevenson in support of the belief in reincarnation. In that context I suggested, for various reasons, that the possession hypothesis is not so persuasive an explanation as the reincarnation hypothesis. Obviously, this is a debatable issue only among those who believe in the possibility of some form of disembodied personal existence. It is not a debate that a strongly committed reductive materialist can take seriously.

At any rate, the question is whether the defense of reincarnation offered in Chapter 1 takes the possession hypothesis seriously enough. We granted that, for nonmaterialists, the possession hypothesis may well seem the most plausible alternative explanation of the data, or at least as plausible. In this chapter we will examine two (of very many) fairly typical possession-type cases,

135

and we will do this for two reasons. The first reason is that these two cases provide solid evidence for belief in some form of disembodied personal postmortem existence. And the second is that, by providing us with a better understanding of the phenomenon, these cases may help us appreciate more fully the reasons why we cannot explain the richer cases offered for belief in reincarnation by urging that they are merely cases of ostensible possession.

In examining the possession cases, the first question we shall ask is whether the best evidence for the occurrence of this phenomenon admits of any plausible alternative explanation that does not require of us belief in the occurrence of possession as defined above. The second question will be whether, granted that possession as so defined does occur, we can convincingly explain the data supporting belief in reincarnation in terms of it. Let us now turn to our two fairly typical cases—one of which is quite well known and discussed, and the other quite recent. The first case is the celebrated Watseka Wonder, and the second we may call the Sumitra case.

The Watseka Wonder

Any reasonably adequate discussion of the evidence for life after death should include a consideration of the famous Watseka Wonder as a striking instance of possession—an instance that allegedly supports the belief in postmortem personal survival. The case was originally presented and described by Dr. E. W. Stevens in 1887 in a paper entitled "The Watseka Wonder: A Narrative of Startling Phenomena Occurring in the Case of Mary Lurancy Vennum,"[1] and C. J. Ducasse discusses it in detail in his 1961 *Critical Examination of the Belief in Life after Death*.[2] The circumstances took place in Watseka, Illinois, and concern two girls. The first girl, Mary Roff, had died at age 18 in 1865. She was said to have suffered from "fits" and was allegedly able to read closed books and the contents of sealed envelopes.

The second girl was Lurancy Vennum, born in April 1864 and over a year old when Mary Roff died. Lurancy seemed quite normal until 1877 when, at age 13, she complained of feeling queer and had a fit, "including a cataleptic state lasting five hours."[3] On later occasions, while in a trance state, she allegedly talked with "angels" or "spirits" of deceased persons. She also seemed to be possessed by various alien spirits, each of whom took turns possessing her. Her sanity was questioned.

The most interesting (according to Ducasse) of Lurancy's "possessions" was that by the mind of Mary Roff. Indeed, Lurancy claimed to be Mary Roff and gave evidence of being homesick and wanting to see her (Mary's) parents and brothers. After a few days, Lurancy was taken to and permitted to live with the Roff family.

While living with the Roffs, she seemed quite happy and knew everybody that Mary Roff had known in her lifetime 12–25 years earlier. She readily identified by name the persons who had been friends and neighbors of the Roffs during Mary's lifetime. During her stay at the Roffs' residence, she recounted hundreds of incidents that had occurred in Mary's natural life and, unlike any reincarnation case, never had any awareness of her identity as Lurancy; she could not identify or recognize any of the Vennum family members or their friends and neighbors. Her identity as Mary while living with the Roffs lasted more than three and a half months, and she was fully accepted as Mary by the family.

Later, her identity as Lurancy returned and she recognized nothing about the Roffs but had all the memories of Lurancy, including the usual recognitions attending her life with the Vennums. Occasionally later on, when she visited the Roffs, the Mary Roff personality would emerge for a short while, and again she would lose her identity as Lurancy.

Clairvoyant Knowledge?

Responding to the charge that this is simply a manifestation of alternating personality, or multiple personality—a personality disorder readily characterized in psychiatry—Ducasse notes that the personality that displaced Lurancy's was (by every test that could be applied) not a dissociated part of her own. Rather, it was the personality, including all the memories, of a particular 18-year-old girl who had died when Lurancy was 14 months old.[4]

Moreover, Ducasse claims that in no way could Lurancy have obtained by normal means the extensive and detailed knowledge that Mary possessed and that Lurancy manifested. The Vennums were away from Watseka (the town in Illinois where both the Roffs and the Vennums lived) for the first seven years of Lurancy's life. When they returned to Watseka, their acquaintance with the Roffs consisted of only one brief call lasting a few minutes made by Mrs. Roff on Mrs. Vennum, and of a formal speaking acquaintance on the part of the two men, until the time when Mr. Roff brought Dr. Stevens (the principal investigator) to the Vennums because of Lurancy's insane behavior.[5]

Can we explain what transpired in this case without endorsing the explanation that the disembodied postmortem personality of Mary Roff "took possession" of Lurancy Vennum's body? If not, then we have good evidence that human personality in some important way and to some important degree survives biological death. Naturally, we have to assume that the case is not a hoax or a fraud. Perhaps we could justifiably discount it if there never was another case similar to it, or if we had no other documented cases like it. But we have many cases similar to it, some even better examined and more recent.[6]

Probably the best known criticism of the possession explanation of the Watseka case comes from Frederick Dommeyer, who writes,

> But why need the "possession" hypothesis be accepted here? Ordinary dreams and the hypnotic trance, not to mention the mediumistic situation, testify to the "dramatizing powers" of the unconscious. Under hypnosis the subject can be caused by suggestion to play the role of another person. On several occasions, the writer has seen hypnotised subjects take on the role of others in realistic fashion. The hypnotist, for example, might suggest that the subject is a Civil War veteran. Without delay, the subject would start telling a tale of his suffering as a soldier, his experiences in battle, etc. Granting such well-known powers of the unconscious to dramatize under hypnosis, and recalling also the remarkable though commonplace dramatizations of man's dream-life, and adding to this the power of retrocognition, we have a nonpossession hypothesis for

explaining the Watseka Wonder case. There is no need for believing that "something" that had earlier been "in" Mary was later "in" Lurancy, i.e., that a mind had somehow gone from one to the other. With that need no longer present, the Watseka Wonder case has no bearing upon the survival issue.[7]

Dommeyer's view, therefore, is that we can equally well explain the facts of the Watseka Wonder case just by supposing that Lurancy Vennum first (somehow or other) clairvoyantly obtained detailed knowledge of Mary Roff and her past life, then subconsciously identified with the dead girl, and finally—owing to the dramatizing power of the subconscious mind—successfully impersonated Mary Roff. But is this a plausible alternative to the possession explanation?

Dommeyer's version suffers from at least one major defect. This defect was noted by Ducasse in the very same journal issue in which Dommeyer's explanation appeared. As Ducasse said,

> Consider for example the case of a person who has no knowledge of theoretical physics. Irrespective of whether he be awake, or in hypnosis, or in a mediumistic trance, he could not possibly enact convincingly the part Einstein would take in discussion with a theoretical physicist present on some technical point in theoretical physics.
>
> The crucial question as regards the Watseka case is whether it is possible, or not possible, for a person P to identify himself unmistakenly to another person Q who had known him intimately for years, by means of his behavior and of the contents, style, allusiveness and responsiveness of his conversations with Q. That it is not possible in only an hour or two is probably true. But in the Watseka case, the Roffs had three and a half months of day-long close observations of the behavior, tastes, skills, knowledge and capacity to make and understand allusions to intimate family matters, possessed by the personality which was expressing itself through the body of Lurancy during those months. And the Roffs testified that those traits were the very same as those which had together been distinctive of their deceased daughter Mary, whom Lurancy had never known.
>
> Let Dommeyer suppose that a young woman who remains constantly masked and muffled somehow comes and lives in his

house; and let him ask himself whether he thinks it would be possible for that woman, through facts perceived extra-sensorily, to enact for three and a half months convincingly to him the part of his own daughter, if that woman's personality were not really that of his daughter. An affirmative answer would amount to saying that no way ultimately exists by which it would be possible for a person whose face and fingers have been disfigured by acid or by fire, to prove his identity to another who had known him intimately for many years. And this, I submit, is virtually beyond belief.[8]

In sum, the very idea that Lurancy could successfully impersonate Mary Roff over a three-and-a-half-month period in the presence of the Roff family is unthinkable even if we were to grant that Lurancy could know extrasensorily every detail of Mary Roff's life. That sort of skill is not imparted with the gift of clairvoyance.

Here again, of course, people sympathetic to Dommeyer's critique may be willing to admit that a large dose of implausibility attends his ESP explanation. But, they say, when compared with the explanation offered in terms of possession, Dommeyer's ESP-cum-subconscious-dramatic-impersonation becomes more acceptable, because there is no independent plausibility to be associated with personal disembodied postmortem existence. To this objection we can only reply by pointing to the mounting evidence offered throughout the pages of this book, and to the degree of plausibility being established herein for the belief in personal postmortem existence. In this context—unless we assume fraud, or hoax, or that the Roffs were quite stupid or ill—Ducasse's objection seems quite forceful and should be decisive.

Normal Knowledge?

Another objection to regarding the Watseka Wonder as evidence for possession was raised by Rodger I. Anderson in a 1980 paper entitled "The Watseka Wonder: A Critical Re-evaluation."[9] Here Anderson argues, after a careful examination of Stevens's original paper, that we cannot rule against the hypothesis that Lurancy acquired her knowledge of Mary Roff and the intimate details of

Mary's life in very natural ways both before and after she went to stay in the Roff household. The families lived in the same town, had contact before the case developed, and might easily have had other contacts not known to the original investigator Dr. Stevens who, as a convinced spiritualist, was hardly the unbiased researcher one might desire. Anderson also asserts that the case was not examined correctly, and that the Roffs only tested Lurancy long after she had taken up residence in the house—and even then the tests were conducted under conditions that made it quite possible for Lurancy to know the answers by normal means. In short, for Anderson and for others also, in spite of the celebrated nature of the case, a careful examination of the report will show that the methods employed to establish it as a case of ostensible possession were too inaccurate to eliminate the real possibility that the intimate information Lurancy had about the Roffs was acquired in normal ways.[10]

Anderson is probably right in claiming that the case as Stevens presents it would never be accepted as a well-verified and well-researched case today. Even so, it is important to note that Anderson does not present any evidence showing that the knowledge Lurancy had of the intimate details of the Roff household was *in fact* acquired by natural means. His point is that the methods of investigation employed do not make this hypothesis at all difficult to entertain—and a good case should never allow as much. If this hypothesis is plausible, then we need only add that Lurancy was subconsciously and dramatically impersonating Mary Roff (with whom she strongly identified for some reason) by means of the knowledge she had acquired naturally. This basic alternative explanation, incidentally, was offered in 1981 by C. T. K. Chari, who sees the Watseka Wonder as nothing more than a case of "alternating personality" combined with successful subconscious impersonation based on knowledge acquired quite normally in ways not appreciated by the original investigators.[11]

Perhaps, in the end, the best way to deal with Anderson's and Chari's objection is to return to the above-excerpted reply of Ducasse to Dommeyer, which implies among other things that, even if—for the sake of discussion—Lurancy had acquired all the pertinent information in natural ways, this would still not account for Lurancy's manifesting deep personality traits and basic ways of acting that only a seasoned impersonator could imitate and then only after seeing and being exposed to Mary Roff herself. Appeals to the phenomenon of multiple personality and the power of the subconscious mind to dramatize seem just a bit too weak to explain how Lurancy acquired all the many subtle behaviors and other personal characteristics that convinced all involved she was indeed Mary Roff. As Ducasse wisely suggested, if one knew all there was to know about the intimate details of Einstein's life (no matter how the information was acquired), one would still need to know how to *act* like Einstein in those very many ways that only intimate family members could recognize as part of Einstein's personality; and one certainly could not do that (no matter how powerful the dramatizing power of one's mind) without at least spending some time with Einstein or watching Einstein. Lurancy Vennum could never have even seen Mary Roff. Not even the best impersonator in the world can impersonate someone knowing only the propositions that are true of that person, nor would such an impersonator succeed in convincing all the members of that person's family that he is indeed not an impersonator but the person himself. So, Anderson's and Chari's alternative explanation—even if true so far as it goes (i.e., that Lurancy knew *all* the facts of Mary's existence)—is immaterial in explaining the actual phenomenon of the case. There has never been any evidence, inside or outside the lab, of ESP's ever accounting for such successful impersonation as was seen in the Watseka Wonder.

Obviously, however, our stance as to whether Lurancy's Mary Roff personality showed the personality traits that were unique to Mary Roff, and not able to be impersonated by even a clever impersonator, would be a function of whether we accept the family's identification of those traits as both unique to Mary Roff and not capable of being impersonated by somebody who had only propositional knowledge of Mary Roff's life, family, and unique personality traits. And, in fact, we have no good reason *not* to accept the family's claim on this matter.

The only other conceivable objection to the possession interpretation of the Watseka Wonder would be the argument offered by Stephen Braude and Jule Eisenbud (in another context)[12] to the effect that, as soon as we admit of the existence of super-psi in terms of either super-PK or super-ESP, we cannot reject an explanation in terms of it without unjustifiably assuming that ESP or PK can only exist in ways that are familiar and well documented in the past. If this argument is correct, then we could certainly explain well the paranormal knowledge as well as the behavioral traits evidenced by Lurancy's Mary Roff personality in terms of ESP on a grand scale. For the many reasons defended in the preceding chapter (as well as for the reasons stated in Chapter 1), however, we have seen that this argument is not persuasive. We need not repeat those reasons. Let us turn to a more recent case not subject to the same sort of objections raised against the Watseka Wonder.

The Sumitra Case

In a 1989 article in the *Journal of Scientific Exploration*, Ian Stevenson, Satwant Pasricha, and Nicholas McClean-Rice describe and discuss what they regard as a rare case of possession with evidence of paranormal knowledge.[13] The case involves two completely unrelated and unacquainted persons whose families lived in widely separated towns and villages, and the relevant testimony justifies believing that they had no contact with each other before the case developed. The following are the main details of the case offered by Stevenson and his associates.

The subject, Sumitra Singh, was a young married woman of about 17 years old when the case developed in 1985. She was living with her husband and their one child in the husband's family home in the village of Sharifpura, in the Farrukhabad district of the State of Uttar Pradesh, India. Early in 1985 Sumitra began to develop episodes of loss of consciousness along with eye-roll movements and clenching of teeth. Sometimes in these trances she would speak, and in July of that year she predicted she would die three days later. Indeed, three days later—July 19—she seemed to die. All who were around her considered her dead; she had no pulse, was apneic, and her face was totally drained of blood like that of a dead person. They were grieving and preparing for her funeral when suddenly she revived in a confused state.

Thereafter the woman began to behave very much like a different person. She no longer recognized the people around her, saying that her name was Shiva and that she had been murdered by her in-laws at a place called Dibiyapur. She rejected Sumitra's husband and child and asked to be taken to Shiva's two children. She stated many details that were subsequently found to correspond with the life of another young married woman, Shiva Diwedi, who had died violently—whether from murder or suicide is not known—at Dibiyapur on the night of May 18–19, 1985, two months before Sumitra's apparent death and revival. Shiva's parental family were convinced that her in-laws had murdered her and then attempted to simulate suicide by laying her body on the railway tracks nearby. Shiva's father, Ram Siya Tripathi, had filed a complaint and so initiated a judicial inquiry.

Sumitra's in-laws said they knew nothing of a Shiva who had died at a place called Dibiyapur. Initially, they thought that Sumitra had gone mad and only later that she had become possessed by a discarnate spirit. But, importantly enough, they made no attempt whatsoever to verify what she was saying. It was about a month before Ram Siya Tripathi learned about Sumitra's statements. This occurred accidentally when he heard a rumor, while he was visiting Dibiyapur, that his deceased daughter had taken possession of a girl in a distant village. Nearly two more months elapsed before he was able to verify this information by having someone from a neighboring village visit Sumitra and her family. The information gathered in this way prompted Ram Siya, accompanied by a relative, to visit Sumitra. Sumitra recognized him and said that she was his daughter. With Ram Siya, she visited Shiva's village during the following days and recognized at least 13 members of Shiva's family and friends.

Stevenson and his associates note that, in addition to Sumitra's statements about the life of Shiva and her recognitions of persons Shiva had known, she showed a marked change in behavior. Sumitra's family belonged to the Thakur caste and they were villagers with very little education; Sumitra herself had no formal education, although she could read and write a little. The Tripathis, on the other hand, were Brahmins and middle-class urbanites. Ram Siya was a lecturer in a college, and Shiva had been educated up to the level of earning a B.A. degree. After her revival, Sumitra's behavior changed from that of a simple village girl to that of a reasonably well educated woman of higher caste and more urbane manners, who could now read and write Hindi fluently.[14]

Shortly after the first exchanges of visits between the families concerned, the case caught the attention of Ian Stevenson and S. Pasricha who, with others, began to investigate the case promptly in mid-October 1985. The method of investigation consisted basically of interviews with informants, "particularly first-hand witnesses of the apparent death of Sumitra and the change in her personality that followed upon her revival."[15] But the investigating team spent almost as much time interviewing the members of Shiva's family. The interviews were conducted simultaneously by various investigators over a two-year period (ending in October 1987), but principally by Stevenson and Pasricha, who spoke with everybody who might in any way be relevant or material to the case. They interviewed 24 members of Shiva's and Sumitra's families, with the more important witnesses among them being interviewed two or more times. Extensive verbatim notes were taken; and during a few special interviews, tape recordings were made either solely or in addition to taking notes. Moreover, the investigators interviewed another 29 persons who were able to furnish background information, especially about communications between the communities involved in the case.

In examining the case, the Stevenson team paid particular attention to the following aspects: the preceding illness, apparent death, and revival of Sumitra; the possibilities for normal communication of information about Shiva's life and death to Sumitra and her family; and the circumstances under which Sumitra after her revival identified Shiva's family in person and in photographs. Informants for Sumitra's side of the case claimed no previous acquaintance with Shiva's family, and members of Shiva's family claimed that they were completely ignorant of Sumitra's family before the case developed. As Stevenson also notes, apart from the long (for India) geographical distances between the families, they were also separated by significant differences of caste, education, and economic condition.[16]

Naturally, from an evidential viewpoint, the informants' denial of prior acquaintance between the two families is important. According to the investigators, strong support for the informants' denial of prior acquaintance derives from the slow and indirect manner in which Shiva's family learned about the personality change in Sumitra. The investigators describe this process in the following way:

> Sumitra's father and her in-laws made no attempt to verify her statements about Shiva. Word about them first reached the neighboring village of Murra, which is 2 km from Sharifpura. From there it traveled to Dibiyapur apparently conveyed by women of Murra who had married and were living there. Ram Siya Tripathi, on a visit to Dibiyapur, heard a rumor that his dead daughter had taken possession of a girl in a distant village called Sharifpura. However, he had never been to Sharifpura and did not even know where it was located. After another two weeks he learned about a man called Ram Prakash Dube, a native of Murra who was living in Etawah, but whom he had not previously known. He asked Ram Prakash Dube to inquire about the truth of the account he had heard in Dibiyapur. The monsoon rains led to further delays. When Ram Prakash Dube next visited Murra, he looked into the story and confirmed its main outlines to Ram Siya Tripathi, who, as we have mentioned, then went to Sharifpura and had his first meeting with Sumitra on Oct. 20, 1985. This was exactly three months after Sumitra's apparent death and revival. We believe that if the families concerned had been previously acquainted or had had any lines of communication through mutual acquaintances, they would have exchanged information about Sumitra's change of personality much sooner than they did. . . .
>
> Members of Sumitra's family said that they had heard nothing about Shiva's death before Sumitra's death, revival and personality change. However, in view of the circulation of some newspapers in their area and of some trading between Sharifpura and Etawah, it is best to assume that they might have learned of Shiva's death and perhaps also learned about some of the allegations of suicide and homicide that figured in the newspaper reports. (There was no radio station in the area. Some television had been introduced at Etawah only [Sharifpura had no electricity], but it only relayed programs from Delhi and broadcast no local news.) The newspaper

reports included some of the names of Shiva's parental family and in-laws. The important question remaining is, therefore, whether Sumitra, after the change in her personality, demonstrated knowledge and behavior corresponding to Shiva's life that went beyond the information available in the newspapers reporting the death of Shiva and the related judicial inquiry.[17]

The published report of this case offers a detailed statement of the life, last illness, apparent death, and revival of Sumitra. It emphasizes that, prior to her apparent death, she had experienced a number of "possession-type" episodes for which her family sought the help of a healer. The investigators do not claim that Sumitra had in fact died before her revival. Also, the report examines the pertinent details of the life and death of Shiva. Here the investigators concur with local authorities in saying that Shiva's death was not accidental; she either was murdered by her in-laws who made it look as though Shiva committed suicide, or else did commit suicide by throwing herself before a railway train.

Most importantly, the report shows a large number of detailed and verified claims made by Sumitra about the life and death of Shiva, and concludes that there is no way of explaining Sumitra's knowledge by appeal to the normal sources of knowledge. Also, Sumitra's behavioral traits distinctly replicated the behavioral characteristics of Shiva even though the two had definitely never met. Thus, impersonation cannot be the explanation for the manifestation of those traits. Without seeking to repeat all the facts of the case, let us look a bit more closely at these two factors as described in detail in the case study.

Stevenson and his associates divide Sumitra's statements into three groups. The first group consists of names of persons and places that the newspaper accounts of Shiva's death and her father's lawsuit had published. The investigators think it extremely unlikely that anyone communicated even the fact of Shiva's death—much less the details—to Sumitra's family. Even so, as noted above, the investigators acknowledge that some newspapers were circulated in the general area of Sharifpura, and so it is possible that Sumitra's family might have learned about Shiva's death through normal channels of information. Therefore, none of the facts that Sumitra related were regarded as paranormally derived if they could be found in the various newspaper accounts of Shiva's death and the circumstances attending it. The second group of Sumitra's statements consists of unverified claims. Sumitra's description of Shiva's death, for example, and the role of her in-laws in the death, remains unverified. The third group of statements includes nicknames and other private affairs not published in the newspapers. This group is the most important because it consists of statements that are verified *and* that there is no normal way for Sumitra to have acquired. On this point the report states,

> We learned of 19 items that we felt justified in placing in this, the important group. These showed that Sumitra had knowledge of: a particular yellow sari that Shiva had owned, a watch that had belonged to Shiva and the box (in the Tripathi home) in which it was kept, the respective order of birth of Shiva's maternal uncles (although one who was younger actually looked older than one of the older uncles), one of Shiva's nicknames familiarly used in the home (Shiv Shanker), the names of two educational institutions where Shiva had studied (Sarvodya College and Sorawal Intermediate College), the pet names of Shiva's two children (Rinku and Tinku), the names of two friends of Shiva who happened to have the same name, and the names of Shiva's two brothers, two of her sisters, two of her maternal uncles, a maternal aunt (by marriage), and a nephew.[18]

Sumitra's uncued recognition of Shiva's various family members and friends is important as evidence of paranormal knowledge, once it had been established that there was no normal way in which Sumitra could plausibly have acquired this information. In talking about how these recognitions were authenticated, the report notes that the method is quite the same as in cases of the reincarnation type. As the researchers note,

> Observers of recognitions in cases suggestive of reincarnation—of which the present case may be considered a variant—frequently vitiate them by asking leading questions or by cueing the subject with glances directed toward the person to be recognized.[19] Nevertheless, there remain several circumstances in which recognitions

may occur that deserve credit as showing paranormal knowledge on the part of the subject. These are: recognitions that the subject makes spontaneously without anyone's having asked him or her to identify another person; recognitions that occur when the subject is confronted with a person and asked a question like: "Do you know who this person is?" or "Tell me who I am"; and recognitions in which the subject immediately afterward adds a statement about some intimate detail, perhaps a nickname, not known outside a small circle of family and friends. We learned of twelve members of Shiva's family and circle of friends whom Sumitra recognized under conditions that we believed excluded cueing.[20]

The report then describes in detail the circumstances of seven of Sumitra's recognitions, six of which were clearly without any cueing at all. Perhaps the most interesting consisted in her recognizing a friend of Shiva's youth, one Krishna Devi Dube. This recognition occurred at Sikandarpur when Sumitra visited her mother-in-law's family in February 1986. More than eight years earlier, Krishna Devi and Shiva had known each other when Shiva used to visit one of her maternal uncles in the nearby village of Kainjari, Krishna Devi's native place. When Krishna Devi married, she moved to Sikandarpur and had not met Shiva for more than eight years before Shiva's death. As the investigators report, when Shiva saw Krishna Devi, she cried, "Jiji! How come you are here? I died and have come into a Thakur's family and am helpless." Shiva, when alive, had called Krishna Devi "Jiji," the word meaning "sister."[21]

Shiva's father, Ram Siya Tripathi, was initially quite sceptical about the alleged possession until he showed Sumitra a family photograph album and she correctly identified (without prompting) 15 of the 17 people shown to her. Later on, Sumitra also correctly identified in person eight members of the family or circle of friends whose photographs she had not seen. Concurrently, Sumitra failed to recognize places, activities, and people that had been very familiar to her, prior to her alleged assumption of the Shiva personality.

Behaviorally, after her revival, Sumitra dressed and in all other ways (including mode of addressing others) acted like a Brahmin—especially toward her new family, which she regarded as inferior because they were Thakurs. She persisted in her belief that she was a Brahmin and acted very much as one would expect a Brahmin to act. Shiva's father also claimed that he recognized in Sumitra certain personality traits very much like the traits of Shiva, namely, a certain boldness and a tendency to joke, which were not traits of Sumitra before her revival.[22]

The Sceptic's Response

In discussing the force of this case, Stevenson and his team of investigators note that there are only four possible explanations of the data: (1) fraud; (2) cryptomnesia (source amnesia) with secondary personality; (3) secondary personality having paranormal knowledge; and (4) possession of Sumitra's body by the deceased Shiva.

Fraud?

The investigators reject the possibility of a fraud perpetrated by Sumitra alone. They assert convincingly that "a barely literate village woman in India could not have obtained detailed accurate information about another woman who lived 100 km away without assistance."[23] So, if the case were a matter of a hoax or fraud, it had to include others.

> If there was a hoaxing team, who composed it? Sumitra's husband, as a man, could move around more easily than Sumitra, but he was not in a position to go to places like Dibiyapur and Etawah in order to search out unpublished details about the life of Shiva. It has been suggested that the exorcist Vishwa Nath, who had access to Sumitra (although probably never alone) before and after her apparent death and recovery, might have obtained information about Shiva and coached Sumitra with the details of which he had knowledge. However, this suggestion also, in our view, fails to take account of the information Sumitra had of the private life of the Tripathi family, and it fails to explain her ability to recognize 23 strange persons in person or in photographs.
>
> Shiva's in-laws at Dibiyapur had all the information included in

Sumitra's statements about Shiva's life and death, but they were already incriminated in Shiva's death and had an interest, therefore, in Shiva's silence. Sumitra's "Shiva personality" was saying publicly that Shiva's in-laws had murdered her, and the in-laws could not be suspected of promoting this view of Shiva's death.

Shiva's parental family also had the information included in Sumitra's statements. Ram Siya Tripathi might have collaborated in a hoax. In talking with us he himself mentioned this possibility. When we asked him whether he thought Sumitra might have learned normally about Shiva he said, "No. If she had done that how could she have recognized me and members of my family?" Then he spontaneously added: "People say I have made this case up, but why would I do that? I am gaining nothing, and my [legal] case [against Shiva's in-laws] will not be improved. Sumitra cannot be a witness. I am not getting my daughter back." We think he is correct on these points.[24]

The investigators grant that Sumitra and her in-laws might have gained a little status from the change in her behavior and from the fact that they had a family member "raised" from the Thakur caste to the Brahmin caste. And Sumitra's husband was probably staying home more and being more attentive to her. But, according to the researchers, these alleged benefits seem too insignificant to justify a fraud of such elaborate dimension.

Cryptomnesia with Secondary Personality?

The investigators also consider the possibility that Sumitra had acquired the information about Shiva in very normal ways but then forgot that she had done so. She would then have had the appropriate information to construct a secondary personality, thereby dramatically and subconsciously impersonating Shiva. This objection (as well as the one about fraud) we have already seen when discussing the sceptic's reply to the evidence for reincarnation—which, not surprisingly, admits of the very same objections precisely because possession is indeed a form of reincarnation. The two alleged phenomena are established by appeal to strongly similar bodies of evidence. At any rate, the researchers quickly note that this sort of objection is fundamentally unacceptable because the information Sumitra had about private or intimate family matters was not in the newspapers and could not plausibly have been conveyed to her by traveling third parties. Besides, no information conveyed by third parties from newspaper accounts of Shiva's death could account for Sumitra's successful recognition of Shiva's family members (whom Sumitra had never seen before) from the album of photographs.

Secondary Personality with Paranormal Knowledge?

With regard to the third alternative explanation in terms of secondary (multiple) personality, the investigators are quick to note that there are very few cases in which secondary personalities show highly refined and accurate paranormal knowledge. Moreover, while it is possible that Sumitra acquired powers of extrasensory perception after her revival (she had none before her revival), this would not explain her sudden ability to read and write very fluently. There is no evidence that telepathy extends to an enhanced ability to read and write. And so, while this objection seems plausible to some, it is ultimately arbitrary or ad hoc.

The authors accordingly close their discussion with the claim that the only plausible interpretation consists in appealing to a type of possession or reincarnation.

Further Reflections on the Sumitra Case

Unlike the case of the Watseka Wonder, the Sumitra case is not susceptible to the criticism that the two families lived close to each other and therefore could have had some contact before the case developed. Also, the Sumitra case cannot be dismissed as having taken place too long ago for us to determine whether the facts are as claimed. The Stevenson research team conducted a methodologically careful and extensive effort to uncover all relevant facts and to subject the data to close public scrutiny and alternative plausible explanations. Does this leave an honest sceptic with any other objections to their conclusion of possession?

A resourceful sceptic might suggest that, even if the facts of the case are as they have been depicted by Stevenson and his associates, still—in the absence of Sumitra's being able to replicate non-propositional skills appropriate to Shiva—there are yet some reasonable grounds for thinking that we are dealing with the phenomenon of a secondary personality with paranormal knowledge of facts not publicly known. As we saw above, the research team discounted this possibility, saying that such an hypothesis would not account for the many photograph recognitions Sumitra achieved without ever having seen the members of Shiva's family. For the sceptic, however, photograph recognitions of the various members of Shiva's family might be explained telepathically, whereas we would never be able to explain telepathically the speaking of an unlearned language, or the playing of an instrument one has never learned to play, or the manifestation of very personal character traits.

In other words, a sceptic might argue that photograph recognitions are more like propositional knowledge than they are like knowing how to do something or other that would prove an identification, even though the subject is demonstrating skill in knowing how to pick out and name people in pictures. In short, one could know telepathically *that* a person of a certain description will be an uncle named Willy, for example. However rare, there are cases of this sort of telepathy. But there is no evidence that anybody has ever learned telepathically *how* to speak a new language, or play a new instrument, or impersonate successfully someone he or she has never met. A sceptic with this kind of objection to seeing possession in the Sumitra case would be looking for evidence that Sumitra's Shiva personality spoke a language Shiva spoke but that Sumitra had never been exposed to, or played an instrument that Shiva played well but that Sumitra had never learned to play, or *strongly* manifested Shiva's personal character traits. It is not so clear as it might be that a sufficient amount of Shiva's personality was manifest in Sumitra's behavior. In the absence of this sort of evidence, then, is our sceptic's objection here telling?

Another sort of objection would have to be raised by the sceptic who denies validity to the phenomenon of mental telepathy or paranormal knowledge. This sceptic's position invariably must, as we saw in Chapter 1, fall back on arguments to the effect either that the investigators missed the crucial piece of evidence showing fraud or hoax, or that—because the methodology employed does not accommodate the requirement of repeatability as it is understood in the context of laboratory experimentation—the results are not empirically respectable. In the end, neither of these arguments is forceful. To suppose that there really must be some sort of fraud or hoax here requires a persuasive argument that has not yet been offered. And the Sumitra case was very carefully examined and documented, with events still unfolding as the investigation was going on. This is certainly not an instance of stale data, in any case.

But for those who do believe in the phenomenon of paranormal knowledge, the objection that calls for proof via identifying skills may seem compelling. Indeed, it may seem reasonable to suppose that, because the limits of ESP have never been tested and shown, we really cannot exclude the possibility that Sumitra's recognition of Shiva's family members in photographs is an instance of telepathy or even telepathic "leakage" from Shiva's father when he showed Sumitra the family album. In spite of its sweet plausibility, however, this objection is basically ad hoc: as a matter of fact, we have no reports (from either inside or outside the lab) of anybody's ever *suddenly* acquiring such an ability. Typically, those gifted with telepathy achieve the levels of accuracy evidenced in Sumitra's case gradually and only after years of practice. Even then, statistically, the results are never so accurate as this. And spontaneous, need-based ESP shows nowhere near comparable accuracy.

In short, our response to the sceptical objection based on ESP is the same response we made back in Chapter 1 when we examined the ESP objection to various reincarnation-type cases. Here, as there, we note that such an objection simply does not fit with everything we know about the origin, nature, and accuracy of ESP and telepathy. For this reason it is not so plausible as the empirical explanation that fits with what we know about ESP and telepathy. At any rate, on the principle that there are (or will be) many cases similar to the Sumitra case, the investigative methodology henceforth will presumably employ photographic identifications (wherever possible) conducted in such a way as to provide little opportunity for telepathic leakage.

Other than the call for more behavioral (and skills) evidence of possession in the Sumitra case, it is difficult to see what other plausible objection one might raise. However, at this point we should examine what logical features seem to distinguish reincarnation-type cases from possession-type cases. This is important if we are to defend the thesis of reincarnation against those who say that the evidence used for reincarnation is indistinguishable from the evidence for spirit possession. True, we already discussed this item when we examined the "possession objection" to the evidence for reincarnation; but it was difficult to do so until we had seen good evidence for possession as well. Let us see if we can now say more clearly what the differences are between the two and whether such differences do indeed make a difference when it comes to distinguishing between evidence for reincarnation and evidence for possession.

Reincarnation and Possession: The Relevant Differences

In Chapter 1 we noted that the most important feature distinguishing reincarnation-type cases from possession-type cases seems to be that the subjects in reincarnation-type cases often, if not typically, identify their current life-experiences as continuous with a life they remember having lived in a different body at a prior time. They say things such as "I remember that, when I was so and so, I was a woman, but now I am a man," or "When I was so and so, I remember that I was bit by a snake on the left leg and the leg turned blue." In such cases, while involved in describing activities, personalities, and events of the remembered past life, the subject is simultaneously aware of the events and persons the personality in the current life would be expected to know. He or she retains, rather than loses, a dispositional awareness and memory of the current personality as affected by the historical events experienced in the current body. In short, in reincarnation-type cases we typically do not see the total personality-replacement phenomenon that occurs in typical possession-type cases. In the latter, the subject asserts an identity of self that seems to exclude consciousness of the memories and personality associated with his or her physical body.

Certainly, too, it is a distinguishing characteristic of possession-type cases that this historical bodily continuity is present while the phenomenon of personality replacement takes place. This is why one describes such cases by saying that "her body was possessed, or taken over, by another personality or spirit." Thus, *reincarnation* involves an historical continuity of mind (or memory at least) that extends the personality into a time earlier than the current body. *Possession* involves an historical continuity of body whose personality is in some crucial way replaced or displaced. But will this way of distinguishing between reincarnation-type cases and possession-type cases allow us to sort the two effectively when it comes to making sure that the evidence for reincarnation is not explained or confused as evidence for possession instead? The answer is yes, all suggestions to the contrary notwithstanding. Let me explain briefly.

Confronted with the distinction just drawn, the proponents of possession as the best explanation for the data in so-called reincarnation-type cases would probably ask this question: "Why not construe the rich spontaneous past-life memory cases for reincarnation simply as cases of possession that take place in children before their own distinct personalities can be clearly discerned?" After all, if possession took place in a child at age two, we would not be able to recognize one of the conditions that presumably counts for its being a case of possession rather than reincarnation, namely, a dramatic change in personality. Children at that age just do not have a very well formed and describable personal identity. Thus, we would not be able to certify that it is *not* a case of possession. So the objection goes.

Further, as if this were not enough, the problem of distinguishing between reincarnation-type cases and possession-type cases is exacerbated by the explicit endorsement made by Stevenson and his associates of the view that no single interpretation fits neatly all cases of ostensible possession. As the authors of the Sumitra case research report note,

> Possession states occur in many other countries, one might almost say in all of them. However we think it unnecessary to review the

unmanageably extensive literature on this subject, all the more so since adequate reviews with further references have been published elsewhere. [25] We should like to record our agreement with Lewis[26] who warned against the futility of trying to find a single interpretation that will fit all cases of ostensible possession. The word "possession" labels many conditions of various types and different origins and processes.[27]

It is also important to remember that, as Stevenson and others will readily agree, some possession-type cases may be very difficult to distinguish from reincarnation-type cases simply because of an ambiguity in the utterances offered by the subject.

In the end, although these challenges are persuasive as a way of undermining the evidence for reincarnation, they are nevertheless overridden by two important considerations, the last of which (interestingly enough) comes to us from Stevenson himself. The first consideration is that, in the most fully developed reincarnation-type cases involving spontaneous past-life memories, the subjects—however young—usually have a clearly defined personality that is not regarded by family members as displaced or replaced when the spontaneous past-life memories begin to emerge. Bishen Chand, for example, did not lose a knowledge of his family members or even some previously discernible behavioral traits acquired in the family of Bishen Chand, after he began to remember the personalities and events in the life of Laxmi Narain (see Chapter 1). So, while it is possible that some of these cases are instances of possession rather than reincarnation, the richer of the reincarnation-type cases just do not have the traits that we usually ascribe to manifest possession.

The second consideration is that—as Stevenson has already noted[28]—in the richer of the reincarnation-type cases, total amnesia invariably settles in after age eight; whereas, in possession-type cases, there is no such predictable time for the possession to end. And when the possession does end, the memories, behavioral traits, and knowledge of the displaced personality return. These two considerations seem sufficient to undermine the claim that the evidence for reincarnation could just as easily be counted as evidence for possession rather than reincarnation, even though in some particular cases we may not be able to distinguish the two as clearly as we would like. Given the second consideration, incidentally, it seems plausible to think that Stevenson would side with our being able, at least in *some* circumstances, to distinguish clearly the evidence for reincarnation from the evidence for possession.

Finally, if the above two considerations are still not sufficient to make the case for distinguishing between reincarnation and ostensible possession, Stevenson claims there is one special feature of a rich (and ideal) reincarnation-type case that would allow us irrefutably to distinguish the two—namely, appropriate body scars, birthmarks, or birth defects.[29] According to Stevenson, these features are important for three reasons. First, they provide (when verified) objective evidence of physical correspondence between the subject and a particular deceased person, thus helping to overcome the problem of correctly identifying the past person. Second, it is unlikely that birthmarks can be produced by psychokinesis on the part of a living person (other than the subject's mother); and so they add to the evidence favoring survival as an interpretation of the cases in which they occur, as opposed to the interpretation of clairvoyance to explain the subject's imagined memories. Third and finally, because such body scars or birthmarks are by definition congenital, they suppose a psychic influence *before* the subject's birth. The word *possession* might be applied to cases of an apparent "taking over" of a body after its birth; but if the possession occurs before birth, then it is what we mean by *reincarnation*.

Conclusion

Even if we can question such past cases as the Watseka Wonder for the reason that the methods of examining and reporting the data do not sufficiently exclude the possibilities of misconstrual, fraud, or a purely naturalistic explanation of the data, nevertheless the case seems persuasive as an instance of ostensible possession. Nobody has shown that such stated possibilities in fact obtained. And there is no way of returning to reexamine the alleged facts in the case. By comparison, it seems that the Sumitra case is much stronger because the rich and detailed data collected, as well as the methodology used in examining them, would likely have unearthed fraud, hoax, bias, or a purely naturalistic origin of the circumstances. Certainly, the methods used in the Sumitra case investigation—methods that were clearly not in practice at the time of the Watseka Wonder—show fairly compellingly that the usual objections to the effect that there might be natural ways to explain the data are quite unfounded.

An equally important point is that in nearly all cultures in all of history there are other cases similar to the Sumitra case. We cannot readily return to examine the data in those cases, of course; but as time progresses, the careful documentation of new cases will no doubt produce more compelling evidence for possession if, as we have argued, the two cases examined above are not unique but represent a fairly common phenomenon. If the Sumitra case is typical of what is out there—and many think that it is—we shall look forward to an increasing number of case studies prepared as convincingly as the Stevenson investigation.

Notes

1. E. W. Stevens, "The Watseka Wonder: A Narrative of Startling Phenomena Occurring in the Case of Mary Lurancy Vennum," *Philosophical Journal*, Religio-philosophical Publishing House, Chicago (1887), pp. 286–316.

2. C. J. Ducasse, *A Critical Examination of the Belief in Life after Death* (Springfield, Ill.: Charles C Thomas, 1961).

3. Ibid., p. 172.

4. Ibid., p. 173.

5. Ibid.

6. For other cases similar to the Watseka Wonder, see E. Bourguignon, *Possession* (San Francisco: Chandler and Sharp, 1976); I. M. Lewis, *Ecstatic Religion: An Anthropological Study of Spirit Possession and Shamanism* (Harmondsworth, Middlesex, England: Penguin Books, 1971); and E. M. Pattison, J. Kahan, and G. S. Hurd, "Trance and Possession States," in *Handbook of States of Consciousness*, eds. B. B. Wolman and M. Ullman (New York: Van Nostrand Reinhold, 1986).

7. Frederick Dommeyer, "Body, Mind, and Death," *Pacific Forum* (1963), pp. 36–37.

8. C. J. Ducasse in *Pacific Forum* (1963), p. 38.

9. Rodger I. Anderson, "The Watseka Wonder: A Critical Re-evaluation," *Theta* 8, no. 4 (Fall 1980), pp. 6–9. See also both the response offered by A. Martinez-Taboas, and the reply to the response offered by Roger Anderson and C. T. K. Chari: "The End of the Watseka Wonder," *Theta* 9, no. 4 (Autumn 1981), pp. 20ff; and finally, the follow-up exchange between A. Martinez-Taboas and R. I. Anderson: "Final Comments on the Watseka Wonder," *Theta* 10, no. 1 (Spring 1982), pp. 23ff.

10. For a full statement of Anderson's reasons for this claim, see "End of the Watseka Wonder," pp. 21–22.

11. See Chari's analysis in ibid., pp. 21ff.

12. See Stephen E. Braude, "Evaluating the Super-psi Hypothesis," in G. E. Zollschan, J. F. Schumaker, and G. F. Walsh, eds., *Exploring the Paranormal* (Dorset, England: Prism Press, 1989); and Jule Eisenbud, *Parapsychology and the Unconscious* (Berkeley, Calif.: North Atlantic Books, 1983), ch. 14.

13. Ian Stevenson, Satwant Pasricha, and Nicholas McClean-Rice, "A Case of the Possession Type in India with Evidence of Paranormal Knowledge," *Journal of Scientific Exploration* 3, no. 1 (1989), pp. 89–101.

14. Ibid., p. 83.

15. Ibid., p. 85.

16. Ibid.

17. Ibid., pp. 85–86 and 87.

18. Ibid., p. 91.

19. Citation in original: Ian Stevenson, *Cases of the Reincarnation Type*, vol. 1: *Ten Cases in India* (Charlottesville: University Press of Virginia, 1975), pp. 39–40.

20. Stevenson, Pasricha, and McClean-Rice, "Case of Possession Type in India," pp. 91–92.

21. Ibid., p. 92.

22. Ibid., p. 97.

23. Ibid.

24. Ibid., p. 98.

25. Citation in original: Bourguignon, *Possession*; Lewis, *Ecstatic Religion*; and Pattison, Kahan, and Hurd, "Trance and Possession States."

26. Citation in original: Lewis, *Ecstatic Religion*, pp. 29–30.

27. Stevenson, Pasricha, and McClean-Rice, "Case of Possession Type in India," p. 100, n. 1.

28. Ian Stevenson, *Children Who Remember Previous Lives* (Charlottesville: University Press of Virginia, 1987), p. 156.

29. This description of the importance of birthmarks for an ideal

reincarnation-type case was offered to me by Stevenson in personal correspondence. I had asked why one would need to have body scars to make a convincing reincarnation case. His answer invokes, among other things, their evidentiary value for distinguishing between reincarnation-type cases and cases of ostensible possession. Presumably, this view has been detailed in the current publication of Stevenson's four-volume work on the subject: Ian Stevenson, *Birthmarks and Birth Defects: A Contribution to Their Etiology* (New York: Paragon House Publishers, 1992).

4

Out-of-Body Experiences

Obviously, if people can literally leave their bodies, then human personality is something distinct from the body itself. The person who leaves her or his body and then returns to it must be something more than just the very complex organism whose properties are revealed by physical science. Such a person would need to be some sort of nonphysical being that lives *in* the body. As we saw earlier, this view about persons has been called "mind–body dualism" or just "dualism." By definition, a materialist—on the other hand—thinks it absurd to suggest that people can literally leave their bodies, because people simply *are* bodies and nothing more.

Interestingly enough, there is ample testimony to the out-of-body experience (hereafter OBE). Moreover, although such testimony is by no means new, the recent and popular tendency to regard it seriously seems quite new. And as a result, a number of intriguing questions have been raised, especially because so many people take these experiences as evidence for mind–body dualism and for some form of personal survival after death.[1]

Most indisputably, the recent popular interest in OBEs was caused by the appearance of Raymond Moody's 1975 book *Life after Life* and, more recently, *The Light Beyond*.[2] The first of these books led to extensive public awareness and attention. In 1981, for example, the Gallup Organization conducted a poll on the issue, revealing that 15 percent of American adults reported having had a near-death experience (hereafter NDE) at some time in their lives. At any rate, in his books Moody gives an account of the

163

general characteristics of the NDE as it has often been described by individuals who have had one. These individuals invariably consider their NDE as compelling evidence for belief in some form of personal survival after death. And while Moody and many others refuse to regard the widespread testimony to such experiences as *proof* of survival, they nonetheless regard them as solid grounds for justifying the belief, because alternative explanations of the phenomenon are unsatisfactory and because science cannot in any event *disprove* that these experiences are glimpses into the life beyond. Whether Moody and the others are right in refusing to regard the best case studies here as proof rather than as compelling anecdotal evidence of something that science cannot disprove is a question we shall examine soon enough.

However, not all OBEs are NDEs (although all NDEs are OBEs). There is plenty of testimony that speaks of OBEs in nonclinical and in nontraumatic or nonstressful contexts. Sometimes, for example, people report having an OBE simply on the occasion of falling asleep.[3] By way of content, these experiences are quite different from the NDEs, even though the strength of the personal-survival evidence they both provide is a function of a characteristic common to both. Let us look at some of the more interesting cases and then discuss their force as evidence for some form of personal survival. In doing so, our basic question will be whether *any* of these experiences provide clear evidence that something essential to human personality leaves the body during an OBE.

The OBE: Involuntary and Voluntary

In the typical OBE report, the person concerned—after falling asleep, or after undergoing some acutely stressful event—suddenly awakens to see her (or his) own body inert. She observes her body as if it were the body of someone else. As a rule, she also observes (usually from an elevated position above the body) other objects in the room. In some cases she perceives quite clearly, and is later able to describe, persons who entered the room while she was "out of her body." She may or may not find herself able to travel from the vicinity of her unconscious body. In his book *A Critical Examination of the Belief in Life after Death*, C. J. Ducasse quotes a certain gentleman who had two such experiences. The gentleman's narration reads as follows:

> The first time it was while in a dentist's chair. Under anesthesia, I had the sensation of awaking and of finding myself floating in the upper part of the room, from where, with great astonishment, I watched the dentist working on my body, and the anaesthetist at his side. I saw my inanimate body as distinctly as any other object in the room. . . . The second time I was in a hotel in London. I awoke in the morning feeling unwell (I have a weak heart) and shortly thereafter I fainted. Greatly to my astonishment, I found myself in the upper part of the room, from where, with fear, I beheld my body inanimate in the bed with its eyes closed. I tried without success to reenter my body and concluded that I had died. . . . Certainly I had not lost either memory or self-consciousness. I could see my inanimate body like a separate object: I was able to look at my face. I was, however, unable to leave the room: I felt myself as it were chained, immobilized in the corner where I was. After an hour or two I heard a knock on the locked door several times, without being able to answer. Soon after, the hotel porter appeared on the fire escape. . . . [A] physician was called in. I saw him shake his head after listening to my heart, and then insert a spoon between my lips. I then lost consciousness and awoke in the bed.[4]

Ducasse goes on to note that, in addition to this sort of case wherein the OBE occurs spontaneously, unpredictably, and apparently involuntarily, there are also cases of *voluntarily induced* OBEs.

A voluntarily induced OBE is sometimes called a "voluntary astral projection" and refers to an OBE that the subject is allegedly capable of inducing fairly regularly and at will. In the past 25 years, the voluntarily induced OBE has been the object of a fair amount of serious experimental research, efforts having been made to devise a suitable method of detecting whether something does in fact leave the bodies of such subjects during the voluntarily induced OBEs. Three such experiments are interesting, though their results vary in evidential impact.

In one well-known laboratory experiment, then, there was an attempt made to determine whether the subject who claimed to be able to leave his body voluntarily did in fact leave his body or, that is, whether *something* left his body and went to the target area. The research was designed and conducted at the Psychical Research Foundation in North Carolina, and the subject (who was also part of the research team) was one Mr. "Blue" (now Keith) Harary.[5] The experiment was conducted in the following way.

Mr. Harary was asked to induce a voluntary OBE and, while in that state, was directed to visit a particular target area outside the room. In addition to monitoring Harary's physiological changes during the experiment, and having target material in another location for Harary to observe while "projecting" (i.e., while out of his body), the research team tried to determine whether any animal, human, or mechanical devices could detect the presence of the "second body" near the target area. Interesting results occurred when the subject's pet kitten was used in the target room as a detector. The kitten was placed in a three-foot deep "open field" container divided into 24 numbered ten-inch squares. During the period when Mr. Harary was not inducing the OBE, the kitten was very active, miaowing often, crossing many squares, and attempting to get out of the container. However, during those periods when Harary was professedly out of his body and visiting the target room, the cat became strikingly quiet and calm. This effect was repeated throughout four experimental sessions. Moreover, an additional experiment using a snake as a detector produced similar effects, but in reverse. The snake was calm during the periods when Mr. Harary was not in the voluntarily induced OBE, but began striking and gnawing against the glass front of his cage during the initial OBE test. Even so, the study concluded that "overall, no detectors were able to maintain a *consistent* responsiveness of the sort that would indicate any true detection of an extended aspect of the self."[6] At best, the significance of this particular animal-as-detector type of result as evidence for something's leaving the body during the OBE is problematic since, even if the result had been consistent, it could be ascribed to intentional *action at a distance* (or PK). For the moment, the Harary research simply illustrates a case of alleged voluntary OBE and an experiment seeking to detect whether anything leaves the body during the OBE.

In another well-known experiment conducted in 1967 and 1968,[7] Charles Tart tested the subject Robert Monroe (well known for his book *Journeys Out of the Body*),[8] who professed a capacity for voluntarily induced OBEs. Tart's experiment consisted in displaying a five-digit number behind and above Monroe while the voluntarily induced OBE was going on. Monroe had no way of being able to see or detect the number from his reclining position. Tart's reasoning was that, if Monroe in fact left his body during these experiences, then he ought to be able to say what the displayed number was when the OBE was over. The experiment was conducted under well-controlled conditions. On nine separate occasions when the experiment was conducted, Monroe failed to identify the number.[9] Certainly, this result would appear to confirm the thesis that *nothing* leaves the body (or at least Monroe's body) during OBEs.

Interestingly enough, however, shortly thereafter Tart tested a Ms. Z, who professed to have regular OBEs during sleep.[10] And indeed, Ms. Z succeeded in correctly identifying the five-digit number on the only occasion in which she claimed to see the number, during a well-controlled set of experiments conducted on four separate nights in Tart's sleep laboratory. This result could not be ascribed to probability, and Tart regards it as compelling evidence of an OBE with paranormal content. Unfortunately, for various reasons, Ms. Z disappeared shortly thereafter and was not available for further experimentation. Even so, hers is a confirmed case in which, after having an OBE, a person identified veridical content that the subject could not have acquired normally. And as we shall now see, this particular result has in fact been successfully repeated by others in the context of a somewhat more elaborate experiment.

That experiment, which is perhaps the most striking recent experiment seeking to show that something leaves the body during some OBEs, was conducted by Karlis Osis and Donna McCormick with the subject Alex Tanous, and the results were reported in 1980 in the *Journal of the American Society for Psychical Research*.[11] The experiment consisted in requesting Tanous to visit a designated target area while he was in his voluntarily induced OBE. The target area was a shielded chamber containing strain-gauge sensors, which were placed in front of the viewing window of an optical image device that displayed visual targets. Tanous was assigned the task of identifying randomly selected targets displayed in the optical image device. Unintentional mechanical effects on the strain-gauge sensors were registered on a Beckman polygraph during the time when the subject was professedly out of body and trying to identify the targets. The experiment consisted of 197 trials and resulted in 114 hits and 83 misses, extending over 20 sessions. Blind measurements were made of the strain-gauge activation levels on the polygraph recordings. These data were sampled so that four two-second intervals were measured immediately before, and four such intervals immediately after, target generation for each trial. As the researchers had predicted, the average strain-gauge activation for the period immediately following target generation—that is, when the subject was reportedly "looking" at the target—was *significantly* higher for trials that were hits than for trials that were misses. The average activation levels over all eight sampling periods showed a significantly higher degree of activation on occasions when hitting occurred. Some researchers regard these results as confirming the view that something does leave the body during some OBEs.[12] Shortly, when we discuss the force of this experiment, we will see why it makes sense to say that it is indeed a successful repetition of the experiment conducted by Tart with Ms. Z. Before that, however, we must say something about the near-death experience (NDE).

The NDE Described: Moody's Model

Perhaps the most popular testimony for OBEs comes from Raymond Moody who, after examining numerous cases of NDEs (no two of them identical in circumstances), offers a model indicating the general elements he found. The presence of the various characteristics is typically a function of the length of time the individual undergoes the experience. Moody describes the prototypical complete NDE as follows:

A man is dying and, as he reaches the point of greatest physical distress, he hears himself pronounced dead by his doctor. He begins to hear an uncomfortable noise, a loud ringing or buzzing, and at the same time feels himself moving very rapidly through a long dark tunnel. After this, he suddenly finds himself outside of his own physical body, but still in the immediate physical environment, and he sees his own body from a distance, as though he is a spectator. He watches the resuscitation attempt from this unusual vantage point and is in a state of emotional upheaval.

After a while he collects himself and becomes more accustomed to his odd condition. He notices that he still has a "body" but one of a very different nature and with very different powers from the physical body he has left behind. Soon other things begin to happen. Others come to meet and to help him. He glimpses the spirits of relatives and friends who have already died, and a loving, warm spirit of a kind he has never encountered before—a being of light—appears before him. This being asks him a question, nonverbally, to make him evaluate his life and helps him along by showing him a panoramic, instantaneous playback of the major events of his life. At some point he finds himself approaching some sort of barrier or border, apparently representing the limit between earthly life and the next life. Yet, he finds that he must go back to the earth, that the time for his death has not yet come. At this point he resists, for by now he is taken up with his experiences in the afterlife and does not want to return. He is overwhelmed by intense feelings of joy, love and peace. Despite his attitude, though, he somehow reunites with his physical body and lives.

Later he tries to tell others, but he has trouble doing so. In the first place, he can find no human words adequate to describe these unearthly episodes. He also finds that others scoff, so he stops telling other people. Still, the experience affects his life profoundly, especially his views about death and its relationship to life.[13]

Moody hastens to add that this narrative is merely a "model," or a composite sketch, of the common elements most frequently found in the reports of such experiences when they have lasted for more than a brief period. People do recount such experiences but leave out various elements found in the composite. However, most of the time, most of the elements are present in such reports; and sometimes all the elements are present.

Two NDE Cases: Reinée Pasarow and Tommy Clack

Consider the example of Reinée Pasarow who reports having had an NDE in May 1967 when she was 17. At the time she was suffering from a massive allergic reaction. The following is her own narrative of the events beginning on the evening when she had the NDE:

> After my mother and I had eaten dinner, an old friend I had not seen for some time dropped by unexpectedly. I was rather embarrassed, because I had been covered with welts and hives for two days as a result of the allergy and looked somewhat grotesque. The swelling became substantially worse, and I had great difficulty in breathing. By the time my mother got me to the car, my friend and she realized that they could never keep my breathing on the twenty minute trip to the hospital. An ambulance was called, but, as none was soon available in our rural district, two fire trucks responded in the meantime.
>
> I was unconscious on the sidewalk in front of our residence, although I was aware of making a tremendous effort to keep breathing. Several firemen were working on me when at last the struggle to keep fighting for my life became too tremendous. I stopped breathing and felt a great relief to be free of the burden of trying to stay alive. I slipped into the dark of a totally unconscious but peaceful realm.
>
> Suddenly, I found myself a few feet outside my body, watching with great curiosity as the firemen gave me mouth-to-mouth resuscitation and violently slapped my legs. I remember them thinking that if they could just get me mad enough, I might come back. My mother was splashing water on my ashen face, and the eldest fireman who was giving me mouth-to-mouth resuscitation kept pleading with me mentally not to leave and seeing his own teenaged daughter in his mind's eye.
>
> Just as suddenly, I found myself viewing this cosmically comic scene from slightly above the telephone wires. I saw a young neighbor boy come out of his house upon awakening from his nap, and I tried screaming at his mother to go and get him before he saw all this. Just as I screamed at her, she looked up the driveway and saw him, and my mother said there was nothing she could do, so she best get her child. One of the firemen commented with a great sigh of failure that I had been without a pulse for three minutes.

I felt a pang of guilt that this poor fireman should feel a failure in my death. He was especially touched because I resembled his own daughter. My mother was dazed, hopelessly without any control over the situation and her shock numbed the onset of grief. I remember saying a prayer for her, in hopes that this would help to see her through the pain, but then I realized that she would come to deal with the situation. I wanted to cry out to them all, my mother, friends and the firemen, that everything was as it should be, that I was fine. I was telepathically aware of everyone's feelings and thoughts, and this seemed a burden, as their pain was as it should be.

Delighted at my newly found freedom, I began to soar. I had become the phoenix, released at last from the limitations of the physical world. I was exhilarated. Everywhere around me there was music; the ether of my new universe was love, a love so pure and selfless that I only longed for more. I became aware of my favorite uncle's presence: we gleefully recognized each other although we were now in an energy, rather than a physical form. He travelled with me for a short time, expressing even more love and acceptance. As a vast light became visible in this sea of light, however, I was magnetically drawn into it. The closer I got to this light (closeness, however, not meant in the physical sense) the more love and ecstacy were mine to experience.

Finally, I was sucked into the light source, not unlike one is swept up in a whirlpool. I became one with the light. As I became one with this omnipresent light, its knowledge became my knowledge. I was in a single instant what my life had been and what had been of meaning in my life. . . . The superficial aspects of my life, what I had accomplished, owned and known, were consumed in that same instant by the energy of the light. However, those acts in which I selflessly expressed love or concern for my fellow men were glorified and permanently inscribed in the akashic record, with total disregard for however humble or fleeting those moments had been. . . .

Suddenly, I was ejected from the light to the other side of this new universe, where I realized I would have to make my way. I recall someone beckoning to me, although the identity of that person still remains a mystery, for also at that moment it was revealed to me that my moment in the cosmic dance was not completed, that there was something for my human race that I must achieve on the physical plane of existence. Coinciding with the moment of that revelation, the light, the universe, or God himself proclaimed IT IS NOT TIME, and that proclamation hurled me from this magnificent universe of love.

I was pushed through a tremendous tunnel of light, through a progressive rainbow of the wavelengths of color, and catapulted back into the physical realm. It was as if the whole process was not just initiated by the proclamation, but was the proclamation IT IS NOT TIME itself.

I found myself, griefstricken and heartsick, again a few feet from my body. I felt as if I had been cast out of paradise, an Eve no longer in the Garden of Eden. The physical realm was coarse and confusing, divided and foreign. A sense of time and space was clamped down upon my being, casting upon my soul a sense of imprisonment and degradation unlike any I had ever known.

The ambulance had arrived, and the attendants were checking for my absent pulse, which still eluded them. I tried to merge again with the body that was once mine but which now seemed like a foreign substance. This required a tremendous effort on my part, and the attendants placing me in the back of the ambulance only made the merging that more difficult. I hovered over my body in the ambulance, and for a brief instant rejoined it. I felt the surge of blood through my veins, and the attendant motioned to the driver that he had a pulse.

The pain of the physical was too much for me to stand, however, and I separated from the body again, hovering both inside and outside the moving ambulance. I watched as the young attendant in the back mouthed DOA to the driver about ten minutes into the drive. My mother's pain at this announcement became my pain, and I was angered at the callousness of the ambulance attendant.

I continued watching from several feet above my body as I was wheeled into the emergency room and the first young doctor was unable to revive me again. . . . At that moment, my personal physician burst into the emergency room in his tuxedo, bag in hand.

"Where is she?" he demanded.

"She was DOA," the young doctor announced. . . .

"The hell she is!" shouted my doctor, a family friend of many years, and got down to the business of determining how many shots of adrenaline I had been given. He ordered that I be given up to six large injections of adrenaline, something the other doctors and nurses obviously considered very dangerous. He proceeded to pump me full of adrenaline and give heart massage until at last a pulse was perceived. It is interesting to note that I was fully aware of what was happening both physically and in the minds of those in the emergency room until I was revived, at which point I was very confused.

To the best of my knowledge, I was without a heartbeat approximately fifteen minutes. The incident left me with some minimal brain damage, the effects of which have been totally overcome, although to this day my reflexes reflect the damage.[14]

As a final example of an OBE that is also an NDE, we can relate the account of Tommy Clack, who on May 29, 1969, was a 22-year-old army captain who stepped on a booby trap while leading his men near Chu Chi in South Vietnam. Clack recounts his story this way:

I remember being hit. I went flying through the air, then hit the ground. I sat up for an instant and saw that my right arm was gone, my right leg was gone and my left leg was off to the left side. I laid back down. I remember thinking what it means to die. I lost my sight, lost all sense of feeling, could feel no pain.

Suddenly I realized that I was up (in the air) looking (down) at myself. I saw them pick me (my body) up, put me on a stretcher. They covered me with a poncho, which means they thought I was dead. I realized then that I was dead. I watched them take me to the helicopter. I got on the helicopter with them and went to the field hospital.

I saw nurses cutting my uniform off, starting an IV. I tried to stop them. I was very happy and peaceful where I was. All of a sudden I was back on the battlefield.

All 13 of the guys killed in action the day before were there. I could not see them but somehow I knew they were there. The guys and I communicated with each other—I don't know how. They were very happy where they were. They wanted me to stay with them.

I felt very peaceful and tranquil. I did not see a physical form (for myself). I was a shape—almost a thought process. There was a bright light there the whole time.

I tried to stop them (soldiers) from picking up those who had died earlier in the day. But they didn't even know that I was there.

All of a sudden I'm back in the operating room. They were

operating on me. I knew they were talking, but I don't remember
what was said. Instantly I was drawn back into my body.[15]

The Sceptic's Response

In turning to critical assessments of all the testimony for OBEs,
it is inevitable that we confront a healthy dose of scepticism. As a
matter of fact, sceptics invariably say that all such testimony can
be explained without our needing to believe that persons *literally*
leave their bodies or that anything at all leaves the body during
such experiences. In the next few pages, we will examine these
frequently offered alternative explanations, and seek to determine
their strength. My own conclusion, as will be seen, is that the
alternative explanations offered by sceptics are quite unconvincing, and sometimes embarrassingly so. Nevertheless, the evidence
purporting that something leaves the body during the OBE could
very well stand to be strengthened in certain ways if we are to feel
rationally *compelled* by it, rather than simply persuaded. But some
of it is sufficiently persuasive to warrant the claim that the dualist's
interpretation is proven sound, and cannot be regarded merely as
a matter of anecdote not capable of being disproven by natural
science.

Hallucination?

Within the medical and psychological communities, the experience of viewing one's image outside the body is known as an
"autoscopic hallucination." This kind of a hallucination occurs
often in cases of drug abuse, epilepsy, liver ailments, cerebral
lesions, brain tumors, alcoholism, or other pathological conditions. Frequently, these sorts of experiences are to be associated
with a state of oxygen deprivation called "hypoxia" or, in this
case, oxygen starvation of the brain. Hence, sceptical minds find
it natural to suppose that people reporting OBEs must have some
mental or physical disorder causing the hypoxia (or similar condition) that induces these autoscopic hallucinations. In the case of

NDEs, the fact of there being stress-induced physiological changes present makes the sceptic's supposition initially attractive.

Ronald Siegel, for example, speaks for many persons when he argues that the NDE and the OBE are exactly the sort of experience we would expect of persons hallucinating as a result of some mental or physical disorder induced by physical stress or the lack of oxygen.[16] Siegel believes that all such reports are as likely to be evidence of hallucination as they are to be evidence that people actually leave their bodies. And the philosopher Paul Kurtz cheerfully agrees:

> There are reasonable physiological explanations for NDEs. We know that when the body is badly injured, the heart stops, the brain is deprived of oxygen and cerebral anoxia occurs. Its effects are well-documented. At first there may be a sense of well-being, probably the result of the brain's endorphin response to extreme trauma. As more neurons are damaged by lack of oxygen, the brain's ability to make critical judgments becomes impaired, reality becomes vague or illogical and hallucinations occur.
>
> Psychopharmacologist Ronald Siegel has suggested that NDEs are similar to the hallucinatory experiences induced by drugs, which are directly related to states of excitement and arousal in the central nervous system and are accompanied by disorganization in the brain's regulation of incoming stimuli. Just as psychedelic drugs can trigger such neuronal frenzy, so too can anesthetics, fever, exhaustion, injuries—and probably the emotional and physiological processes involved in dying. The bright light often associated with NDE is a common hallucination and may be the result of some optical peculiarity, such as phosphenes, that arises during an altered state of consciousness. The light may also result if the central nervous system mimics the effect of light on the retina. Siegel notes that he is able to create the tunnel experience in volunteers.[17]

In the same article, incidentally, Kurtz also claims that there is tremendous variability in the details of what the NDE experience amounts to. The basis for his saying this is that some people interviewed by the psychologist Kenneth Ring did not testify to having had in their NDE all the features Moody delineates in his composite picture of the NDE model.[18]

As Kurtz notes, another and quite plausible explanation of the

NDE is that a process of "depersonalization" may be at work. In this view, the NDE is construed as a psychological reaction to the prospect of facing imminent death—a coping or compensatory mechanism used to struggle with a stressing, traumatic situation.[19]

Finally, consistent with the views expressed by Siegel and Kurtz, others have recently proposed a purely neurobiological model that seeks to explain the nature of the NDE as based on a "temporal lobe dysfunction, hypoxia/ischemia, stress, and neuropeptide/neurotransmitter imbalance."[20] In this model, the NDE is seen as an experience subjects have during hallucinatory experiences sometimes induced by acute forms of stress and not unlike those hallucinatory experiences typically produced in temporal lobe epilepsy.

Are Siegel, Kurtz, and the proponents of the neurobiological model correct in claiming that we have a plausible alternative explanation for the NDE when we consider it a hallucinatory experience caused either by stress-induced pharmacological changes or some basically simple form of oxygen deprivation? It is important to note that this alternative explanation need only be plausible. Its proponents need not say, or prove, that NDEs (or OBEs) are *in fact* hallucinatory experiences; they need only assert that such an alternative explanation is *as plausible as* the explanation that something leaves the body during these experiences. Some proponents might go on to assert that all NDEs (or OBEs) are in fact just such hallucinatory experiences; but in order to undermine the NDE (or OBE) as evidence for a form of dualism supportive of some form of personal survival, proponents of this alternative explanation need only assert that their position is as plausible as any proposed. The question is whether that is so.

Reply to the Hallucination Objection

Surely, there are indeed reported OBEs and NDEs that admit of the alternative explanation offered by Siegel, Kurtz, and the proponents of the neurobiological model. Take, for example, the philosopher Sir Alfred J. Ayer's recent NDE as reported in the *Manchester Guardian Weekly*.[21] At age 77 Ayer's heart stopped for four minutes in a London hospital. When restored to conscious-ness, he claimed that his "thoughts had become persons," and thereafter wrote a 2,000-word account in which he claimed now to have, as a result of this experience, "rather strong evidence that death does not put an end to consciousness."[22] The lifelong atheist went on to describe his experience, which was reported in the *Guardian* in the following way:

> "I was confronted by a red light; exceedingly bright and also very painful even when I turned away from it. I was aware that this light was responsible for the government of the universe. Among its ministers were two creatures who had been put in charge of space." The ministers, however, were not doing their job properly, which meant that "space was slightly out of joint." The painful red light was a warning that the laws of nature were not working properly. Ayer "felt that it was up to me to put things right." Drawing on an Einsteinian space/time analogy, he tried to communicate with the guardians of the universe. "This elicited no response. I became more and more desperate, until the experience suddenly came to an end."[23]

The *Guardian* goes on to note that the typical reaction to Ayer's experience consisted in claiming, as did Sir Hermann Bondi, that it was a fine example of hallucination caused by oxygen depriva-tion of the brain.[24] Ayer's account also interested Colin Blake-more, professor of physiology at Cambridge. Blakemore was quoted as saying that, in heart arrest, the first part of the brain to go out of kilter during oxygen decline is the temporal lobe, which organizes interpretation and judgment. "I think what happened to Freddie Ayer was that lack of oxygen disordered the interpretative methods of his cortex which led to hallucinations."[25]

Assuming that the *Guardian* report is reasonably accurate, we have no reason *not* to think that Ayer was suffering from halluci-nations caused by oxygen deprivation. In this case, Bondi's expla-nation coincides with the explanation offered for all NDEs by Siegel, Kurtz, and the proponents of the neurobiological model. Indeed, there is very little in the report to justify seeing Ayer's NDE in any other way, notwithstanding his own profession of newfound belief.

Notice that Ayer never said he was aware of leaving his body, hovering above it, going through a tunnel, having a sense of peace, and seeing a white light. As a matter of fact, his description is very unlike any description offered by most people who have reported such experiences, as shown in the composite model offered by Moody. The language used by Ayer is highly suggestive of just the sort of hallucinations that never appear in the typically characterized NDE. Who, after all, has ever said that his or her thoughts became persons, or that "the painful red light was a warning that the laws of nature were not working properly," or that "it was up to me to put things right"? Indeed, the story Ayer told is like no NDE ever reported that even roughly fits the model Moody describes. But might not the NDE as described in the composite model be hallucinatory for precisely the same reasons we all believe that Ayer's experience must be hallucinatory?

In the end, the single most persuasive reason why the hallucination hypothesis will not work generally as a plausible alternative explanation is that, while it may fit some cases like that of A. J. Ayer, it cannot fit the richer cases. In the richer NDE and OBE cases, the subject reports immediately afterward on events that occurred during the OBE or the NDE and at a considerable distance from the subject's body while the subject's body was being watched by independent witnesses. These are the important cases. These are the ones we cannot explain away by saying that the subject must have been (or may have been) hallucinating, because what they testify to we can independently confirm as having happened while the subject was having the OBE. In such cases, as we shall see, the content of the testimony is veridical and could not have been acquired in normal ways (leading some researchers to appeal to ESP, although the resemblances between ESP and the knowledge acquired during OBEs falls short of explaining the latter phenomenon, as will be discussed later in the chapter).

Before going any further in assessing the hallucination hypothesis, a logical point is in order. Proponents of the NDE or OBE as offering persuasive evidence for something's leaving the body during these experiences need not and should not argue that every reported NDE or OBE is nonhallucinatory, or that every reported

NDE and OBE is plausible evidence for something's leaving the body. Rather their claim should be, and typically is, that there are clean cases in which the NDE or OBE cannot be explained on the grounds that it might well be a hallucinatory experience; and those are the cases—however many or few there may be—that offer evidence for the view that during some NDEs and OBEs something leaves the body.

Although it might seem unnecessary to have made this last point, it is nonetheless worth making because one researcher, Susan Blackmore, has criticized the appeal to the most highly evidential cases on the grounds that this rules out the majority of OBE cases (which do not include ESP-like claims that contain veridical information) and in so doing offers "a very shaky criterion" for examining the OBE experience.[26] Certainly, as an astute reviewer of Blackmore's thesis has noted,[27] if one's purpose is to examine the OBE as a psychological phenomenon only, then any definition of the OBE that covers only those cases with ESP-like claims and veridical content would be too restrictive; but if one's purpose is to examine the OBE phenomenon to determine whether it offers evidence for something's leaving the body during the OBE, then one may conclude that indeed the OBE does offer such evidence but only in those cases with ESP-like claims containing veridical information that could not have been acquired normally. Excluding such cases as potential sources of evidence for something's leaving the body during OBEs simply begs the question in favor of the view that OBEs are based solely on imagination and hallucination. In short, the very idea that one does not need to explain the richer cases because they are not like those in which one need only appeal to hallucination is an arbitrary way of refusing to consider just those cases that can prove something leaves the body in OBEs. And what could possibly justify such a procedure?

Blackmore ultimately denies that the highly evidential cases exist anyway;[28] but her refusal to consider such cases in principle for the reason stated is unjustifiable. Thus the question is whether there really are such cases—and if there are, whether they provide the evidence the dualist needs against the hallucination hypothesis. Let us examine this question.

In one of the cases described early in this chapter, for example, the subject—Mr. Alex Tanous—claimed to be able to "project" voluntarily to distant areas. In the presence of other persons, he lay down during 20 different sessions and projected voluntarily to an area assigned or targeted by the researchers, who meanwhile were attending him closely and monitoring his bodily states. Mr. Tanous knew nothing about the target area to which he was directed; he was also asked to observe the visual targets in an optical image device in the general target area. Later when he "awoke" in the room with the researchers (who had never left his side), Tanous would—more often than not—describe correctly the visual targets in the general target area. The fact that his descriptions were accurate in 114 out of 197 attempts shows that his success was hardly a matter of luck or chance. It also shows, of course, that the content of his OBE cannot be explained as hallucinatory. This is also true of Tart's experiment with Ms. Z, another case described earlier. Some sceptics such as Susan Blackmore discounted the experiment with Ms. Z because it was not repeated. But—*with regard to the content of the OBE and the claim that the content is hallucinatory*—why isn't the experiment conducted by Osis and McCormick with Alex Tanous a way of repeating the same experiment conducted by Tart with Ms. Z? The experiment is the same experiment not because it has the same subject, or even different researchers with the same subject. It is the same experiment because, even with a different subject and different researchers, we can use roughly the same method to determine whether the content of specific OBEs is or is not hallucinatory. In short, we are at liberty to regard the Osis–McCormick experiment as a repetition of the same experiment conducted by Tart. And the results are clear. Later on we will confront again the so-called failure-of-repeatability argument that seeks to dismiss all evidence for personal survival on the grounds that the evidence is merely anecdotal (and nonscientific) because nonrepeatable in the way evidence must be repeatable to establish scientific truth. For now, however, let us continue our discussion of the hallucination hypothesis.

Can we explain Tanous's general accuracy in these experiments and still hold—along with Siegel, Kurtz, and proponents of the hallucination model—that his experience is simply a hallucination? How could Tanous *describe* (as indeed he did) the visual targets in the target area during his OBE if he were simply hallucinating? Surely, then, the claim that all OBEs are classifiable as autoscopic hallucinations is false. And to any suggestion that we need to repeat these sorts of experiments before accepting the implications, we would answer that this experiment with Tanous was itself a suitable (but better) repetition of the experiment conducted by Tart with Ms. Z.

And if that is not enough, there are other cases in which the subjects accurately describe sensory events occurring during their OBEs and *near* their bodies. In these cases—as with Renee Pasarow, whose story was quoted earlier—the numerous witnesses testify that the subjects were clinically dead or in some other way physically incapable of seeing what they nevertheless accurately describe. Dr. Michael Sabom, for example, relates an instance in which one of his patients had undergone cardiac arrest.[29] The patient was rolled into the operating room to undergo recovery procedure. He was on his back and faced toward the ceiling throughout the procedure. Later the patient accurately described tile patterns on the floor of the operating room. He also described other characteristics of the room—characteristics that could not be described unless we suppose that the subject had seen the room from some position other than the one in which his body was lying throughout the recovery procedure.

Moreover, in *The Light Beyond* Moody documents a number of cases in which patients, claiming to have had the NDE, subsequently report in great detail the substance of conversations held in rooms on the other side of the hospital between family members waiting for the outcome of the operation. One patient claimed, on waking from cardiac arrest, that during the resuscitation procedure she left her body and went to the waiting room where she saw her daughter in mismatched plaids. The family verified that the daughter was indeed in the waiting room, with mismatched plaids.[30] Could the experience be hallucinatory when in fact what the subject testified to was independently confirmed by a number of people and when we know that the subject physically went nowhere near the waiting room? Moody also tells of another case in which a woman claims to have left her body in the resuscitation area and traveled to the hospital lobby. There she saw her brother-in-law, who was responding to a business associate whom he happened to meet and who had asked him why he was in the hospital. The patient said she heard the brother-in-law say, "Well, I was going out of town on a business trip. But it looks like Jane is going to kick the bucket. So, I better stay and be a pallbearer." A few days later when she was recovering, the brother-in-law came to visit. She told him that she had been in the room when he spoke to his friend, and then erased any doubts when she went on to say, "Next time I die, you go off on your business trip because I'll be just fine."[31] And Moody relates a number of other instances in which, upon resuscitation, the subject correctly testified to events taking place at some remote distance while the patient was in a complete state of cardiac arrest.[32]

Surely, these OBEs undermine the view that the subjects in all OBEs (including NDEs) are simply hallucinating. The patients Moody was writing about testify to *actual* events that were taking place at remote distances from them. Why do the proponents of the hallucination hypothesis ignore these cases and concentrate more on those of the sort we found described in the *Manchester Guardian*? It may be that the cases reported by Moody are considered "anecdotal" and, for that reason, not so strong as the cases reported by Tart, and by Osis and McCormick. But are they merely anecdotal if such cases occur frequently and are reported by observers who have nothing to gain from lying or hoax? If so, then the belief that there were dinosaurs is anecdotal, too. Generalizing from the weak cases that really *are* hallucinations of the autoscopic sort involving hypoxia is a matter of ignoring those very many other cases, which keep occurring in both experimental and nonexperimental contexts, that we cannot plausibly explain under the hallucination hypothesis but to say that such cases do not exist.

So—while some OBEs and NDEs bear striking similarities to what are usually considered autoscopic hallucinations—still, many of these experiences cannot be explained as hallucinations. In these more important cases, the OBE subject describes independently verified facts that we have no way of explaining how he or she knows. If these people did not leave their bodies (but only mistakenly believe that they did), how shall we account for their knowing what took place some distance away when numerous observers testify that their bodies never moved?

Of course, where people report OBEs and do *not* testify to facts that can be independently verified as having occurred some distance from their bodies (during the OBEs), the view offered by Siegel, Kurtz, and the proponents of the hallucination hypothesis would be reasonable. It is probably because most OBEs and NDEs are like these cases that the explanation in terms of autoscopic hallucinations suggests itself. For example, in Moody's *Life after Life* there is not even one case cited in which the subject testifies to the *independently verified* occurrence of some event that took place during the NDE outside the immediate area of his or her body—say, in another room beyond earshot or beyond the sight of others in the room during the NDE. The important cases—the ones that do not lend themselves to explanation in terms of autoscopic hallucinations—are just those in which the subject's testimony extends to true claims about independently verifiable events that took place while the subject was independently observed to be sensorily incapacitated in the extreme and at a place beyond the customary sensory reach of the event to which the subject testifies. And there are many confirmed instances of such nonhallucinatory OBEs.

ESP plus Physiological Change?

When the attempt to explain all NDEs and OBEs as hallucinatory experiences fails, the sceptic sometimes moves to a more subtle alternative explanation. We then get something like the following explanation.

People who have OBEs (including those who have NDEs), and who as a result of such experiences have knowledge of events beyond their ordinary sensory capacity, need not have left their bodies at all. Rather we can suppose that in these states the subjects undergo dramatic changes in brain chemistry. These changes activate—unbeknown to the subject—whatever neurological mechanisms cause the phenomenon of clairvoyance. In these states, then, *the subjects mistakenly believe they are in those places or situations that they correctly perceive clairvoyantly.*

Given this explanation, we must consider as illusory the subject's claims about leaving his or her body; whereas the subject's claims about seeing what is independently verified must be viewed as the product of clairvoyance induced in and through physiological change.

For example, suppose Smith reports having an OBE while others are watching his body. And suppose he claims, on waking (so to speak), that he visited his cousin Sam 300 miles away, and that during the visit (he noticed the time on Sam's clock) Sam was eating anchovies and reading a new novel by Robert Ludlum. We investigate the matter and find that Sam was indeed eating anchovies and reading a new novel by Robert Ludlum at the time Smith said he was doing these things. Given the present explanation offered by the sceptic, we need not assume that Smith left his body. We need only suppose that Smith is clairvoyant on these kinds of occasions, but mistakenly believes he leaves his body to secure the information he has. In other words, the subject hallucinates leaving his body but does not hallucinate the facts he claims to know, because he has acquired correct knowledge clairvoyantly. (Obviously, this alternative explanation would not be offered by anyone who did not believe in clairvoyance as a purely natural phenomenon.)

Reply to the ESP-plus-Physiological-Change Objection

Does this ESP-plus-physiological-change explanation fare any better than the hallucination hypothesis?

Not really. For one thing, it seems arbitrary to select certain items for clairvoyance and other items for hallucination. Why should we count as clairvoyant hits those items that are independently verified, but write the rest off to illusion or hallucination? The sceptic's answer, of course, will be that we must appeal to clairvoyance only to explain the independently verified facts, and that the person's being at some place removed from his or her body is not one of them. As predictable as this answer may be, however, it still does not seem to justify the conclusion that all the rest of the testimony—beyond the verified facts—is readily explicable under the hypothesis of illusion or hallucination. It still seems an arbitrary and simple refusal to consider anything as evidence for the subject's claim to have left his or her body.

More importantly, the present explanation does not quite fit the more interesting cases of OBE. For example, consider again the Osis–McCormick experiment with Alex Tanous. In this case the data compiled by the strain-gauge sensors indicate very clearly that, while the subject was trying to identify the visual targets, unintentional significant mechanical effects were being registered (and illustrated on a Beckman polygraph). How could this result occur if in fact something had not left the body of the subject during the voluntary OBE? There seems to be no way of explaining these effects while saying the subject's belief that he left the body was hallucinatory. And if the data from the strain-gauge sensors show (as they certainly seem to) that something left the body during the OBE, then we cannot plausibly claim that, while the subject's other beliefs were nonhallucinatory, nevertheless the subject's belief that he left the body was hallucinatory. Indeed, the Osis–McCormick experiment represents the most important kinds of cases because—however rare they may be—they do not admit of ready disposal by appeal to ESP (or clairvoyance) plus illusion. Does the sceptic have any arrows left in the quiver?

Clairvoyance, Illusion, and Action at a Distance?

But if the results of the Osis–McCormick experiment offer the strongest kind of evidence that something actually does leave the body during some OBEs (and these results certainly seem to), then the sceptic may still have one last reply. He or she may seek to account for the effects on the strain-gauge sensors by saying that we have ample evidence of persons' moving objects at a distance—and to explain these effects, therefore, we do not need to suppose that Alex Tanous left his body.[33] Such a sceptic would still need to grant clairvoyance as a way of explaining the independently verified facts the subject knew but could not have learned in normal ways. Thus, the sceptic might seek to discount the Osis–McCormick results as evidence for something's leaving the body during some OBEs, and instead explain these results by appeal to *clairvoyance* (to account for the subject's knowledge), *illusion* (to account for the subject's claim to have seen his own body and to have been someplace where his body was not), and *action at a distance* (to account for the subject's ability to produce mechanical effects on the strain-gauge sensors in the target area). Would such a response be persuasive?

Even if, for the sake of discussion, we were to grant the phenomenon of action at a distance—sometimes known as psychokinesis, or PK—this last of our sceptic's responses would not be plausible as an alternative way of explaining the Osis–McCormick results. And basically, the reason is that, in all known (or alleged) cases of PK or action at a distance, there is an *intentional* component. People do not produce effects consistent with action at a distance (or general PK) unless they have a deliberate intention to do so. In the Osis–McCormick experiment with Tanous, the effects on the strain-gauge sensors were—as the researchers note—unintentional because Tanous was not asked to move anything and did not know that the strain gauge was in the target area. Therefore, our sceptic who believes in clairvoyance cannot explain the effects on the strain-gauge sensors by appeal to PK or action at a distance.

Naturally, if our sceptic now says this shows only that there is, or might be, a new form of PK or action at a distance—namely, a kind that does not require an intentional component—we would have no trouble seeing the reply as ad hoc, and of a kind with the argument that, because nobody has ever established the limits of psi or PK, the strain-gauge effects could be accounted for by some property we do not now know about. Even if we were to admit that there is evidence for some unintentional PK, what evidence do we have—either in the lab or outside—that this unintentional PK works *in a regular way* consistent with the data in the Osis–McCormick experiment? Here again—as we pointed out in each of the preceding chapters—while we cannot deny that it is *possible* that super-ESP and super-PK exist in ways we cannot understand, we cannot simply assume that, whenever we have data that do not fit with everything we now know about PK or ESP, it must be the unconfirmed and unconfirmable result of super-ESP or super-PK at work in the world. Such a policy, in the absence of some sense of what could be used to falsify explanations of this sort in particular cases, would constitute an explanatory deus ex machina whose primary function would seemingly be to guarantee that nothing should ever count as empirical evidence for postmortem personal survival.

Then, too, the sceptic might well be inclined to assert that, until the Osis–McCormick experiment is repeated with the same results by independent researchers, we are at liberty to ignore the data that purportedly require us to believe something leaves the body in some OBEs. To this objection, two replies are in order. First—although the importance of its claims does suggest the strong desirability of repeating the Osis–McCormick experiment—for reasons indicated above in this chapter, the Osis–McCormick experiment *is* a repeat of the Tart experiment with Ms. Z and, as such, strongly refutes the hallucination hypothesis as an explanation of the content of the OBE in general. We can simply no longer justify the claim that what people testify to in their OBEs is hallucinatory in nature, or that all OBEs are hallucinatory experiences. Some have veridical content that the subject could not have acquired in any normal way. Second, it should be clear then that, *when* the Osis–McCormick experiment is repeated and confirmed using the same strain-gauge test for unintended mechanical effects in the target area, there shall be no plausible alternative but to explain these results as evidence that in some OBEs something leaves the body.

Finally, the last possible objection to the Osis–McCormick experiment as establishing that something leaves the body during these nonhallucinatory experiences consists in throwing out the whole experiment for the reason that the strain-gauge effects were probably unreliable. This has in fact been suggested by a few critics such as Susan Blackmore[34] and H. J. Irwin,[35] both of whom cite the criticism offered by Julian Isaacs.[36]

Julian Isaacs expressed reservations about the Osis–McCormick results for three reasons. His first reason was that, in his own research on psychokinetic metal bending (PKMB), he found strain-gauge instrumentation to be subject to "artifactual signals" because airborne electromagnetic interference cannot be eliminated by normal electrostatic screening. He goes on to state that

> even the steel sheeting used by Osis and McCormick was probably too thin and did not enclose a sufficient volume to act as an effective shield. . . . It is therefore somewhat disturbing to find no account in their paper of any test procedures used to evaluate the integrity of their strain-gauge system against this form of artifact. Nor do they use any of the precautions normally employed in PKMB research, such as a "dummy channel" which registers main interference, and which is identical to the "live" channel except that it is terminated on its input end by a resistor instead of a strain gauge.[37]

Isaacs concludes that "there was probably an unchecked source of error variance in the Osis–McCormick data."[38] The second reason for his reservations was that the size of the kinetic effects Osis and McCormick obtained were too small.

> They were working with a signal-to-noise ratio of about one and a half times unity! While the use of appropriate statistical methods can on a formal level justify this procedure, no other worker in strain gauge PKMB experimentation that I know of would attempt to use data of this signal-to-noise ratio. Further, the miniscule scale of signals in the Osis–McCormick data reinforces the problems generated by electromagnetic interference, because less interference is needed to register as "kinetic effects."[39]

Isaacs's third reason consists in asserting that, even if—for the sake of discussion—Osis and McCormick did detect some weak ("micro") PKMB effects, it is quite possible that all three members of the experimental team (Osis, McCormick, and Tanous) unwittingly produced the nonintentional micro-PKMB effects.

> Typically, such group effects occur during moments when some or all of the members are experiencing emotion, a change in focus of attention, or relaxation after a period of tension. . . . In the Osis–

McCormick experiment, in which no one was consciously trying to produce PK, the sequence of events occurring during Tanous's target-identification procedure provided an effective situation for eliciting micro-PKMB from all three participants because the procedure had a built-in tension-creating/relaxation sequence of operations.[40]

Replying to Isaacs's criticisms, however, Osis and McCormick observed that, first and foremost, there is a remarkable difference between research on psychokinetic metal bending or PKMB and OBE research. Metal bending as a psi phenomenon usually involves strong effects—hence, the term "macro-PK"—as opposed to the minute "micro-PK" effects usually observed in laboratory experiments. PK metal bending, they remark, often produces permanent deformation of target material and is said to involve structural changes in the metal. Osis and McCormick go on to note that—while their research and Isaacs's both involve using the strain gauge—they had no reason to associate macro-PK with the out-of-body experience, and there is no laboratory evidence suggesting that one ought to. Thus, they justify their not using strain-gauge techniques appropriate for measuring macro-PK effects, saying that Isaacs's technical criticisms are quite inappropriate because based on a faulty analogy between the two experiments.

> Our experiment was aimed at the same low-level "micro" effects that are customarily obtained in PK and ESP research and which are usually just slightly above chance or noise level. Signal to noise ratios of five to one and better are rare in psi research. The magnitudes we obtained (base to peak measurements) are within the range of others most often reported in our field.[41]

Second and more importantly, Osis and McCormick take issue with Isaacs's suggestion that the strain gauge in their experiment may have been influenced by electromagnetic transients, and thus the results undermined.

> Isaacs speculates about the nature of "noise" factors in our experiment. Even if artifacts were indeed mainly coming from "airborne electromagnetic transients caused by switching of mains powered

equipment" (which we have reason to doubt), that would not alter our findings. Not the source but the noise patterns are relevant. We compared strain-gauge activation levels during two kinds of trials:

1. Hits—trials in which Alex Tanous correctly identified the target pictures displayed by the optical image device;
2. Misses—trials in which incorrect responses were given to the target pictures.

Provided that it affected hit and miss trials alike, the comparison would not be hampered even if the "noise" had shown nonrandom fluctuations. We did not find any patterned "noise" source related to hitting and missing. Isaacs is right in that our shielding did not eliminate all electrical noise. No equipment is noise free, but our shielding of the cubicle was indeed effective in diminishing it.[42]

And third, with regard to Isaacs's suggestion that the three experimenters might have produced the desired effects noninten-tionally for the reasons stated above, Osis and McCormick note that in the exploratory period before the experiment they tried to produce such effects, but to no avail.

We did indeed try, in our exploratory period, to exert a psi influence but had no noticeable results. We were very much motivated to find local subjects living in the New York area besides Tanous, who lives in Maine. In our exploratory trials with these potential subjects we did not obtain results justifying inclusion in a formal experiment. In other words, the strain gauge effects are apparently not depen-dent on our presence, but on that of Alex Tanous.

Concerning Isaacs's suggestion that "possibly all three members of the experimental team . . . were in fact involved in the production of non-intentional micro-PKMB effects," we would like to reiterate the aforementioned point: no such results were achieved in explor-atory work with subjects other than Tanous. Even if this had not been the case, Isaacs's statement regarding the "release-of-effort" effect is somewhat far-fetched. While the structure of our experi-ment could be construed as having an inherent "tension-creating/ relaxation sequence of operations," which is supposedly ideal for the production of unintentional PKMB in groups, we would logi-cally have expected the strain-gauge effects to have appeared after the "release of effort," either while Tanous was giving his verbal response to the target or after having done so. Following Isaacs's assumption, we would certainly *not* expect effects to occur in the eight seconds prior to the generation of the tension-producing stimulus (the target) or immediately thereafter, when the experimenters were awaiting Tanous' response. A similar argument might be applied to Isaacs's attribution of the results to experimenter's retroactive PK.[43]

Osis and McCormick close their reply with the observation that, if their own PK were the unintentional source of the strain-gauge effects, then we would ordinarily expect their PK effects to coincide with their expectancies regarding where the strain-gauge effects would probably occur in the sequence. They note, however, that the experimenters initially expected to obtain effects only *after* target generation and possibly only during the time Tanous was verbally responding. They certainly did not anticipate significant strain-gauge activation in periods *prior* to target generation. They conclude that their alleged micro-PKMB abilities could not possibly have been the source of the strain-gauge effects.[44]

The above exchange between Isaacs and Osis and McCormick is well worth citing because it shows fairly conclusively why Isaacs's reservation about the strain-gauge effects are unacceptable. It also raises the disturbing question of how scientists such as Susan Blackmore and H. J. Irwin can cite Isaacs's criticisms as offering good grounds for setting aside, or disparaging, the importance or the validity of the experiment, without even attempting to assess or discuss the relative merits of the reply offered by Osis and McCormick. Doubtless, the experiment does need to be repeated with another gifted and willing subject. But that is certainly no reason for refusing to look at the compelling reply Osis and McCormick have made to Isaacs's "far-fetched" critique of the experiment—especially when the reply occurs in the same journal, immediately after Isaacs's piece. To date, I know of no response made by Isaacs to the reply offered above by Osis and McCormick.

It is important to note also that, even if—for any reason whatsoever—the strain-gauge effects were unreliable, the experiment would still count for establishing that there are some nonhallucinatory OBEs wherein the knowledge the subjects acquire cannot be explained by appeal to normal ways of knowing and acquiring knowledge. In this respect, as has been said earlier, the experiment is a successful repetition of the Tart experiment with Ms. Z. As such, it shows that if there are other reasons for thinking that the knowledge obtained could not have been acquired by clairvoyance or ESP, then the experiment would—even without the strain-gauge effects—support the view that something had to leave the body during these experiences.

Incidentally, at this point it is equally important to note that, while the hallucination hypothesis stands strongly refuted by the large number of OBEs in which there is verified veridical content the subject could not have acquired in normal ways, we cannot—even independently of the Osis–McCormick strain-gauge results—plausibly explain the knowledge the subject has in these OBEs by appeal to clairvoyance or distant viewing. In nonhallucinatory OBEs, there are aspects of *autoscopic description* that defy explanation by appeal to clairvoyance as we generally understand it.

For example, in cases described above (as well as others reported by Dr. Sabom and others), the *subjects describe the environment in a way that is only consistent with viewing the environment from an elevated position above the body of the subject.* As a matter of fact, this is a typical feature of descriptions of events offered by subjects whose OBEs have veridical content that the subject could not have acquired in normal ways. Frequently, if not invariably, people reporting OBEs and NDEs describe in detail the pattern and colors of floor tiles, for example.[45] Clairvoyant descriptions associated with distant viewing, however, do not typically have this feature. Contrary to what some have suggested who would wish to explain OBEs as an ESP phenomenon, there is no clear evidence—either inside or outside the lab—showing that distant viewing typically has this feature. And if clairvoyant descriptions, or descriptions found in distant viewing, do not typically have this feature while reported OBEs and NDEs do typically have this feature, then it seems reasonable to conclude that we have here two different types of description not readily assimilable to each other, thereby rendering them two distinct phenomena. Besides, the features of descriptions offered in OBEs and NDEs are precisely what one would expect from subjects who had actually left their bodies, whereas the absence of those features is precisely what one would expect of subjects who were successfully practicing clairvoyance as it is standardly described.

Inability to explain this autoscopic aspect of nonhallucinatory OBEs by appeal to clairvoyance or distant viewing undercuts the force of the alternative explanation offered by those who appeal to ESP (clairvoyance) in explaining how the subject comes to have the knowledge she or he has acquired in these OBEs. It is, of course, remotely possible that there is some form of ESP (clairvoyance) that we do not know about, and that would account for the autoscopic along with the verifiable descriptions in these nonhallucinatory OBEs. But as things presently stand, we have precious little evidence (either in the lab or outside) of the existence of such a form of clairvoyance; and so, any appeal to it as a possible way to explain the data is purely ad hoc and gratuitous.

Furthermore, if we combine this reasoning with the results of the strain-gauge data in the Osis–McCormick experiment, it is difficult to avoid the conclusion that the best available explanation of how the subjects come to acquire their knowledge in these nonhallucinatory OBEs is simply that they must have left their bodies and must have been in the target area—and in that place, directly acquired the knowledge, without the normal use of their bodies. This, of course, is precisely what the subjects in OBE and NDE experiences claim, and it is not what subjects involved in distant viewing or clairvoyance claim.

Surely, it would be erroneous to base the whole of the dualist's view of OBEs on the inability of certain sceptical explanations to account for autoscopic descriptions in nonhallucinatory OBEs by appeal to clairvoyance.[46] Nevertheless, the inability to account for these autoscopic features is a serious problem for the sceptic who seeks to appeal to clairvoyance or distant viewing as a source of the subject's knowledge.

Besides, even if it should turn out that there is a form of clairvoyance that allows for these autoscopic features, that would only mean we must now decide between clairvoyance and personal presence in the target area as a way of explaining the subject's knowledge. Of the two, the only one that fits the strain-gauge data of the Osis–McCormick experiment is the latter because, for all the reasons noted above, we cannot account for such data by appeal to nonintentional PK or action at a distance. Therefore, even if there were a form of clairvoyance that lent itself to the sorts of descriptions we find in nonhallucinatory OBEs, it would add very little weight to the nondualist view that in these experiences nothing leaves the body.

And I know of no other alternative hypothesis that the sceptic could offer to explain the OBE without adopting the dualist's position. (I am assuming, of course, that the strongest cases are amply documented and that the data are not just fraudulently fabricated to fit a logically ideal case of what it would take to sustain the dualist's interpretation of the nonhallucinatory OBE or NDE. I am also assuming that in the stronger cases the knowledge the subject acquires while ostensibly under the OBE cannot be explained by appeal to telepathy. Frequently, what is reported and independently verified is nothing anyone near the subject could know.)

Conclusion

Certainly, then, the evidence just examined favors the dualist's view on the nature of those OBEs we have called "nonhallucinatory OBEs." As a matter of fact, the evidence at hand strongly warrants our endorsing some form of mind–body dualism that eschews a pure reduction of human personality to bodily existence as we know it. In short, contrary to what some people have suggested, we have in these best cases enough in the way of "proof" to justify a rational belief in some form of postmortem personal survival. Even so, in the interest of stimulating further experimentation, we may well be prompted to ask what it would take to undermine this conclusion.

The answer seems simple enough. If the Osis–McCormick experiment should, for any reason whatever, prove to be incapable of repetition, we *might* need to abandon the dualist hypothesis as the most plausible explanation. I say "*might*" because there would still be the claim that we cannot explain the special autoscopic features in such OBEs by appealing to the sorts of descriptions we are familiar with in ESP or distant viewing. But even if such an abandonment were in order, it would by no means imply endorsing the kind of simpleminded materialism that comes with the hallucination hypothesis. For even if we failed to repeat the Osis–McCormick experiment (including the strain-gauge effects), and found some plausible way to account for the special autoscopic features of descriptions in nonhallucinatory OBEs, we would still have abundant testimony and evidence (both experimental and nonexperimental) that some OBEs are nonhallucinatory; and those are the ones in which the subject acquires paranormally a knowledge of something taking place at some distance from her or his body. At that point, the sceptic could move to the ESP hypothesis as a way of explaining how that knowledge is acquired, and abandon dualism by simply construing ESP as a purely natural phenomenon rooted in some emerging property of the brain. Thereafter the subject's claim that she or he "left the body" during the OBE could plausibly be viewed as the hallucinatory part of the otherwise nonhallucinatory OBE.

On the other hand, repetition of experiments similar to the Osis–McCormick procedures involving unintended strain-gauge effects would, for all the reasons indicated above, further entrench the justification for thinking that human beings (or at least some human beings) are distinct from their bodies and, under certain circumstances, manage to leave them and acquire knowledge without their use.

Finally, some researchers have suggested that if we could monitor the brain activity of subjects in both voluntary and involuntary OBEs, and if a monitored subject's EEG reading were determined to be flat during the time of the nonhallucinatory OBE, then this would prove conclusively that the subject's independently confirmed reports about what was taking place some distance from her or his body could not be the product of either ESP (clairvoyance) or hallucination, because both of those phenomena would require the presence of some brain activity in the subject during the OBE. Further, the satisfaction of this last requirement would also make it impossible to explain by appeal to action at a distance (or PK) how the subject in a voluntary OBE is able to have a detectable physical effect in the target location. In other words, this requirement would have been satisfied in the Osis–McCormick experiment if Osis and McCormick had determined that, whenever the strain-gauge effects showed up, Alex Tanous's EEG was flat or very low. Interestingly enough, some researchers claim that this has already been established on a grand scale during experiments that utilized the medical monitoring of those who have had NDEs;[47] but their claim has not yet been substantiated.

Naturally, too, were this requirement to be satisfied, there might still be objections that the EEG is measuring only a certain kind of brain activity and, thus, that the flat EEG does not provide the crucial evidence for the dualist's view. How one could know that there is another kind of energy (natural energy) in addition to that measured by the EEG would be questionable, of course; and appeal to its existence to determine the force of the flat EEG would be quite arbitrary.

For most of us, then, an *ideal OBE* supportive of dualism could be either a *voluntary* OBE that meets these four conditions:

1. the subject is antecedently directed to visit a distant location and then return to describe the location correctly;
2. the subject's brain waves are monitored by EEG during the OBE and are determined to be flat (or very, very low) during the OBE experience;
3. after the OBE, the subject accurately reports on the details of the environment visited and offers autoscopic descriptions fitting the details of the environment and indicative of an elevated viewpoint; and
4. reliable strain-gauge effects are recorded at the site the subject is asked to describe during the OBE when the subject's reports are nonhallucinatory.

Or else it could be an *involuntary* OBE that meets these three conditions:

1. the subject's vital functions cease and brain activity is monitored, with the EEG reading flat (or very, very low) during the OBE;

2. after the OBE, the subject reports on events that took place during the OBE at some distance from his or her body, and these reports are independently verified by third-party witnesses of those events transpiring during the time of the flat (or very, very low) EEG reading; and

3. the events reported and described by the subject having the OBE are not predictable by appeal to general probabilities.

Notice that in the involuntary idealized case, while it would certainly be confirmative, the subject need not describe the area around his or her body in ways that indicate a viewpoint above the body. It is enough to show that the subject was not hallucinating the content of his or her reports, and that the content cannot have been the product of ESP, clairvoyance, or lucky guesses, with the EEG flat or very low. Here again, it would be enough that the EEG be flat and the subject's report on the details of the target area be accurate and not generally predictable; for then the epistemic content of the subject's report could not be explained either by appeal to chance or by appeal to forms of clairvoyance.

Of course, if the Osis–McCormick results with the strain-gauge effects were regularly repeated, then one would not need to present evidence of a flat EEG reading while the subject is in the OBE. But it would seem to be of further confirmatory value if it were present.

It has also been suggested that we may well want to add to our list of idealizing conditions for the voluntary OBE the further condition that the subject *appear* to an independent observer (or observers) stationed at the designated place of visit. And surely, if this were to occur, we could not explain it by appeal to action at a distance if the subject's EEG were determined to be flat during the OBE. But if the subject's EEG were not flat, it is difficult to see how we would rule against this phenomenon's being an instance of *actio in distans* or telepathy. It has been claimed in the popular press that some people are capable of making others (at a distance) "see" what the subject wants them to see.[48] But there is no solid evidence of this. Further, it is difficult to see how this added condition would be necessary if all the others were satisfied. Indeed, the satisfaction of this condition would not provide any

different or stronger evidence than what is provided by the failure
to be able to explain the subject's unintentionally moving a strain
gauge during an OBE while the EEG is flat. Moreover, for those
who think that the existing evidence tips the scale in favor of the
dualist position, the flat (or very, very low) EEG requirement
would even be unnecessary. Like the call for an apparition, the flat
EEG seems too strong a requirement because we do not generally
find it in voluntary OBEs even when all the other idealizing
conditions are satisfied. But, for those like myself who feel that
the earlier cited evidence for the dualist's interpretation of the
OBE could be stronger, the further requirement that the subject's
EEG be flat during the OBE would present more compelling
evidence.

The virtue of seeking evidence in terms of the idealized voluntary OBE is that it is experimentally feasible; but in no case yet
reported are we demonstrably able to satisfy the flat EEG requirement. And seeking evidence in terms of the idealized involuntary
OBE is also problematic because it is so difficult to get EEG
readings on patients (or others) in critical arrest while trying to
save them from dying. In practice, the failure to secure flat (or
very, very low) EEGs should not be viewed as failure to confirm
the dualist's view, because it is not a *necessary* condition. Even at
that, however, it is clear that, should we be able to secure the flat
reading, the dualist's view of OBEs would be more strongly
supported.

Amid all of this speculation, then, one thing is certain. Until
such ideal cases—whether voluntary or involuntary—have been
well documented and repeated frequently under controlled conditions, we cannot claim to have conclusive evidence warranting the
dualist's interpretation of the nonhallucinatory OBE, but we can
certainly claim that the dualist's interpretation is more rationally
warranted than any alternative interpretation presently available.

Notes

1. See Raymond Moody's *Life after Life* (Covington, Ga.: Mockingbird Books, 1975), and *Reflections on Life after Life* (New York: Bantam

Books, 1978); Ronald Siegel, "Accounting for 'Afterlife' Experiences," *Psychology Today* (January 1981), pp. 65ff; Robert Monroe, *Journeys Out of the Body* (New York: Doubleday, 1971); Michael Sabom, *Recollections of Death: A Medical Examination* (New York: Harper and Row, 1981); John Hartwell, Jane Janis, and Blue Harary, et al., "A Study of the Physiological Variables Associated with Out-of-body Experiences," paper presented at the Parapsychological Association Convention, New York, 1974, and published in *Research in Parapsychology 1974*, eds. J. D. Morris, W. D. Roll, and R. L. Morris (Metuchen, N.J.: Scarecrow Press, 1975), pp. 127–29; Janet Mitchell, "Out-of-body Vision," *Psychic Magazine* (April 1973), pp. 44–47; S. Muldoon and H. Carrington, *The Projection of the Astral Body* (New York: Samuel Wieser, 1970); Robert Crookall, *The Study and Practice of Astral Projection* (New York: University Books, 1966); Robert Crookall, *Out-of-the-body Experiences* (Hyde Park, N.Y.: University Books, 1970); Kenneth Ring, *Life at Death: A Scientific Investigation of the Near-death Experience* (New York: Coward, McCann, and Geoghegan, 1980).

2. Moody, *Life after Life* (cited in note 1); and Raymond Moody, *The Light Beyond* (New York: Bantam Books, 1988).

3. See, for example, Crookall, *Out-of-the-body Experiences*.

4. Originally from *Revue Metapsychique* (May/June 1930), and cited by C. J. Ducasse in *A Critical Examination of the Belief in Life after Death* (Springfield, Ill.: Charles C Thomas, 1961), pp. 161–62.

5. R. L. Morris, S. B. Harary, J. Janis, J. Hartwell, and W. G. Roll, "Studies of Communication during Out-of-body Experiences," *Journal of the American Society of Psychical Research* 72 (1978), pp. 1–22. See also Hartwell, Janis, and Harary, et al., "Study of the Physiological Variables"; R. Morris, "PRF Research on Out-of-body Experiences, 1973," *Theta*, no. 41 (Summer 1974), pp. 1–3; and Muldoon and Carrington, *Projection of the Astral Body*.

6. Morris, Harary, Janis, Hartwell, and Roll, "Studies of Communication," p. 22.

7. Charles T. Tart, *Psi: Scientific Studies of the Psychic Realm* (New York: Dutton, 1977).

8. Monroe, *Journeys* (cited in note 1).

9. Tart, *Psi*, p. 43.

10. Charles Tart, "A Psychophysiological Study of Out-of-the-body Experiences in a Selected Subject," *Journal of the American Society for Psychical Research* 62, no. 1 (January 1968); and the case study reprinted in Martin Ebon, *The Signet Handbook of Parapsychology* (New York: New American Library, 1978), pp. 173–200.

11. Karlis Osis and Donna McCormick, "Kinetic Effects at the Ostensible Location of an Out-of-body Projection during Perceptual Testing," *Journal of the American Society for Psychical Research* 74 (July 1980), pp. 319–29.

12. Ibid., p. 319.

13. Moody, *Life after Life*, pp. 21–25, and reprinted in James Humber and Robert Almeder, *Biomedical Ethics and the Law* (New York: Plenum Publishing, 1979), pp. 627–28.

14. From *Vital Signs* 1, no. 3 (December 1981), pp. 4–7.

15. From the *Atlanta Constitution*, January 18, 1982. This case is also related by Sabom in *Recollections of Death*.

16. Siegel, "Accounting for 'Afterlife' Experiences."

17. Paul Kurtz, "Brushes with Death," *Psychology Today* 22, no. 9 (September 1988), p. 15.

18. See Ring, *Life at Death*.

19. Kurtz, "Brushes," p. 15.

20. Juan C. Saavedra-Aguilar and Juan S. Gomez-Jeria, "A Neurological Model for Near Death Experiences," *Journal of Near-death Studies* 7, no. 4 (Summer 1989), pp. 205–22, quote at p. 205.
Incidentally, a close examination of the neurobiological model indicates that the proposed explanation based on the model fails because, among other things, it does not make predictions sufficiently precise to refute the hallucination hypothesis. Presumably, any model that does not specify the precise conditions under which the desired phenomenon (supposed explained by the model) will occur, or what specific effects will count for undermining the proposed explanation, cannot plausibly support an alternative explanation.
Also, any reflective epistemologist will surely be amused by the attempt to determine the veridicality of what is reported in the OBE by determining the neurobiological causes of the beliefs. It is often difficult to convince psychologists (in particular) that the truth of a belief has fundamentally nothing to do with the way in which the belief comes about. But this is a very long story that we need not tell now. For a longer discussion on this point, see R. Almeder and F. Hogg, "Reliabilism and Goldman's Theory of Justification," *Philosophia* (December 1989); and Robert Almeder, *Blind Realism* (Lanham, Md.: Rowman and Littlefield, 1991), pp. 60–92.

21. *Manchester Guardian Weekly*, September 11, 1988, p. 21.

22. Ibid.

23. Ibid., p. 15.

24. Ibid.

25. Ibid.

26. Susan Blackmore, *Beyond the Body: An Investigation of Out-of-body Experiences* (London: Heinemann, 1982), p. 59.

27. See the review of ibid. by Emily Williams Cook in *Anabiosis* 4, no. 1 (Spring 1984), p. 101.

28. Blackmore, *Beyond the Body*, pp. 60ff.

29. Sabom, *Recollections of Death*, p. 25. See also Ring, *Life at Death*, p. 66.

30. Moody, *Light Beyond*, p. 14.

31. Ibid., p. 15.

32. Ibid., p. 16.

33. See William K. Stuckey, "Psychic Power: The Next Super Weapon," *Harpers* (January 5, 1977), pp. 47–55.

34. Blackmore, *Beyond the Body*, p. 147.

35. H. J. Irwin, *Flight of Mind: A Psychological Study of the Out-of-body Experience* (Metuchen, N.J.: Scarecrow Press, 1985).

36. Julian Isaacs, "On Kinetic Effects during Out-of-body Projection," *Journal of the American Society for Psychical Research* 75 (1981), pp. 192–94.

37. Ibid., p. 192.

38. Ibid., p. 193.

39. Ibid.

40. Ibid.

41. Karlis Osis and Donna McCormick, "The Authors Reply to Mr. Isaacs," *Journal of the American Society for Psychical Research* 75 (1981), pp. 195–97.

42. Ibid., p. 195.

43. Ibid., p. 196.

44. Ibid., p. 195.

45. See Sabom, *Recollections of Death*, pp. 73ff; and Ring, *Life at Death*, p. 46.

46. Indeed, it has been claimed that some clairvoyants are able to describe certain phenomena from whatever viewpoint they are asked. This ability has been attributed to Ingo Swann, for example. See Stuckey, "Psychic Power," p. 48.

47. In Dina Ingber, "Visions of an Afterlife," *Science Digest* (December 1980), pp. 95ff, it is claimed by the author that in 1979 a Dr. Schoonmaker released the results of long-term research in which there were 55 cases of NDE wherein flat EEGs were established.

48. Sheila Ostrander and Lynn Schroeder, *Psychic Discoveries behind the Iron Curtain* (New York: Bantam Books, 1976), pp. 120ff.

5

Communications from the Dead

Some people claim that dead persons occasionally communicate with the living through persons called *mediums*. Fascinated by this claim, philosophers and scientists continue to examine mediums and mediumship as a possible source of evidence for some form of personal survival after death. In this chapter we shall examine a specific form of mediumship—trance mediumship—and point to some case studies that provide persuasive evidence for some form of personal survival. We shall also see a number of cases that *seem* quite powerful but that fail when confronted by the serious sceptic. Before going further, however, let me say something very briefly about *trance mediumship* and *possession mediumship*.

Trance Mediumship

A trance medium is a person (usually female) who enters voluntarily into a trance state—a conscious but sleeplike state such as deep hypnosis. While in this altered state of consciousness, she supposedly receives information from deceased persons and conveys the information to others (usually relatives or friends of the deceased) sitting in her presence. In this most common form of trance mediumship, the medium uses her own mental states and vocal organs to convey consciously information she receives from the deceased.

But in another kind of trance mediumship, the medium enters voluntarily into a trance state and her personality is "taken over" or "replaced" by the personality of a deceased person. In this second and rare form of mediumship, the personality taking over the personality of the medium is called the *control*. The control possesses and then "uses" the body and vocal organs of the medium to speak directly to the *sitters* (those present at the trance), usually about their deceased relatives or friends. In this form of mediumship—unlike in the more common form—since the personality of the medium is apparently totally replaced by the personality of the deceased, the medium speaks and acts in ways totally characteristic of the deceased but quite foreign to her normal personality. After the trance is over, the medium usually has no conscious recollection of anything that transpired during the trance.

Obviously, this rarer form of mediumship is also a form of ostensible possession, not at all unlike the form we discussed in Chapter 3; and to the extent that we have valid instances of this form of mediumship, we also have valid instances of the sort of ostensible possession defined in Chapter 3. The principal difference seems to be that, in the typical case of ostensible possession, the subject does not voluntarily induce it, and it typically lasts over an extended period of time or occurs in unexpected ways lasting over sometimes long and unpredictable periods of time. Whereas, in mediumship, the form of ostensible possession involved seems to be voluntarily induced by the subject, who allows the possession to take place for a limited period of time for some specific purpose or other.

Sometimes, too, during a séance of this possession type, a succession of deceased persons will emerge or (to use Ian Stevenson's phrase) "drop in" and speak through the medium. And each of them will manifest the individual traits supposedly characteristic of that deceased person before death.

In the literature, this general phenomenon wherein the personality of the medium under trance is replaced by the personality of a deceased person is sometimes referred to as "ostensible possession" or, more often, simply "possession mediumship."[1]

The Language Cases

So much for the preliminaries. The important question is whether we have any strong cases of possession mediumship that provide convincing evidence for personal survival. We will begin by looking at a number of cases I call *language cases.* These cases allegedly involve possession mediumship plus xenoglossy. As examples of what *would* be logically sufficient to establish survival on the basis of possession mediumship they are very convincing. When we come to assess their evidential impact, however, we shall see that there are good reasons for being very cautious in accepting these language cases. Even so, independently of these language cases, we have other well examined cases of possession medium-ship that certainly do succeed in providing convincing evidence for survival.

The Greek Case

In 1905 the *Annales des Sciences Psychiques* reported a case in which a medium under trance spoke a language of which, in her normal state, she was entirely ignorant.[2] This would be a case allegedly involving both possession mediumship and responsive xenoglossy. The medium was a Ms. Laura Edmonds, the daugh-ter of the distinguished Judge John Worth Edmonds, president of the New York State Senate and later judge of the Supreme Court of New York. Judge Edmonds was widely regarded as a person of unquestionable integrity and considerable intelligence.

At one time the Judge had undertaken the study of psychical research to demonstrate the worthlessness of the activity and the foolishness of those who took such phenomena seriously. We can imagine the depth of his concern when his daughter Laura, a fervent Catholic capable of speaking her mother tongue and French only, began to shine as a developing medium.

Anyway, as the case is reported, one evening a Mr. Evangelides, a Greek, visited the Edmondses. At a sitting (a séance) held later that evening, Laura—in trance—was controlled by a friend of Evangelides named Botzaris, who had died earlier in Greece.

According to Judge Edmonds, this control (Botzaris) spoke in modern Greek to Evangelides and informed him that his son, whom Evangelides still supposed was well and alive in Greece, had recently died. Evangelides wept at this news and could scarcely believe it. But the fact of his son's death was subsequently confirmed. Judge Edmonds, who submitted an affidavit testifying to the above, made the following observations:

> To deny the fact is impossible, it was too well known; I could as well deny the light of the sun; nor could I think it an illusion, for it is in no way different from any other reality. It took place before ten educated and intelligent persons. We had never seen Mr. Evangelides before; he was introduced by a friend that same evening. How could Laura tell him of his son? How could she understand and speak Greek which she had never previously heard?[3]

The Welsh Case

In *Towards the Stars* Dennis Bradley tells of a séance involving himself and friends with the famous (and much criticized) American medium George Valiantine on February 27, 1924, at Bradley's house in Dorincourt, England.[4] Present at the sitting were Dennis Bradley, Mrs. Dennis Bradley, Newman Flower, Harold Wimbury, Mr. and Mrs. Caradoc Evans, Miss Queenie Bayliss, and the medium George Valiantine. During the sitting Mr. and Mrs. Evans, who had attended earlier sittings, renewed a discussion with a deceased friend, a Mr. Edward Wright. After a while, however, a new voice—claiming to be that of Mr. Evans's father—came forward. Then the following exchange occurred:

Caradoc Evans: Do you want me?
Voice: Yes.
Caradoc Evans: Who are you?
Voice: Your father!
Caradoc Evans: Father! Can't be. How do you know that I am
                here? Who told you?
Voice: Edward Wright.

Caradoc Evans: Well, look, if you are my father, *siaradwch a fy yn eich iaith.*
Voice: *Beth i chwi am i fy ddeyd?*
Caradoc Evans: *Eich enw, wrth gwrs.*
Voice: William Evans.
Caradoc Evans: *Yn le maro chwi?*
Voice: *Caerfyrddin.*
Caradoc Evans: *Sir?*
Voice: *Tre.*
Caradoc Evans: *Ble mae'r ty?*
Voice: *Uch ben ye avon. Mae steps—lawer iawn—rhwng y ty ar rheol. Pa beth yr ydych yn gofyn? Y chwi yn mynd i weld a ty bob tro yr rydych yn y dre.*
Caradoc Evans: *Nhad . . .*

TRANSLATION

. . . speak to me in your own language.
Voice: What do you want me to say?
Caradoc Evans: Your name, of course.
Voice: William Evans.
Caradoc Evans: Where did you die?
Voice: Carmarthen.
Caradoc Evans: Shire?
Voice: Town.
Caradoc Evans: Where is the house?
Voice: Above the river. There are steps—many steps—between the house and the road. Why do you ask me? You go to see the house every time you are in town.
Caradoc Evans: My father . . .[5]

Before going on to our third language case, it is worth noting that the medium in this case, George Valiantine, neither spoke nor understood a word of Welsh.

The Hungarian Case

In 1939, the *Psychic News* (published in London) carried an account of Dr. Nandor Fodor's first encounter with a case of possession mediumship.[6] Dr. Fodor had arrived unexpectedly in New York on the day before this particular séance, and his good friend William Cartheuser had introduced him to the medium Arthur Ford just before the sitting.

When the séance began, Ford went into trance, and a control named Fletcher spoke through him. After a while, Dr. Fodor asked Fletcher if he could bring forth somebody who would speak Hungarian, Dr. Fodor's native tongue. Fletcher said he would try. After a period of silence—Dr. Fodor's account continues—

I hear a voice. Cold shivers run down my back. It sounds like a distant cry. It is repeated. Someone is calling my name.

"Who—who is it? Whom do you want?" I ask hoarsely in my native tongue.

The call is more explicit: "Fodor—*Journalist!*"

The last word shakes me to the core. It is pronounced in German. It is the only German word my father ever used. He used it only when he spoke about me!

I stammered an answer. Craning my neck in the dark—I listened with strained nerves to tatters of a terrific struggle for expression.

"Edesapa—edesapa—" (Dear father—dear father—)

The voice vibrates with emotion. It makes me hot and burning. I sound unnatural to myself: *"Apam? Apam?"* (Father, dear?)

"Iges. Edes fiam—" (Yes, dear son—)

I cannot describe the minutes that followed. From beyond the Great Divide somebody who says he is my father is making desperate efforts to master some weird instrument of speech, and trembles with anxiety to prove his presence by speaking in his native tongue:

"Budapest—nem ertesz? Enekelek—Magyar Kislany vagyok." (Budapest—don't you understand?—I will sing—)

I don't know the song. Two lines rhyming. Have I heard them before? I recognize the pet name of my eldest brother, to whom my father was very attached.

The voice comes from near the ceiling. But it comes nearer at my request. It is still struggling for words.

Fletcher takes pity and explains: "Your father wishes to tell you that he died in January 16. It is for the first time he tries to speak. That makes it very difficult for him."

The interruption brings relief. The voice becomes much clearer. It gives me a message about my mother and sister.

Then: *"Isten aldjon meg, edes fiam."* (God bless you, my son.) Sounds of kisses—Silence—

The voice speaks again in Hungarian: *"Esti Ujsag."* (*Evening News.*)

My wife screams.

Esti Ujsag was the newspaper on which her brother was employed before he died.

"Sanyika?"

"Yes."

I feel her trembling with excitement.

The voice is youthful and explosive. It speaks as my wife's brother would. He knows all about the family and is always about. He has but one regret: *"Szegeny Vilmis basci!"* (Poor Uncle Vilmos.)

"Why, what is wrong with Uncle Vilmos?"

"He is not well, he will go blind."

We receive the prophecy in dead silence.

My experience was more unusual than that of the majority. I was a foreigner on the staff of a foreign daily in New York. I had few friends, they were all new ones. None of them knew about my old country relations. Yet the statements about my family were correct.

The voice spoke in Hungarian. Plain as the words were, my native tongue offers a variety of expressions for the relationship between father and son.

The voice made no mistake. My father was in the habit of using the *very* words.

He had forgotten his German years before. It was no more spoken at home. The only word retained was *"journalist."* He was very proud of his boy, the journalist. The Hungarian equivalent of *ujsagiro*. He never used it. He preferred the German term.

The reference to the date of his death was not correct. He did not die on January 16. But he was buried on that day.

Uncle Vilmos, as predicted, went blind—and committed suicide! I know him as Uncle Villy. Vilmos (the proper name) left me uneasy. I had the matter out with my mother-in-law two years later when I revisited Budapest. She opened her eyes wide.

"Why, didn't you know? My boy alone in the family called him Uncle Vilmos. He was Uncle Villy to everybody else!"[7]

Once again, we should note that the medium, Arthur Ford, neither spoke nor understood Hungarian. We can now turn to the last of our language cases.

The Chinese Case

In *Psychic Adventures in New York* Dr. Neville Whymant tells of the time he was invited by Judge W. M. Cannon to attend a sitting with the medium George Valiantine.[8] Judge Cannon told Dr. Whymant that voices had spoken in foreign tongues—European and Oriental—at previous sittings; and because Dr. Whymant (who, before coming to New York, had lectured in Chinese for many years at Oxford) spoke 30 dialects and languages, his attendance was desired in order that he might comment on the voices that none of the others could understand.

Dr. Whymant later confessed that he had found himself amused by the prospect of uncovering an ingenious hoax. Moreover, when Whymant met Valiantine, he formed the opinion that this medium was basically stupid, unlettered, and distinctly incapable of any form of acting. (Incidentally, this is the same controversial George Valiantine who was the medium in the Welsh case discussed above.)

As usual, the séance began with the Lord's Prayer followed by some singing; and then the first voices started coming through the entranced Valiantine, speaking of very personal matters to sitters other than Whymant. A voice spoke in Italian, and Whymant was kind enough to translate it for one of the sitters. Then, according to Whymant's narration, there suddenly came

a weird, crackling, broken little sound which at once carried my mind straight back to China. It was the sound of a flute, rather poorly played, such as can be heard in the streets of the Celestial Land but nowhere else. The next sound seemed to be a hollow repetition of a Chinese name, *K'ung-fu-T'zo,* "The Philosopher-Master-K'ung," the name by which Confucius was canonized. I was not sure I had heard aright and I asked in Chinese for another opportunity of hearing what had been said before. This time without any hesitation at all came the name, *K'ung-fu-T'zo.* Now, I thought, this was my opportunity.

Chinese I had long regarded as my own special research area, and he would be a wise man, medium or other, who would attempt to trick me on such soil. . . . It was difficult to discover what was said next, and I had to keep calling for a repetition. Then it burst upon me that I was listening to Chinese of a dialect not now spoken in any part of China. As the voice went on I realized that the style of Chinese used was identical with that of a Chinese classic edited by Confucius 2500 years ago. Only among scholars in archaic Chinese could one now hear that accent and style, and then only when they intoned some passage from the ancient books. In other words, the Chinese to which we were now listening was as dead colloquially as Sanskrit or Latin. I thought suddenly of a supreme test. There are several poems in the *Shih King* (Classics of Poetry) which have baffled the commentators ever since Confucius himself edited the work and left it to posterity as a model anthology of early Chinese verse. Western scholars have attempted in vain to wrest their meaning, and Chinese classical scholars versed in the lore and literature of the ancient empire have long ago given up trying to understand them. I have never read any of these poems myself, but I knew the first lines of some of them through seeing them so often while looking through the book for others. At this moment it occurred to me that if I could remember the first line of them I might now get a chance to astonish the communicator who called himself "Confucius." I asked if the "Master" would explain to me the meaning of one of those long, obscure odes. Without exerting conscious choice I said, *"Ts'ai Ts'ai chuan ehr,"* which is the first line of the third ode of the first book (*Chow nan*) of the Classics of Poetry. I certainly could not have repeated another line of this poem, for I did not know any of the remaining fifteen lines; but there was no need or even opportunity, for the voice took up the poem and recited to the end. I had a pad of paper and a pencil and I made notes of what the voice said and jotted down keys to the intonation used.

In declaiming the ode the voice had put a construction on the verses and made the whole thing hang together as a normal poem. Altogether there were about sixteen sittings at which I assisted in exactly the same fashion as that detailed in the first sitting. The self-styled Confucius was very regular in its incidence. Fourteen foreign languages were used in the course of the sittings I attended. They included Chinese, Hindu, Persian, Basque, Sanskrit, Arabic, Portuguese, Italian, Yiddish (spoken with great fluency when a Yiddish and Hebrew speaking Jew was a member of the circle), German, and modern Greek.[9]

Dr. Whymant went on to note that only the Chinese can pronounce correctly Confucius's name, and Whymant was abso-

lutely convinced that the owner of the voice had to be Chinese—
and a Chinese scholar at that. Whymant even asked the voice,
"What was your popular name when you were fourteen years
old?" Not only was the reply correct, but it was uttered with the
proper intonation; according to Whymant, this sort of information is known only to experts in the Chinese language. And
Whymant—with his 25 years of research on the language spoken
in Confucius's time (some 2,500 years ago)—claimed that scholars
agree there are only about a dozen sounds known to have been
used in the time of Confucius. These archaic sounds were uttered
by the voice with whom Whymant spoke.

The day after the first sitting, Whymant went to the library to
check on the poetic diction supplied by the communicating entity.
As a result of this investigation, Whymant discovered an error and
concluded that either he had misheard or misquoted the entity, or
the entity made a mistake in reciting the poem. But at the next
sitting—before Whymant had an opportunity to say anything—
the voice came forth and said, "Speaking the other day, this
clumsy, witless one stepped into error. Too frequently, alas, he
has done this; and the explanation he gave was a faulty one. Listen
now to the reading of the passage about which the illustrious
scholar inquired." Whymant then noted that the true reading
followed and corrected the faulty reading.

Before discussing the force of all these language cases as evidence for some form of personal survival, let us recount a few
other cases that have been the subject of painstaking investigation.

The Mediumships of Mrs. Piper and Mrs. Willett

Among the trance mediums most examined and discussed in
the early days of the Society for Psychical Research (founded in
England in 1882) were Mrs. Leonora Piper and Mrs. Willett.
Although, as we shall see, the principal investigator of Mrs.
Piper's mediumship had serious reservations about the extent of
her authenticity, I include here a discussion of her mediumship
because it is by no means clear that Mrs. Piper's mediumship
failed as a source of evidence for personal survival. Indeed, there

is good reason to think her mediumship succeeded as a source of such evidence. Moreover, the examination of Mrs. Piper's mediumship underscores the force of the case made on the basis of Mrs. Willett's mediumship—a mediumship not at all vulnerable to a strong sceptical response.

Mrs. Leonora Piper

The American philosopher William James was quite active in the Society for Psychical Research, serving as its president in 1894 and 1895. He also helped to found the American branch of that society, later to become autonomous as the American Society for Psychical Research. James was introduced to Mrs. Leonora Piper, the Boston medium, in 1885; his interest in her mediumship continued over a 25-year period up to his death in 1910. In a report issued in 1909 and entitled "Report on Mrs. Piper's Hodgson Control," James undertook to collate all the results of Mrs. Piper's sittings in America in which Richard Hodgson figured as her alleged control.[10] Hodgson had been a close friend of James and also one of the early founders of the American Society for Psychical Research. Prior to his sudden death in 1905, Richard Hodgson had himself examined the mediumship of Mrs. Piper and had concluded, for reasons we shall note later, that Mrs. Piper's activities could be explained only by appeal to some form of personal survival after death. He often claimed that, if he should die while Mrs. Piper was still alive and functioning as a trance medium, he would come back as her control and speak to his friends through her. After his death in 1905, he began to appear as her control, replacing the former control named Phinuit. As discussed below, James examined her mediumship both when Phinuit was the control and then later when Hodgson was the control.

When William James and his wife first went to one of Mrs. Piper's séances back in 1885—and considerably before the period of the Hodgson control—they gave her no information about themselves and said nothing while Mrs. Piper was in trance and Phinuit (who was supposed to be a French physician) spoke to the

Jameses about matters that William James and his wife subsequently felt certain nobody but they could have known. Indeed,
in a letter he wrote to his friend F. W. H. Myers, James said that
after his first two visits with Mrs. Piper he was initially convinced
that either she was possessed of supernormal powers or else she
knew the members of his wife's family by sight and had, by some
lucky coincidence, become acquainted with the information she
divulged.[11] But he went on to note that later—as a result of
numerous sittings with her, and because of their growing personal
acquaintance—he came to believe that she had supernormal powers, after all.[12] In a report James filed with the Society for Psychical
Research in 1886, he wrote,

> This lady can at will pass into a trance condition, in which she is
> controlled by a power purporting to be the spirit of a French doctor,
> who serves as intermediary between the sitter and deceased friends.
> This is the ordinary type of trance mediumship of the present day.
> I have myself witnessed a dozen of her trances, and have testimony
> at first hand of twenty-five sitters, all but one of whom were
> introduced to Mrs. P by myself. . . .
>
> Fifteen of the sitters were surprised at the communications they
> received, names and facts being mentioned at the first interview
> which it seemed improbable should have been known to the me-
> dium in a normal way. The probability that she possessed no clew
> as to the sitter's identity was, I believe, in each and all of these
> fifteen cases, sufficient. But of only one of them is there a steno-
> graphic report; so that, unfortunately for the medium, the evidence
> in her favor is, although more abundant, less exact in quality than
> some of that which will be counted against her.
>
> Of these fifteen sitters, five, all ladies, were blood relatives, and
> two (I myself being one) were men connected by marriage with the
> family to which they belonged. . . . The medium showed a startling
> intimacy with the family's affairs, talking of many matters known
> to no one outside, and which gossip could not possibly have
> conveyed to her ears. The details would prove nothing to the reader,
> unless printed *in extenso* with full notes by the sitters. It reverts,
> after all, to personal conviction. My own conviction is not evidence,
> but it seems fitting to record it. I am persuaded of the medium's
> honesty, and of the genuineness of her trance; and although first
> disposed to think that the "hits" she made were either lucky

coincidences, or the result of knowledge on her part of who the sitter was and of his or her family affairs, I now believe her to be in possession of a power as yet unexplained.[13]

But James was quick to add that, even though Mrs. Piper had knowledge not acquired in normal ways, he did not see enough evidence to establish that Mrs. Piper was in contact with deceased persons. He thought that Phinuit—Mrs. Piper's supposed control at the time—was in fact a fictitious entity subconsciously created by Mrs. Piper. James's reasons for this latter conclusion were twofold. First of all, Phinuit was supposed to be a French physician, but his French was limited to a few salutations and small phrases; and Phinuit did not understand or respond when James addressed him in French. Second, Mrs. Piper failed three crucial tests put to her by James. (In the most interesting test, a Mrs. B on her deathbed wrote a letter, sealed it, and gave it to her sister, who did not know the contents. Nor did anybody else know the contents. After Mrs. B died, the letter was carried to William James by Mrs. B's sister. James in turn took the sealed letter to Mrs. Piper, who identified its author but failed three times to get the written message correct, even though the deceased Mrs. B was supposedly telling the entranced Mrs. Piper what the message was.)

At any rate, after James's friend Richard Hodgson died in December 1905, people were claiming that Hodgson had taken over as Mrs. Piper's control. Intrigued, William James once again investigated Mrs. Piper's mediumship, and his investigation resulted in the earlier mentioned "Report on Mrs. Piper's Hodgson Control," published in 1909. For this last report, James studied the transcripts of the various sittings in which Hodgson was said to be in control. By January 1908 there had been 75 such sittings.

James once again concluded that, from a purely logical point of view, the Hodgson control could well be a fictitious entity created and dramatized by the subconscious mind of Mrs. Piper. James admitted that the Hodgson control did manifest paranormal knowledge; and everybody admitted that the Hodgson control showed many individuating personal characteristics and traits of Hodgson.[14] However, James still felt that the evidence was not strong enough. There had been numerous personal contacts between Mrs. Piper and Hodgson before he died. As a result of these personal contacts, Mrs. Piper could, James felt, be subconsciously dramatizing his personality and furnishing it with information acquired by ESP.

Others have been quick to criticize James's findings for somehow overlooking the important evidence that would have shown that Mrs. Piper communicated with deceased persons.[15] This evidence occurred after Phinuit was the alleged control but before Hodgson allegedly took over, during the control of one George Pellew (G.P.). It was principally this period of séances when G.P. was the control (1892–1905) that ultimately convinced Hodgson and others that Mrs. Piper was indeed then controlled by a discarnate personality, although they agreed with James and others both that Phinuit was a fictitious entity subconsciously dramatized by Mrs. Piper and (later on) that the Hodgson control might also be fictitious for the reasons James stated. Briefly, the evidence is as follows.[16]

George Pellew had been a young man of philosophical and literary talent who had been killed in New York two weeks before he became Mrs. Piper's control. Five years earlier, Pellew had—under a pseudonym—attended one and only one sitting with Mrs. Piper. According to A. Gauld, out of 150 sitters who were introduced to G.P. during the sittings, G.P. recognized 29 of the 30 who had been known to the living Pellew.[17] (The thirtieth, whom G.P. recognized after an initial failure, was a young person who had "grown up" in the interval.) G.P. conversed with each of them in an appropriate manner and showed an intimate knowledge of their careers and of his own supposed past relationships with them. According to Gauld, rarely did G.P. slip up badly in these matters, as he sometimes did when discussing certain philosophical questions that had interested him during life.[18]

It was during this time that Hodgson came to believe that Mrs. Piper's controls were sometimes what they claimed to be, namely, surviving disembodied persons.[19] Presumably, the reason was that G.P.—in identifying the 30 people known to him when alive, and in describing his own personal (and sometimes intimate) relationships with them—manifested a very systematic, coherent, and personal set of memories that one would have expected of Pellew. Also, it seemed unlikely that Mrs. Piper was successfully drama- tizing the personality of Pellew. because she had met him only once briefly, five years earlier, when he sat with her anonymously. Unlike the Phinuit control, G.P. was not demonstrably fictitious. Unlike the Hodgson control, Mrs. Piper had no knowledge of George Pellew. when he was alive. And how could Mrs. Piper have had such a memory and succeeded in dramatically imperson- ating somebody she had hardly met in a way that convinced 30 people who were intimate with Pellew. before he died? Under the circumstances, it is not hard to understand why Hodgson thought Mrs. Piper's G.P. control was indeed a disembodied surviving person. Even so, James never explicitly agreed, even when he had an opportunity to do so.[20]

Later, we will return to examine the force of both James's and Hodgson's conclusions about the mediumship of Mrs. Piper. At that time we will study more closely the possibility of explaining the G.P. material by appeal to the super-psi hypothesis.

Mrs. Willett

Unlike Mrs. Piper and other mediums, when the English medium Mrs. Willett went into deep trance she did not lose control of her body as if she were asleep or in a swoon. She would sit up and talk in a natural way and in the first-person singular. There was no appearance of her body's being used by the deceased personality that spoke through her. So, while clearly a trance medium, she was not the usual kind of possession medium.

Back in 1885 Mrs. Willett had married a landed proprietor from Neath. Her husband's sister was the wife of F. W. H. Myers, one of the founders of the Society for Psychical Research and the author of *Human Personality and Its Survival of Bodily Death*.[21] Mrs. Willett, a person of notable achievement, was well educated and took a prominent part in public affairs, particularly in South Wales. For example, she served as chairman of the arts and crafts section of the national Eisteddfod in 1918, and later in 1920 was made a justice of the peace for Glamorganshire, being the first

woman to occupy that office there. In 1922 she was appointed by
the British government as a delegate to the assembly of the League
of Nations. In terms of the history of her mediumship, Mrs.
Willett became a member of the Society for Psychical Research
soon after F. W. H. Myers (whom, by the way, she had never met)
died in 1901, and then—for lack of interest—resigned in 1905.
However, in 1908 she suffered a death in the family and decided to
take up automatic writing—an activity she had dabbled in as a
young girl. In 1909 Mrs. Willett's mediumship bloomed, and
continued for a number of years.[22] She died in 1956.

What is important about Mrs. Willett's mediumship is that the
alleged postmortem persons of F. W. H. Myers and Edmund
Gurney—both of them founders of the Society for Psychical
Research—seemed to communicate through Mrs. Willett and
requested that one of the sitters be their friend G. W. Balfour, a
keen psychic researcher and president of the Society for Psychical
Research from 1906 to 1907. When alive, Myers and Gurney were
avid philosophers, widely read in philosophy, psychology, and
theology. Balfour had engaged in numerous philosophical discussions with both Myers and Gurney before they died.

With Balfour and others present on June 4, 1911, Mrs. Willett
went into a deep trance. There ensued the first of a series of
sittings characterizable as lively philosophical discussions between
Balfour, the sitter, and both Myers and Gurney, the communicators.[23] Commenting on the content of these discussions, C. D.
Broad noted that all the ostensible communications were "plainly
the product of a highly intelligent and cultivated mind or minds,
with a keen interest in psychology, psychical research and philosophy, and with a capacity for drawing subtle and significant
distinctions."[24] Moreover, whatever the source of the utterances,
the communicators showed a thorough acquaintance with the
views and terminology of Myers's book *Human Personality and Its
Survival of Bodily Death.*

It is worth emphasizing that the séances produced a high level
of sophisticated philosophizing between the sitter and communicators.[25] Typically, for example, Balfour would examine leisurely
the record of a sitting, and then at the next sitting make criticisms
or suggestions and ask for explanations. The Gurney communi-

cator would then speak to the issues raised and try to clear up the obscurities. Sometimes the Gurney communicator would accept, and sometimes vigorously reject, Balfour's suggestions and interpretations. Some of the sittings—those held on October 8, 1911, January 21, 1912, and March 5, 1912—were purely philosophical and sound like the transcript of an Ivy League graduate seminar on classical philosophy.[26]

Before determining the strength of these communications as evidence for personal survival, we must keep in mind two crucial considerations. First, Mrs. Willett knew little philosophy and had even less patience for all that kind of talk. When not in trance state, and when subsequently shown a transcript of the sittings, Mrs. Willett could not understand the content. For example, one typical sentence—uttered by the communicator on May 24, 1911—is this: "The Absolute labors to attain self-consciousness through the myriad of self-created sentient beings."[27] When shown this script some time later, Mrs. Willett did not know either the origin or the point of the script. Second, even though Balfour and others were convinced that the Myers and Gurney communicators acted and spoke in ways uniquely characteristic of Myers and Gurney when they were alive, Mrs. Willett had met neither one of them. As we shall see, these two considerations, when combined with the content of the communications, make it impossible to explain the sittings as an instance of the medium's subconsciously impersonating people she had previously met and communicating information obtained through ESP. At any rate, Balfour came to believe that he was indeed in communication with the departed spirits of both Gurney and Myers, and that no other hypothesis could explain the data so well.

We can now turn to another case—a famous "cross-correspondence" case (involving more than one medium), frequently discussed in the literature and generally thought to be a good source of evidence for belief in personal survival.

The Edgar Vandy Case

The Edgar Vandy case is similar to many other cases examined at length by various investigators.[28] Discussed by C. D. Broad,[29] this English case was originally sent to the Society for Psychical Research by Mr. George Vandy. It concerns sittings held by George Vandy and his brother Harold with various mediums in 1933 shortly after the death of their brother Edgar on August 6 of that year. The records of the case, along with other correspondence and papers, had been locked away for a number of years as a result of conditions arising from World War II. These papers came into the possession of George Vandy in 1953, and he submitted them to the Society for Psychical Research shortly thereafter.

Edgar Vandy, a 38-year-old engineer, had visited an estate in Sussex with a friend whose sister was a secretary to the owner. On arriving at the estate, Edgar and his friend decided to swim in the private pool and thus changed into swimming apparel in the bushes 200 feet distant from the pool. Edgar, who finished dressing first, entered the water considerably earlier than his friend, whose view of Edgar entering the pool was blocked by bushes.

When Edgar's friend reached the pool some two or three minutes later, Edgar was drowning. Although the friend caught hold of Edgar, he could not hold his grip, and Edgar sank to the bottom—whereupon the friend went to seek help. Edgar's death was clearly due to drowning. Medical evidence further indicated that he had fallen while entering the pool, struck his jaw, and lost consciousness before drowning. But various conflicting hypotheses about the way Edgar died were offered, all of them consistent with the available facts of the case. Dissatisfied with the results of the official inquest, George Vandy thought it likely that trance mediums might be able to illuminate some of the details attending his brother's death.

Accordingly, George Vandy wrote to Drayton Thomas, a distinguished psychic researcher, for a "proxy sitting" with the medium Mrs. Leonard.[30] He also requested the names of other mediums with whom he himself might have sittings.

A *proxy sitting* occurs when an *experimenter* (in this case, Mr. Thomas) receives in writing from some person—usually a complete stranger—a few distinctive facts about a certain recently deceased individual who also is completely unknown to the experimenter. The specified facts are usually sufficiently clear to allow the experimenter to determine that the medium is indeed referring to the individual in question, if she should happen to do so during his next sitting with her. The experimenter writes down (or tapes) the information that the stranger has sent him, memorizes it, and then sends a copy of it to an officer of the Society for Psychical Research to be filed without being opened. The experimenter meditates and tries to contact the deceased, and asks for cooperation. Thereafter the experimenter visits the medium and has a sitting with her. She is told nothing of the contents of the filed paper, or of the reason for that particular sitting, though she is aware of the general idea of proxy sittings. Sometimes under these circumstances the medium supposedly contacts the person answering the description submitted to the sitter about the deceased individual, and proceeds to supply further specific details that are highly characteristic of that person and not applicable to anyone else.

The only relevant fact George Vandy offered was that he wanted to obtain information about a brother who had died recently, and that some doubt remained in the minds of relatives about the cause of death. No names or other details were given. He did not mention that the death was not due to natural causes.

Thomas agreed to the proxy sitting and recommended three reputable mediums. George Vandy arranged for either himself or his brother to have sittings with the three mediums recommended. So as to protect the results of these sittings, the following safeguards were taken to prevent the mediums from gaining relevant information by normal means before the sittings, and to prevent unwitting conveyance of information by leading questions during the sittings.

1. In making an appointement with the medium, the intending sitter always gave a fictitious name and address.
2. All correspondence making appointments was preserved for future reference.
3. To each sitting the sitter took with him an experienced shorthand typist, chosen by himself and unknown to the medium. The name of the deceased Edgar Vandy was never mentioned

to the medium, and the person employed as typist was not always the same. The shorthand writer wrote an exact report of everything said at the sitting. The notes were typewritten and then sent to the sitter, who annotated them immediately after receiving them.[31]

We need not repeat the fascinating content reports and analysis generated by the six sittings that were thus conducted under very careful conditions. They are readily available in the literature.[32] Suffice it to say that many facts about Edgar Vandy's death (as well as about a machine he had invented and was secretly perfecting) were revealed in a way that defies explanation in terms of the normal ways of knowing.

For example, the following four themes were common to all six sittings, in terms of the information conveyed by the medium about the deceased: (1) that Edgar *fell* and in particular that his head was hit and damaged; (2) that *one or more* persons were present at the scene of the tragedy; (3) that likely they could and should have saved Edgar's life, but failed to do so through cowardice and incompetence; and (4) that Edgar wished to shield them. Common to exactly five sittings (all five nonproxy sittings) were two other references: (1) to water and drowning, and (2) to Edgar's death's being a strangely unlucky event that might easily have been avoided. Finally, common to two sittings were these two themes: (1) that the death was not because of suicide or culpable carelessness on Edgar's part, and (2) that Edgar experienced a feeling of dizziness just before or in close conjunction with the accident. In Broad's analysis, then, there are—in all—eight themes, some of them highly specific and characteristic of the deceased and the circumstances of his death.[33] These themes occurred in sittings in which both the medium and the sitter varied. For the sake of brevity I shall overlook the frequency and precise nature of the information conveyed about the machine Edgar Vandy had invented and was secretly perfecting.[34]

Before going on to describe one last case, it seems timely to reexamine the above cases with a sceptical eye.

The Sceptic's Response

How shall we regard the language cases, the cases involving the mediumships of Mrs. Piper and Mrs. Willett, and the Edgar Vandy case? In terms of providing evidence for some form of personal survival after death, how strong are these cases? Which, if any, offer us compelling evidence for personal survival? How would the sceptic see them?

In these next few pages I shall urge that the sceptic can justifiably disregard the evidence offered in the Edgar Vandy case. Also, there is good reason to be very cautious in accepting at least two of the language cases as offering good evidence for postmortem personal survival. However, the sceptic may well have no adequate response to the evidence offered for survival in examining Mrs. Willett's mediumship, Mrs. Piper's mediumship, and one of the language cases, namely, the Greek case. In other words, on the evidence from possession mediumship, the Greek case and both Mrs. Piper's and Mrs. Willett's mediumships may establish the existence of some form of postmortem personal survival. But there remains a problem with the evidential strength of the Greek case, as well as with the mediumship of Mrs. Piper.

Let me explain why all this is so, and in so explaining I will discuss the cases in an order different from the way in which they were introduced. The discussion will go a bit more smoothly if we examine them in this sequence. So, beginning with the Edgar Vandy case and proceeding through the mediumships of Mrs. Piper and Mrs. Willett to the language cases, let us now examine the force of the sceptic's best response to each case. Thereafter we will discuss a quite recent report—the Berger experiment—that adds something to the credibility of the evidence from mediumship.

. . . To the Edgar Vandy Case

In evaluating the force of the Edgar Vandy case, the philosopher C. D. Broad denied that the results of the proxy sittings could be a matter of coincidence.[35] He thought it incredible that the amount and kind of agreement found among the statements made by the various mediums at the various sittings could be pure chance. So, for Broad, we must either suppose (without direct evidence) an elaborate fraud in which the experimenter and the subjects must have collaborated, or we must admit that the case is evidence of paranormal knowledge. Broad then goes on to conclude that the most natural and simplest way to explain the Vandy case is to suppose that some people survive their death. Many people would agree with Broad's assessment.

But no serious sceptic would ever accept Broad's conclusion. After all, even if the Vandy case does provide evidence for belief in paranormal knowledge, still it would not follow that the most natural, or simplest, hypothesis to explain the data is the hypothesis of personal survival after death. Broad's conclusion does not follow, because in fact the Vandy brothers failed to get so much as one grain of new and verifiable information about the question that was troubling them and for which they instituted the series of sittings. In itself, this failure is quite significant. It shows that we can explain the cross correspondences, and the ability of the various mediums to ascertain the relevant facts pertinent to Vandy's death, by appeal to clairvoyance (or telepathy) plus the subconscious dramatizing power of the medium's mind. That is, the mediums could have been picking up the information through ESP and a little telepathy, and then subconsciously personating and dramatizing the information in the predictable way. Or so the sceptic would argue, and the sceptic seems quite persuasive here. Cases like the Vandy case—however impressive they may be—still do not appear to be strong enough to carry the hypothesis of survival if we grant the fact of clairvoyance, telepathy, and subconscious personation.

Also the sceptic can further argue that, even if the mediums in the Vandy case *had* turned up some verifiable fact not already known by somebody connected with the case, it would by no means follow that we must accept the hypothesis of personal survival in order to explain the facts. We could still hold onto the explanation that appeals to clairvoyance plus the subconscious dramatizing power of the medium's mind.

... To Mrs. Piper's Mediumship

What is interesting about the mediumship of Mrs. Leonora Piper is that William James's sceptical conclusions are quite strong. Doubtless, our own sceptic would share James's opinion on the value of her mediumship as a source of evidence for personal survival. Indeed, the assessment that James made offers the best possible argument favoring the sceptic's position. James, of course, granted that Mrs. Piper could (and did) communicate verifiable facts that she had no normal way of knowing. He even granted that the alleged Hodgson control manifested predictably the flamboyant manners and unique characteristics of his friend Hodgson. However, James still felt that, from a logical point of view, paranormal knowledge plus the dramatizing powers of the medium's subconscious mind would be sufficient to explain the data.

If Mrs. Piper had never met Hodgson, then James might have had difficulty explaining how the medium could so successfully impersonate Hodgson as to convince the deceased man's intimate friends that it was indeed Hodgson talking through Mrs. Piper. But inasmuch as Mrs. Piper had known Hodgson for a long time before his death, James did not feel that the evidence warranted belief in personal survival. Thus, William James showed us that the medium's ability while in trance not only to provide verifiable information unknown to anybody connected with the case, but also to do it in a way that leads people to believe it is the deceased conveying the information, is simply not strong enough evidence for belief in some form of personal life after death.

This last point is important because some people continue to think that, if only we can show that the medium revealed some relevant and verifiable fact unknown to anyone connected with the case, then we have good evidence for believing that the medium was in touch with a disembodied spirit. (Hodgson himself seems to have made this same mistake before he died, when he went on record as believing that Mrs. Piper was in communication with the dead.)[36] The uncovering of such a fact would certainly rule against telepathy as a way of explaining how the medium knows it, but it would not rule against simple clairvoyance as an alternative explanation.

However, as we noted above in the section where the case was first introduced, James's analysis of Mrs. Piper's mediumship inexplicably failed to grasp the relevance of the evidence offered in the G.P. communications. Apparently, James felt that if the Phinuit and the Hodgson controls were fictitious entities, then the chances were pretty good that the G.P. control was also fictitious. But the important point is that the G.P. communications were quite different in two relevant respects.

First of all, the remarkable memory evidenced by G.P. when communicating with the 30 people known to George Pellew before death seems to defy explanation in terms of telepathy precisely because of its overall accuracy, fecundity, systematicity, and attention to intimate detail. It is of course logically possible that Mrs. Piper was telepathically picking up all this information from the former friends of Pellew when they showed up unannounced. If so, this would certainly turn out to be a case of supertelepathy. But neither in the lab nor outside have we ever yet seen any case of telepathy like it. An appeal to ESP or super-psi in explaining how Mrs. Piper acquired this knowledge would require evidence of ESP or super-psi working this way in cases outside the one in question. Otherwise, as mentioned in earlier chapters, such an appeal would be arbitrary and dogmatic because rooted in a hypothesis that is not verifiable either experimentally or otherwise.

Second, and more importantly, even if G.P.'s communications to and identifications of Pellew's friends constituted a fantastic case of telepathy only, we would not be able to explain by appeal to the subconscious dramatizing power of the medium's mind why his friends accepted the person of G.P. as Pellew. It is implausible to think that Mrs. Piper was successfully impersonating somebody she had met briefly five years earlier—someone who sat with her anonymously. And it seems equally arbitrary to suggest that all of the friends may have had such a strong desire or need to believe that Pellew was the control that they were deluded into believing that G.P. had the same personal traits that George Pellew had before death.

Certainly, there are interesting cases in which the medium acquires a great deal of information clairvoyantly or telepathically and then, through the subconscious power of the mind, constructs a fictive persona to retail the information as if it were coming from a discarnate person. The Cagliostro case—at least as it is described and examined by Jule Eisenbud—seems to be one good example of just such a case.[37] But those types of cases are clearly distinct from the type in which the communicator professes to be a deceased person communicating with former friends who agree that the communicator has the personality traits unique to their friend before death. In this latter type, if we can establish both that the medium never knowingly met the alleged communicator before death and that there is no reason to suppose the former friends had some need to believe they were communicating with their deceased friend, then we have no plausible way to explain how the medium can be successfully impersonating someone the medium has never met. Here again, being able to impersonate successfully a person one has never met is not a demonstrable or verifiable property of ESP in any of its forms. Outside of such cases, has anybody ever demonstrated an ability to impersonate successfully someone they have never met—and in a way that convinces those who know intimately the person impersonated?

Thus, while James could plausibly explain the Phinuit and the Hodgson communications by appeal to ESP plus the subconscious dramatizing power of the medium's mind, that same explanation would not work at all with the G.P. control. If all Pellew's former friends accepted—as they did—the G.P. persona as acting in character, then the persona was either a successful impersonation (either consciously or subconsciously) on the part of the medium, or else the postmortem person of the deceased George Pellew communicating through Mrs. Piper. But because Mrs. Piper never knowingly met George Pellew before his death, we cannot explain G.P. as a successful impersonation on the part of Mrs. Piper. To suggest that the successful impersonation of an unknown person is readily explained in terms of ESP or super-psi is to assert, without benefit of proof, the existence of a property that cannot be demonstrated to exist either experimentally or observationally outside the case in question. For this reason, Mrs. Piper's me-

diumship—at least in the case of the G.P. communications—offers
persuasive evidence for personal survival. Any explanation offered
in terms of ESP is empirically meaningless because dogmatic and
not falsifiable either by experimental or nonexperimental evidence.

The survivalist, on the other hand, is willing to state what
would constitute evidence falsifying the survivalist hypothesis. To
be more specific, if we should find that Mrs. Piper had (contrary
to the evidence offered in the case) an intimate or well-established
relationship with George Pellew before he died, then the case
could be set aside for the same reason James set aside the evidence
from the Hodgson communications. Similarly, we *might* reject the
survivalist interpretation of the G.P. material if we suddenly found
somebody who could successfully impersonate someone they had
never seen or heard. Finally, if we could determine that in fact all
of G.P.'s former friends had a strong desire or need to believe that
they were communicating with the postmortem personality of
George Pellew, then we would have good reason to question the
survivalist interpretation. Otherwise, we have no option but to
accept the G.P. communications as evidence for personal survival.

What evidence—experimental or otherwise—would the proponents of the ESP hypothesis (whether normal or super) accept as
good grounds for setting aside the ESP hypothesis? Failure to
answer this question puts the antisurvivalist in the position of
being dogmatic.

It is difficult to explain why James, who was extremely acute in
analyzing the Phinuit and the Hodgson material, did not take the
G.P. material as persuasive evidence for the view that, while Mrs.
Piper's mediumship generally failed to provide anything more
than compelling evidence for paranormal knowledge, nevertheless
the G.P. communications established personal survival. Possibly,
as we suggested above, James felt that if two of her controls were
fictitious, then the likelihood would be that the third must also be
fictitious. However natural that conclusion might appear, it is not
supported by a close examination of the G.P. material.

We should also note here that, while James argued in favor of
the sceptical position with regard to Mrs. Piper's mediumship,
nevertheless he also argued that when *all* the evidence for belief in

personal survival is considered, then it seems quite reasonable to hold to the belief in personal survival.

If we suppose Mrs. Piper's dream-life once and for all to have had the notion suggested to it that it must personate spirits to sitters, the fair degree of virtuosity need not, I think, surprise us. Nor need the exceptional memory shown surprise us, for memory seems extraordinarily strong in the subconscious life. *But I find that when I ascend from the details of the Piper Case to the whole meaning of the phenomenon, and especially when I connect the Piper case with all the other cases I know of automatic writing and mediumship, and with the whole record of spirit-possession in human history, the notion that such an immense current of human experience, complex in so many ways, should spell out absolutely nothing but the word "humbug" acquires a character of unlikeliness.* The notion that so many men and women, in all other respects honest enough, should have this preposterous monkeying self annexed to their personality seems to me so weird that the spirit theory immediately takes on a more probable appearance. The spirits, if spirits there be, must indeed work under incredible complications and falsifications, but at least if they are present, some honesty is left in the whole department of the universe which otherwise is run by pure deception.[38]

. . . To Mrs. Willett's Mediumship

When we turn to consider the cases relating to Mrs. Willett's mediumship, however, the sceptical response William James offered against Mrs. Piper's mediumship holds no water. There is a crucial difference between the two. Like Mrs. Piper, Mrs. Willett could provide information not known by anybody connected with the case; and like Mrs. Piper, Mrs. Willett's communicators spoke directly to relatives and friends in a way convincingly characteristic of the traits of the communicator before death. However, unlike the material relating to Mrs. Piper's Phinuit and Hodgson controls, we cannot explain the Willett case by appeal to ESP plus dramatic subconscious impersonation, because in the Willett case the high-level philosophical discussions that took place between the controls Gurney and Myers and the sitter Balfour reflected an acquired skill—the skill of philosophizing well. Once again, as was said in our discussion of possession in Chapter 3, knowing *how to* philosophize well—like knowing *how to* speak a foreign language or *how to* play a musical instrument—is not something we can know by clairvoyance or telepathy. We can clairvoyantly or telepathically know *that* something or other is so; but we cannot, for all the reasons mentioned in Chapter 3, clairvoyantly or telepathically know *how to* speak a language, play an instrument, or philosophize. This basic point, when combined with the fact that Mrs. Willett *never* met either Gurney or Myers, would seem to tip the scales in favor of the belief in personal survival. Underscoring these considerations, C. D. Broad offered the following reflections on the Willett case:

> The mere utterance, by the lips and the pencil of a woman of Mrs. Willett's normal range of interest and knowledge, of a long coherent series of statements of this kind, in the form of conversations by the deceased Gurney and Myers with the living Lord Balfour, about topics that had been the main interest in life of the ostensible communicators, is a fairly startling fact.
>
> Suppose we altogether rule out the suggestion that Myers and Gurney in some sense survived bodily death and were the deliberate initiators of these utterances. We shall then have to postulate in some stratum of Mrs. Willett's mind rather remarkable powers of acquiring information from unread books or the minds of living persons or both; of clothing it in phraseology characteristic of Myers and Gurney, whom she had never met; and of working it up and putting it forth in a dramatic form which seemed to their friend Balfour to be natural and convincing.[39]

For Broad, presumably, ascribing all that to the mind of Mrs. Willett is just a bit too much to accept.[40]

To the above argument, however, a predictable response on the part of an antisurvivalist will consist in asserting that there is quite a difference between knowing how to philosophize well and knowing how to speak a foreign language or play an instrument well. Knowing how to philosophize well is more like knowing how to write a good poem or piece of prose than it is like speaking a foreign language or playing an instrument well. By implication, even if knowing how to speak a foreign language fluently or play an instrument well cannot be acquired via ESP, it by no means follows that knowing how to philosophize well cannot be the product of ESP. Indeed, it seems quite possible that Mrs. Willett at some level of consciousness was capable of philosophizing at the level shown in the sittings with Balfour when Myers and Gurney ostensibly communicated. Recall, for example, the case of Pearl Curran, a poorly educated St. Louis housewife who, during quasi trances, assumed the character of "Patience Worth."[41] Patience was quick, witty, and capable of spontaneously composing well-regarded poems and novels in highly saxonized English. Her achievements were generally considered far beyond Mrs. Curran's normal conscious powers, but certainly not beyond those of her subconscious mind. As Ian Stevenson has noted,[42] few (if any) students of her case have thought that Patience Worth qualified as a discarnate spirit. Most regard her simply as evidence for a multiple personality disorder (MPD) combined with paranormal abilities. And, given that there is not much relevant difference here between philosophizing well and writing poems well, there would consequently be no justification for our considering Mrs. Willett any differently than Pearl Curran.

There are two possible replies we might give to this antisurvivalist objection. The first is simply to grant the objection but then still argue for the survivalist interpretation of Mrs. Willett's mediumship, solely on the grounds that there is no way of explaining by appeal to ESP how she could be dramatically impersonating—to the satisfaction of surviving friends—people she had never met. The only response left on the part of the antisurvivalist would be to appeal to super-psi as a way of explaining how Mrs. Willett could succeed in doing this. At that point, for all the reasons stated in discussing the sceptical response to Mrs. Piper (as well as earlier), I would urge that there is no demonstrable or verifiable evidence—either experimental or nonexperimental—that would justify such a response. So, even if we gave up the idea that knowing how to philosophize well is a skill that cannot be acquired via ESP, the survivalist interpretation of Mrs. Willett's mediumship could still be well defended.

The second reply we might give would be to argue either that composing fine poems and philosophizing well really are different in that the latter is not a skill one can acquire by appeal to ESP, or else that composing excellent poems and philosophizing well are identical in that neither can be explained by appeal to ESP. If we take the first alternative, the poet might well object that knowing how to write an excellent poem is certainly as demanding as knowing how to write·a sound argument. If we take the second alternative, it would seem to follow that, the poetry of Patience Worth being sufficiently skilful, Patience Worth—regardless of what her students think—must be a discarnate person. *This* philosopher's inclination is to opt for the second alternative and leave the question of whether Patience Worth is a discarnate person up to those who are able to judge whether the quality of the poetry involved is sufficiently high to warrant the conclusion. Ceteris paribus, this would apply as well in the case of Mrs. Willett's mediumship. In other words, if it seems maximally implausible (as Broad so asserts) that the level of philosophical discourse manifested in the exchanges among Gurney, Myers, and Balfour could not be attained except after years of solid practice, so to speak, then we would judge that it is not an activity we can explain by appeal to ESP. There are, of course, certain problems one might have in determining whether a particular piece of poetry or philosophy is of the requisite level—problems we do not seem to have in determining whether someone is playing the banjo skilfully or speaking Urdu fluently. But, given the argument of the preceding paragraph, we need not enter into that discussion now, though one might indeed argue that it is no more difficult in principle to pick out a good philosopher or a good poet than it is to pick out a good banjo player or a fluent speaker of Urdu.

In the end, Broad concludes cautiously that many quite well attested paranormal phenomena strongly suggest persistence of the psychical aspect of a human being after death, and that a few also strongly suggest the full-blown survival of a human personality.[43] As we noted above, William James came to much the same conclusion after his examination of Mrs. Piper, even though his verdict on her mediumship as a source of belief in personal survival was negative.[44] The important point is that the basic difference between a survivalist interpretation of some forms of mediumship, and the interpretations that see those forms of mediumship as instances of multiple personality disorder (or subconscious dramatic impersonation) plus ESP, rests crucially on the fact that—for the many reasons mentioned above and in earlier chapters—the survivalist sees no justification for appealing to ESP (either normal or super) as an explanation of behaviors that are not demonstrably the product of ESP as we understand it in cases outside the ones in question. We need not repeat those reasons here.

. . . To the Language Cases

Finally, in each of the language cases introduced earlier in this chapter, the ability of the medium to convey to the sitters information unknown to anybody connected with the case, and to convey the information in a foreign language demonstrably not learned (or understood) by the medium, would surely be very strong evidential justification for the belief in some form of personal survival after death. Unfortunately, there are good reasons why we should not accept the evidence offered in the Chinese case, the Hungarian case, and the Welsh case.

To begin with, the medium in both the Welsh case and in the Chinese case was the controversial George Valiantine, who was more than once implicated in fraud. The medium in the Hungarian case was Arthur Ford, who had also been implicated in fraud.[45] Of course, nobody has in fact *shown* that either Valiantine or Ford was acting fraudulently in these language cases. The argument simply asserts that if there is good reason to think they acted fraudulently in some instances, then in the absence of strong evidence showing that they did *not* act fraudulently in these cases (the Welsh case, the Chinese case, and the Hungarian case) we should not use these cases as evidence. The point is well taken and, because none of these language cases was closely examined for fraud at the time, we should be reluctant to offer them as good evidence.

On the other hand, however, if we are to feel comfortable in discounting *these* cases, we need to show how it would be possible for the medium to act fraudulently in conveying fluently in an allegedly unlearned language information known only to the sitters and some information unknown to the sitters. In the Welsh case, for example, Valiantine would need to have learned Welsh secretly and would also need to have learned an incredible amount of detail about both Mr. and Mrs. Caradoc Evans before even attempting to answer in detail the questions Evans would ask of his father in Welsh. Is it plausible to think Valiantine could have learned all this detail (even as to where Evans's father had lived) and enough Welsh to answer fluently those questions Evans did ask of his father? Possible, yes; plausible, no. Is it possible that Evans had an auditory hallucination that was undetectable to any of the other sitters? In the absence of any recorded transcript of what transpired and in the absence of extant testimony by others at the session agreeing that Welsh was spoken in the way described by Caradoc Evans, and in the absence of his getting from the medium any information he did not already know, it certainly seems possible. Is it plausible? It seems more plausible to suppose that the whole case was fabricated by Valiantine and all the sitters who testified to the events. But that in itself also seems quite implausible because, apart from the fact that all the sitters and Valiantine had nothing much to gain from such a fraud, the probability is pretty high that the fraud would be discovered sooner or later simply because there were so many people involved.

As for the Chinese case, Ian Stevenson[46] and W. H. Salter[47] have concluded independently that Dr. Whymant may very well have suffered from auditory illusion, because, among other things, there was no other verification of the xenoglossy involved. Naturally, if some reason does exist for thinking Whymant tended to that sort of auditory hallucinations (he claimed that he had gone to 16 sittings and that 14 foreign languages had been used, although nobody else verified as many), then the explanation offered by Stevenson and Salter makes sense. Otherwise, what makes the Chinese case questionable anyway is that nobody other than Whymant testified to the events as described by Whymant; and even Whymant had to admit that the recorded transcript was untranslatable, because hardly audible.

Typically, in foreign language cases (xenoglossy cases) under Valiantine's mediumship (and this extends to the Welsh case also), only one person at the sitting has a knowledge of the alleged language used. With regard to the two cases we have considered, the Welsh case seems more plausible than the Chinese case; but even here the plausibility of the Welsh case would require some independent verification or argument that Welsh was actually spoken by the medium. Nobody other than Evans himself testified explicitly to that fact, and nothing else about the case suggests that he must have been right. The real problem is that neither of these cases was examined in the way they would be examined today.

In the Hungarian case, Arthur Ford was the medium, and Ford was generally known to have kept files of information about potential sitters. Nevertheless, because Dr. Fodor arrived unexpectedly from Europe and was invited at the last moment to Ford's séance, it is not likely that Ford had the opportunity to prepare a file on Fodor—or to learn Hungarian. Also, could Fodor really have suffered an auditory hallucination in thinking that somebody was speaking to him in Hungarian? If so, his wife also suffered the same hallucination, because she by implication testified to the use of Hungarian in the sitting when her deceased brother allegedly spoke to her. Of course, Ford could have acquired a knowledge of the facts unknown to the sitters (such as when Fodor's father died or, what nobody could have known, that Uncle Vilmos would go blind, etc.) via ESP. But as we have noted several times already, Ford could not have acquired a capacity to speak reasonably fluent Hungarian via any known type of ESP. And as we have just seen, it seems implausible to suggest that Fodor suffered an auditory hallucination, because we would need to suppose that his wife suffered the same hallucination. It seems more plausible by far that the whole thing was a hoax committed by Ford, William Cartheuser, and the Fodors. Here again, however—entertainment value aside—what would these people have gained from such a hoax, and is it not probable that such a fraud would have been detected sooner or later? This case seems much stronger than either the Welsh case or the Chinese case because, when we do try to suppose that the medium was not speaking the foreign language, it takes a good deal more to prove the point here. Even so, it would be nice to have a recorded transcript of the sitting.

Finally, of all the language cases discussed in this chapter, the Greek case seems the most convincing and acceptable as evidence from mediumship for survival. This is because the medium involved was never implicated in a fraud, everybody involved signed an affidavit, and it is very implausible that Mr. Evangelides was deluded in thinking Greek had been spoken during the session in question. Let me explain.

One critic of this case has suggested that because Evangelides was the only person who knew any Greek in this case (the Judge in his affidavit claimed that none of the ten people at the session knew Greek), there is no independent verification of the fact that fluent Greek was spoken by the medium.[48] We must remember, however, that nobody denied Evangelides spoke in Greek and, as a result of the conversation he had with the medium, came to believe what was in fact true, namely, that his son had died. This piece of information was not conveyed in English; and when the information was given to him, Evangelides broke down and wept. The critic of this case would have us believe Evangelides was hallucinating the belief that the medium was also speaking in Greek—even though, while conducting a conversation in Greek with the medium, Evangelides came to acquire veridical information about the death of his son, information unknown to him or anybody else in America before the séance. In this view, Evangelides did not hallucinate the content of what was conveyed to him; he was merely hallucinating the belief that the content was conveyed to him in Greek during his conversation with the medium in which he himself was speaking Greek and (as everybody else said) the medium was not speaking English. If we were to accept that the sceptic is right here, we would need to suppose what has never occurred in the history of humankind, namely, that two people could have a conversation in two different languages and that one of them could acquire from the other, via this conversation, veridical information about an event that neither could have known about. Had Evangelides not acquired veridical information as a result of the conversation that he conducted in Greek with the medium who (as the others testified) was not speaking in English, it might make some sense to suppose that the medium had not spoken Greek. As it is, however, the supposition that the medium was not speaking Greek—that only Evangelides was speaking Greek—is maximally inconsistent with supposing that Evangelides acquired, via his conversation with the medium, veridical information that nobody in the group could have known.

What these last reflections also show, incidentally, is that a language case can be established even when we have only one person at the sitting who claims to know the language the medium allegedly speaks. Of course, here again, it is possible that this case was fully contrived by all the participants as a wonderful hoax. But if so—again—apart from entertainment, what would be the gain for the participants? Would the entertainment value be worth the risk of discovery for somebody such as Judge Edmonds? Moreover, if, as in the Greek case, such a hoax took place before at least ten sitters (all of whom signed an affidavit), the probability seems very high that we would sooner or later detect it. Accordingly, we can indeed regard the Greek case as a strong piece of mediumship evidence for some form of personal survival after death.

To summarize our results thus far: for all the reasons mentioned above, some of the evidence from Mrs. Piper's mediumship, all of the evidence from Mrs. Willett's mediumship, and the Greek case offer compelling evidence for postmortem personal survival—with the possible further inclusion of the Hungarian case. The Welsh case, the Chinese case, and the Vandy case all seem flawed in some important way. Finally—in spite of all that we have just said in favor of the Greek case—after discussing the Berger experiment (which we shall now do), we will return in our conclusion to the one disturbing consideration or problem that tends to threaten the force of the Greek case, namely, that possession mediumship in the past 35 years does not seem to have produced any language cases like it. For the moment, however, let us examine the Berger experiment to see whether it has uncovered any more evidence for survival based on mediumship.

The Berger Experiment

In his recent book *The Aristocracy of the Dead: New Findings in Post-mortem Survival,* Arthur Berger presents empirical evidence from trance mediumship for postmortem survival.[49] Berger's work is unlike any other piece of evidence based on mediumship, because it allows more fully for repeatability of the experiment. It also deals with trance mediumship not involving possession.

Berger's General Strategy: The Ideal Communicator

After sorting through a number of case studies of alleged postmortem communicators, Berger generalizes from the strong cases (i.e., cases wherein the communicator succeeds in fully identifying himself through a trance medium and in providing information that does not admit of alternative explanation by appeal to normal processes or telepathy) and offers a profile of the ideal communicator. According to Berger, in the strong cases all the communicators had certain common characteristics prior to death, ranging across personality traits and similarity of death experiences. After a long and detailed analysis, Berger concludes with a "thumbnail sketch" of what these strong-case communicators had in common before death.

> From the analyses that were made covering three areas of inquiry and two population samples it became possible to make tentative findings concerning factors thought related and those believed unrelated to good communication. A mass study therefore confirmed, falsified and left up in the air many of the related factors. All these results may now be taken into account and the various factors related, verified, falsified and still remaining to be checked may now be collected and composited into the following thumbnail sketch of the ideal communicator:
> A male who persists in the pursuit of his interests and endeavors, he is an artist, or has an aptitude for poetry or music. His attitude toward the possibility of survival after death will be heavily tinged with scepticism or doubt. When he dies, his death will be painful or unpleasant, and he will die leaving work unfinished.

No disposition should be made of his body until at least two days have elapsed after his death.

Any efforts at communication with him should be made in the home of a medium who speaks the language he spoke and who had been a stranger to him.[50]

Naturally, this profile assumes, among other things, that we have indeed been successful in the past in communicating with postmortem discarnate persons. But this point is irrelevant because Berger claims that if he has picked the right characteristics, then—however he may have come by the profile (and at least one reviewer, Emily Williams Cook, claims his methodology is extremely careless and flawed)[51]—we now have a selection procedure for determining which persons are likely to be good communicators after they die; and if with this selection procedure we generally succeed in communicating with such persons after death, we will then have a verifiable and repeatable hypothesis for survival. Or so it would seem.

To test his hypothesis, Berger and his associates then proceeded to select a person who had recently died and who also ostensibly satisfied the characteristics outlined in the composite thumbnail sketch of an ideal communicator. A classic experiment was undertaken to establish contact through the phenomenon of trance mediumship. If Berger was right about the relevance of the characteristics in his thumbnail sketch, then he should be able to achieve verified communication with the recently deceased. And in the same way, we ought to be able to repeat the experiment successfully in the future, provided we are dealing with competent mediums. Of course, as any logician will note, Berger could also be quite wrong in his hypothesis about the ideal communicator and still establish contact with somebody thought to be the target communicator. But more on this later.

The Experiment: One, Two, Buckle My Shoe

In seeking to establish contact with a deceased subject who closely corresponded with the ideal type, Berger conducted the classic cross-correspondence experiment. The deceased subject in the experiment was William Lee Petty III (known as Lee), who was killed at the age of 25 on Friday, March 14, 1978, on Interstate 10, near Baton Rouge, Louisiana, when the small car he was driving crashed into the rear of a parked truck. Two dogs in the car were killed with him. The description of Lee given by his mother Catharine fitted that of the model communicator. The experiment was very closely monitored, and great care was taken to prevent leakage of information to any of those involved in it. The experiment consisted of two parts. This is the way Berger describes his own experiment:

> First, I had to initiate it. There was ample precedent for my doing so. Many cross-correspondence experiments were begun by experimenters. Sir Oliver Lodge, for example, asked the purported communicator, Hodgson, through one medium to send a message to another, and the "Lethe" case began when the experimenters Dorr and Lodge asked the dead Myers, "What does the word 'Lethe' suggest to you?"
>
> If there were reason to believe that Lee Petty was communicating at any mediumistic session with Mrs. Petty as sitter, a question would be put to him to ask him if he would agree to take part in an experiment. If he agreed, I would proceed to the second phase. Mrs. Petty would be excused from the session and the experiment would be described to the communicator. The experiment was to consist of three numbers, one of which was the sum of the other two. The communicator was to select these three numbers and not to reveal them to me at the time the experiment was proposed. At a later time, however, he would take the initiative to convey one number to another medium with whom those who loved him might be sitting, a second number to still another medium with whom they might be sitting and the third number to a third medium under similar circumstances. Neither the sitters nor the mediums knew anything about the nature of the experiment. They did not know that the experiment had anything to do with numbers so that the meaning of the numbers would not be understood by any of them. But when the communications were connected, they would be seen to be relevant to the experiment. If the third number received by a medium was the sum of the two smaller numbers received by each of two other mediums, the experiment would be a

success. The actual numbers would be left to the ingenuity and plan of the communicator. I would not be present at any of the sittings but at the end would see if the results could be tied in.[52]

In February 1983, Mrs. Catharine Petty arrived in Florida for the initial part of the experiment. Berger arranged two appointments with mediums in the Hollywood, Florida, area. The mediums were strangers to Mrs. Petty; they knew nothing of her or her family. And at no time were the identities of these mediums disclosed to Mrs. Petty. The session held with the first medium failed because Mrs. Petty was not at all convinced that her son had communicated during the sitting. Berger and his coexperimenter Joyce Berger (JB) were also sitters at the first meeting.

The second appointment with a different medium was held on the following evening in the general vicinity of Pompano Beach. On this occasion Berger and JB met Mrs. Petty at a predesignated spot some 30 miles from her hotel in Pompano Beach. They blindfolded her and drove her through a number of streets for quite some time in order that she not know where they were going. At the appointed hour they reached the home of the designated medium, Serraine Diane Newman (SDN). Berger left JB and Mrs. Petty in the car and went into the home of the medium to arrange a proper seating. Berger then returned to the car and led Mrs. Petty—still blindfolded so that she could not see the name or the address of the medium—into the house. After they entered, the blindfold was removed as they entered the room where the medium SDN sat with her back to Mrs. Petty, who sat behind SDN. Mrs. Petty remained there during the entire sitting, and at no time during the sitting did Mrs. Petty say anything. At no time during the sitting did the medium see Mrs. Petty, nor did Mrs. Petty ever see the medium's face. Berger sat facing the medium where he could also see Mrs. Petty and JB, who sat beside Mrs. Petty.

Mrs. Petty was to nod or shake her head, depending on whether she thought the material expressed was right or wrong. Berger thus left it to Mrs. Petty to judge the evidential weight of what the medium said. If she thought the medium was getting a number of successful hits, she was to nod to Berger or write him a note so that he would know whether there were any reasonable grounds for continuing the experiment. If Mrs. Petty did indicate that the medium was in contact with Lee, then Berger would ask Mrs. Petty to leave the room and he would go on with the next phase of the experiment, which consisted in asking (through the medium) the deceased Petty if he wanted to participate in the experiment.

As things progressed, however, in this second sitting also, Mrs. Petty was not at all convinced that the medium had established contact with her deceased son. Once again, precautions were taken as Mrs. Petty and the Bergers left the second sitting. The medium remained seated; and JB escorted Mrs. Petty to the door, replaced the blindfold, and took her to the car. Thereafter, Mrs. Petty was driven to the original rendezvous point, and the blindfold removed; she then returned to her hotel.

On the following day, however, Mrs. Petty decided after reflection that there had been some evidential statements made by the medium, but she was still not very sure that Lee had communicated. So another meeting was arranged, with the same procedures; and after that meeting Mrs. Petty—looking over the notes she had made in this and the previous sitting with SDN—was convinced that Lee had been communicating after all. Accordingly, a third meeting was arranged with SDN. By this time, however, Mrs. Petty had to return to her home in Louisiana; Berger continued on with the experiment, having finally been given the nod to do so.

JB and another observer returned to SDN's home for this third session. They provided the medium with personal objects Lee had owned and asked SDN to try to establish communication with Lee Petty. When JB felt that the communicator might be Lee, she asked the communicator if he would participate in the experiment. As described by Berger in the quote above, the communicator was to give three numbers to three different mediums. The third number must be the sum of the first two. He could choose any numbers he wished, and was not at that time to tell JB what numbers he had in mind. The communicator agreed.

To assure themselves that Lee had been the communicator at this sitting, a transcript of the meeting (with all reference to the experiment left out) was sent to Mrs. Petty, who said in writing that she believed Lee was indeed the communicator during the sitting in question. The first phase of the experiment was complete.

Continuing to the next phase, Mrs. Petty was then to make arrangements with mediums of her own choice so as to try to establish contact with Lee. If willing, the sitters were to be herself, Lee's sisters, his father, and Lee's girlfriend. Mrs. Petty selected seven mediums, all unknown to Berger and JB—who, prior to the conclusion of the experiment, never had any dealings of any kind with the mediums selected. Tapes were made of all the mediumistic sessions with Mrs. Catharine Petty and with Ms. Parish (Lee's girlfriend) and of the sessions with JB.

At one sitting held with the English medium Donald Galloway for Ms. Parish (who taped the sitting) in the offices of the Louisiana Society for Psychic Research on March 25, 1983, the medium said in the middle of the session that he was getting something strange from the communicator.

> I'm getting a strange thing here. (Pause. Then half whispering.) One, two, button my shoe. One, two, button my shoe—I don't know what sense to make of it, but Lee's saying very audibly "One, two, button my shoe." I think that when I was a kid there was a poem—a popular song called that. One, two, button my shoe. What's he doing with his shoes? He's trying to make a play on (inaudible). One, two, buckle my shoe. I really don't know what that means.[53]

Later that day at another sitting with Galloway but held for Catharine Petty, numbers came up again. The taped transcript reads as follows:

DG: Now also, a very strange thing here because he's— (Talking under his breath.) Just a minute— (Now in a low whisper.) 1,2,3; 1,2,3; 1,2,3; 1,2,3; 1,2,3; 1,2,3; I don't know. He's not beating time. 1,2,3; 1,2,3; 1,2,3; 1,2,3; 1,2,3.
CP: There are three other people that own the farm.
DG: Are there? Oh, all right. 1,2,3; 1,2,3. Just like that.[54]

There were other sittings at which various things were said. But the relevant data consist in the fact that the communicator revealed to one medium two numbers ("One, two, buckle my shoe") and then, to the same medium on another occasion, three numbers— the third of which is the sum of the first two, which had been revealed on the earlier occasion. Does this count as a successful experiment favoring postmortem survival? Predictably, opinions vary.

Evaluation of the Experiment

Berger is quick to note that, from a legalistic viewpoint, the experiment was a failure because the communicator did not perform precisely as he had agreed to. He was supposed to give one number to one medium, another to a second, and a third to a third; and one of the numbers was to be the sum of the other two. Instead, he gave two numbers to one medium, and then three numbers to the same medium at a later time—though, indeed, one of the numbers given on the second occasion *was* the sum of the two that were given on the first occasion and again repeated on the second occasion. Even so, there is good reason to think that, assuming there was no fraud involved here, the experiment was a success. The contract was substantially satisfied in that numbers were given on separate occasions and in that one of the numbers was the sum of the first two given on a previous occasion. But would the sceptic accept that conclusion?

For the nonsceptic—that is, for one who believes the evidence here favors postmortem personal survival rather than some alternative explanation—it is easy enough to see how through a predictable bit of cognitive dissonance, resulting from Lee's not being an ideal "ideal" communicator, the communicator may have easily misunderstood the directions. He might have thought that the core of the instructions was to make sure that the third of the numbers given on a separate occasion be the sum of the first two given earlier. A very plausible and easily understood mistake. The interesting point is that, if we too understand (or allow that Lee understood) the core of the instructions as being to give numbers the third of which is the sum of the first two, then we can dismiss the discrepancy between the results and the strict set of instructions as an incidental effect of such a plausible misunderstanding. Indeed, if that *were* the main line of the instructions, and if there were no other explanation in terms of fraud or chance available for the numbers coming up as they did, then the result of the experiment would have an awesome ring of truth to it even though, technically, the experiment failed. And it does have an awesome ring of truth to it. Nonetheless, in the absence of repeated instances of the experiment (either with the same communicator or with another), the sceptic may quite reasonably be a bit hesitant to accept the conclusion. This sort of experiment needs to be repeated frequently if we are to regard it as robust support from mediumship for the existence of some form of personal survival after death.

However—barring fraud on the part of Berger and the others (and we know that some sceptics will make that charge because the number of people involved is fairly small)—the deviant results of the experiment do make it impossible for the sceptic to say that the results came out positive only because Berger, or somebody else, in some fashion leaked the nature of the experiment in such a way that we can explain the results by appeal to telepathy or normal ways of knowing. Indeed, if the medium had known about the details of the experiment, the results would not have been so ambiguous with regard to Lee's technical failure to follow the instructions he allegedly agreed to follow. If fraud, or normal ways of knowing, were involved, we would expect somewhat less ambiguous results. (On telepathy, more in a moment.)

Might the two series of numbers have come up purely as a matter of coincidence—satisfying, purely and simply as a matter of coincidence, what a liberal interpretation of the core of the instructions were? Berger is justifiably dismissive of this alternative explanation.[55] Indeed, to all but a mathematician committed to the technically acceptable view that even the infinitely implausible or improbable event occurs occasionally, the suggestion that these numbers popped up coincidentally seems implausible. And soon, if Berger's general thesis about the ideal communicator is sound, this coincidence objection should be settled anyway because, presumably, we will see more cases similar to the Petty case; generally repeating its results would undermine the plausibility of the appeal to coincidence. Until then, the best available explanation seems to be that some form of postmortem survival is established by the experiment.

Incidentally, as suggested earlier, Emily Williams Cook has asserted that the success of such an experiment should not be taken to imply an endorsement of the "ideal communicator theory."[56] As a matter of fact, anybody who looks closely at the data from which Berger establishes the criteria for the supposedly ideal communicator cannot help but notice that the sample is much too small and biased at the outset. Nevertheless, what is interesting about Berger's experiment is not the so-called hypothesis of the ideal communicator, but that it is a way of establishing the legitimacy of communication. One could very easily reject—as indeed one should—the ideal communicator theory but still accept the work that supposedly follows from it, as a desirable experiment for successful communication. Naturally, if Berger's criteria for an ideal communicator were always followed and if successful communication were established more often than not, then we might want to accept Berger's criteria and argue that his criteria were right even though he himself never established them by any empirically reliable methodology. Those who are inclined to regard the experiment as interesting and potentially significant find it easy to suppose also that Berger was just plain lucky in selecting Lee as an ideal communicator, despite the fact that the methodology he used in generating the so-called criteria for being an ideal communicator was conspicuously defective.

In the end, of course, it does very little good to argue over whether the experiment was a success or not. If it really was a good experiment, we will be able to repeat it in other cases and, in time, get better results. This is one of the intriguing features of Berger's proposal: in light of the hypothesis as to what counts as an ideal communicator, the thesis is empirically and experimentally falsifiable. Still, there is good reason to think that the Berger experiment as evidence of establishing contact with a postmortem discarnate person was a success, and that alternative explanations in terms of chance, fraud (which has not been established), or telepathy on the part of the mediums involved are unconvincing.

Incidentally, as to the question of telepathy on the part of the medium, Donald Galloway could not have gotten the appropriate knowledge relevant to the experiment from either of the sitters because neither of them knew what the specifics of the experiment were. The only way the medium could have found out was by reading the Bergers' minds, but the Bergers never even saw or met Galloway. And, in fact, none of the mediums in Louisiana had been told that they were the object of an experiment. Telepathy is therefore out of the question as an alternative explanation.

So, our sceptic can only claim that the experiment failed because the instructions were not followed precisely, as the experimental protocol required. But even then, the sceptic must explain the sequence of numbers in terms of chance or coincidence; and that explanation, as we have just argued, is logically possible but very implausible given the specific nature of the instructions.

In future cases, it *might* help to have the communicator repeat back through the medium just what he or she takes the instructions to be. As things presently stand, the conclusion that Berger's experiment establishes postmortem personal survival is, as Berger would probably agree, by no means robustly confirmed. If we had a number of cases like this—as we do in the research on reincarnation—then the data would be more robustly supportive. One can discern the same arguments arising from Berger's research that arose from some of Ian Stevenson's early cases (see Chapter 1). When the cases get richer and more frequent, the sceptical response will get weaker.

What does seem promising and important about Berger's research, however, is its provision of a clear and repeatable testing procedure that will presumably, sooner or later, yield solid results. Perhaps it is in the nature of the phenomenon that any kind of ideal communicator will not always be reliable with respect to following some specific set of instructions that would allow us a robustly confirmed belief in postmortem survival. Nonetheless, we have here a line of research that seems more promising than the sort of language cases discussed earlier, because the language cases seem to have disappeared—curiously enough.

On that score, though, one might conduct a Berger-like cross-correspondence experiment in which some notable communicator would be asked to speak in a foreign language that we all know he spoke, in such a way that he would complete a famous sentence—uttering, say, one word to each of no fewer than three mediums. Once again, as in the Berger experiment, only the experimenter would know the specifics (and a sealed copy delineating them would be sent to an independent agency prior to commencement of the experiment).

Conclusion

Although the Greek case and possibly the Hungarian case—two of the instances of possession mediumship presented in this chapter—seem to offer strong evidence for personal survival, we cannot overlook the fact that these particular cases were not the object of the close scrutiny and investigation such cases would undergo today. More importantly, even though the sceptic has not in any way shown that these cases are in fact instances of fraud, deceit, or error, the occurrence of such language cases in the context of possession mediumship seems to be too rare to support a theory of survival. Indeed, over the past 35 years of careful research, the attempt to find such cases has produced meager results. Apart from the instances of xenoglossy we saw back in Chapter 1—cases that were not really possession mediumship—I know of no compelling language case in possession mediumship that has been successfully examined and professionally documented during the past 35 years. The sceptic is only too willing to tell us that this situation is less a testament to the rarity of such cases than it is a reason for seriously doubting the authenticity of cases like the Greek case and the Hungarian case. Therefore, these two cases should be viewed as having a legitimate but limited force until we can find and document new cases having the same features.

In the meantime we still have the evidence provided by the study of both Mrs. Piper's and Mrs. Willett's mediumships. Even here we must admit that—however strong the evidence—it is probably not strong enough by itself to carry a full-blooded conviction. On the principle that extraordinary beliefs require extraordinary evidence, the sceptic will want more mediumship evidence for the belief in some form of personal survival. Nevertheless, the evidence provided by the mediumships of Mrs. Piper and Mrs. Willett seems quite compelling, and there is no reason *not* to accept it as good evidence for survival. Again, it would be nice to have a more recent case with the same features.

The Berger experiment—in spite of all the qualifications noted above—seems to provide the sort of supplement necessary to carry a full conviction in mediumship as a source of evidence for personal survival. If repeated in the way suggested above, positive results of this type of experiment would be strongly confirmatory.

In the end, then, even if we cannot find any more language cases like the Greek case, we still have the results of Mrs. Piper's mediumship, Mrs. Willett's mediumship, and the Berger experiment. We must add to this the fact established above that the only way we can justifiably dismiss the Greek case is to suppose implausibly that everybody involved was part of a hoax. The sceptic has not demonstrated this to be true in either the Greek case or the Hungarian case. Certainly, the fact that we apparently have not had any such cases to investigate in the past 35 years must be taken seriously when the sceptic has difficulty in accepting the evidence based on language cases. Be that as it may, if what we have here does not seem robust enough evidence based on possession mediumship to make postmortem personal survival a sure thing, it does make survival more likely than not. It also makes very clear what sort of evidence for survival the dualist should be looking for when examining the phenomenon of possession mediumship.

Doubtless, if there are contemporary language cases with the same logical features as the Greek case (and I hope such cases come to our attention as a result of publishing this book), then the evidence from mediumship will be—or ought to be—considerably more persuasive for everybody. And if we can find more recent cases of mediumship similar to that of Mrs. Piper and Mrs. Willett, then the case for survival based on mediumship will be very compelling, if not conclusive.

Notes

1. In another type of mediumship, the medium—without entering a trance state—claims to have direct conscious contact with deceased disembodied spirits. But I am not here concerned with this type of mediumship. For a fuller discussion of various kinds of mediumship, see C. D. Broad, *Lectures on Psychical Research* (New York: Humanities Press, 1962), pp. 253ff. These different kinds of mediumship have been the subject of careful and formal investigation ever since the founding of the Society for Psychical Research (SPR) in 1882. Indeed, extensive case studies of mediumship and of specific mediums have appeared, and are continuing to appear, in the *Proceedings of the Society for Psychical Research*. See, for example, Mrs. Henry Sidgwick, "A Contribution to the Study of the Psychology of Mrs. Piper's Trance," *Proceedings of the Society for Psychical Research* 28 (1915), pp. 1–645. See also Gardner Murphy, "An Outline of Survival Evidence," *Journal of the American Society for Psychical Research* 39 (January 1945), pp. 2–34, and "Difficulties Confronting the Survival Hypothesis," *Journal of the American Society for Psychical Research* 39 (July 1945), pp. 67–94, and "Field Theory and Survival," *Journal of the American Society for Psychical Research* 39 (October 1945), pp. 181–209; Stephen Braude, "Mediumship and Multiple Personality," *Journal of the Society for Psychical Research* 55, no. 813 (October 1988), pp. 177–93; Hornell Hart, *The Enigma of Survival* (New York: Rider Press, 1959); and W. H. Salter, *Zoar* (London: Sidgwick and Jackson, 1961).

2. *Annales des Sciences Psychiques* 15, no. 317 (1905).

3. Ibid.

4. Dennis Bradley, *Towards the Stars* (London: T. Werner Laurie, 1932), pp. 208ff.

5. Ibid., p. 54. After the sitting, Evans gave Bradley the conversation in Welsh and the translation in English. Bradley, of course, never spoke Welsh.

6. *Psychic News,* London (November 1939).

7. Ibid.

8. Neville Whymant, *Psychic Adventures in New York* (London: Morley and Mitchell Kennerly, 1931).

9. Ibid., pp. 36.

10. William James, "Report on Mrs. Piper's Hodgson Control," *Proceedings of the Society for Psychical Research* 23 (1909), pp. 2–121. A copy of James's 1909 report is available in Gardner Murphy and Robert

Ballou, *William James on Psychical Research* (New York: Viking Press, 1960), pp. 144ff.

11. William James to F. W. H. Myers, letter reprinted in the *Proceedings of the Society for Psychical Research* 2 (December 1890), pt. 17.

12. Ibid. See also Murphy and Ballou, *William James on Psychical Research,* p. 104.

13. Murphy and Ballou, *William James on Psychical Research,* p. 97.

14. See ibid., p. 149, where several testimonies are cited, including that of Dr. Charles Bayley, an intimate friend of Richard Hodgson: "Such expressions and phrases were quaintly characteristic of R.H. in the body, and as they appear, often rapidly and spontaneously, they give the almost irresistible impression that it is really the Hodgson personality, presiding with its own characteristics. To appreciate this fully, of course, one would have to have known him as intimately as I did."

15. See, for example, A. Gauld, *Mediumship and Survival: A Century of Investigation* (London: Heinemann, 1982), pp. 50–85.

16. Ibid.

17. Ibid., p. 54.

18. Ibid., p. 60.

19. Ibid., p. 66b.

20. See James's review of Hodgson's second paper in Burkhardt, Bowers, and Skrupskelas, eds., *The Works of William James, Essays in Psychical Research* (Cambridge, Mass.: Harvard University Press, 1986), pp. 186ff.

21. F. W. H. Myers, *Human Personality and Its Survival of Bodily Death* (London: Longmans Green, 1903).

22. The early phase of Mrs. Willett's mediumship was the subject of a long and important paper authored by G. W. Balfour in the *Proceedings of the Society for Psychical Research* 43 (1935), pp. 43–318.

23. As C. D. Broad has noted about the Willett sittings with Balfour, the sittings covered three topics: (1) the conditions under which the communicators were working in communicating through Mrs. Willett; (2) the processes involved in such communication in general, and the special procedures involved in conducting a cross-correspondence (several mediums) experiment; (3) their views on certain philosophical questions about the nature of human personality, its survival of bodily death, and the relation of the human individual to the Absolute. C. D. Broad, *Lectures on Psychical Research* (London: Routledge and Kegan Paul, 1962), p. 296.

24. Ibid., p. 297.

25. Ibid.

26. Much of the transcripts can be found in ibid., pp. 290ff.

27. Ibid., p. 298.

28. See the *Proceedings of the Society for Psychical Research* 39, no. 691 (1926).

29. Broad, *Lectures,* pp. 359ff.

30. Ibid., p. 353.

31. Ibid., p. 354.

32. Ibid., pp. 360ff.

33. Ibid., pp. 350ff.

34. Ibid., pp. 355ff.

35. Ibid., pp. 356ff.

36. Because he could not explain by appeal to telepathy her ability to provide facts unknown to anybody at the time of the sitting, Hodgson mistakenly concluded that Mrs. Piper must be in communication with the dead; see J. Mishlove, *Roots of Consciousness* (New York: Random House, 1975), p. 87. Mrs. Henry Sidgwick, however, did not make this mistake. For Hodgson's discussion, see *Proceedings of the Society for Psychical Research* 13 (1897); and for Sidgwick's discussion, see Sidgwick, "Contribution to the Study" (cited in note 1 above).

37. Jule Eisenbud, *Parapsychology and the Unconscious* (Berkeley, Calif.: North Atlantic Books, 1983), pp. 227–43.

38. As quoted in Murphy and Ballou, *William James on Psychical Research,* p. 147 (emphasis added) and see also p. 209.

39. Broad, *Lectures,* p. 313.

40. With such considerations in mind, Broad—at *Lectures,* pp. 425ff—concludes his treatment on mediumship with the following:

Many mediumistic communications, which take the dramatic form of messages from the surviving spirit of a deceased human being, imparted to and reported by the medium's "control," plainly do not warrant us in taking that aspect of them literally. Often they require no more radical assumption than telepathic cognition, on the medium's part, of facts known (consciously or unconsciously) to the sitter or to other human beings known to him. . . .

Not withstanding such cases as these, I think it unplausible to claim that all well-attested cases of ostensible possession of a medium by the spirit of a certain deceased human being can be explained by telepathy from persons still alive in the flesh and dramatization on the part of the entranced medium. I am thinking now of cases where the medium speaks with a voice and behaves with mannerisms which are recognizably reminiscent of the alleged communicator, although she never met him in his lifetime and has never heard or seen any reproduction of his voice or his gestures. . . .

Now it seems to me that any attempt to explain these phenomena by reference to telepathy among the living stretches the word "telepathy" till it becomes almost meaningless, and uses that name to cover something for which there is no *independent* evidence and which bears hardly any analogy to the phenomena which the word was introduced to denote. *Prima facie,* the cases in question are strong evidence for the persistence, after a man's death, of something which carries traces of his experiences, habits and skills, and which becomes temporarily united during the seance with the entranced medium's organism.

But they are also *prima facie* evidence for something more specific, and surely very surprising indeed. For they seem to suggest that dispositions to certain highly specific kinds of *overt bodily* behavior, e.g., speaking in a certain characteristic tone of voice, writing in a certain characteristic hand, making certain characteristic gestures, etc., are carried by the x-component when it ceases to be incarnate, and are ready to manifest themselves whenever it is again temporarily united with a suitable living human body. And so strong do these dispositions remain that, when thus temporarily activated, they overcome the corresponding dispositions of the entranced medium to speak, write and gesticulate in her own habitual ways.

Nevertheless, it seems to me that *most* of the well-attested mediumistic phenomena which are commonly cited as evidence for the survival of a deceased human being's personality, do not suffice to support so strong a conclusion.

41. For discussion on the Patience Worth material, see Irving Litvag, *Singer in the Shadows* (London: Macmillan, 1972); Casper Yost, "The Evidence in Telka," in W. F. Prince, ed., *The Case of Patience Worth* (New Hyde Park, N.Y.: University Books, 1964), pp. 356–69; Braude, "Mediumship and Multiple Personality"; and Ian Stevenson, *Xenoglossy* (Charlottesville: University Press of Virginia, 1974), p. 23.

42. Ian Stevenson, in correspondence with the author.

43. Broad, *Lectures,* pp. 425ff. (See note 40 above.)

44. See Murphy and Ballou, *William James on Psychical Research,* p. 147. (And see note 38 above.)

45. See H. Salter's "The History of George Valiantine," *Proceedings of the Society for Psychical Research* 40 (1932), pp. 389–410.

46. Stevenson, *Xenoglossy,* pp. 10–11.

47. Salter, *Zoar.*

48. See Michael Coleman's review of *Beyond Death* (by Robert Alme-

der), *Journal of the Society for Psychical Research* 55, no. 815 (April 1989), p. 372.

49. Arthur Berger, *The Aristocracy of the Dead: New Findings in Post-mortem Survival* (Jefferson, N.C.: McFarland, 1987).

50. Ibid., p. 149.

51. See Emily Williams Cook's review of *Aristocracy of the Dead* (by Arthur Berger), *Journal of Parapsychology* 53 (1989), pp. 72–78.

52. Berger, *Aristocracy of the Dead,* p. 152; notations in the original have been omitted.

53. Ibid., p. 155.

54. Ibid., p. 156.

55. Ibid., p. 158.

56. Cook's review, cited in note 51 above.

6

The General Picture

It is a field in which the sources of deception are extremely numerous. But I believe there is no source of deception in the investigation of nature which can compare with a fixed belief that certain kinds of phenomenon are impossible.

William James commenting on paranormal research, 1886

If we had *only* the best available evidence from recent reincarnation studies, or *only* the best evidence on apparitions of the dead and cases of possession, or *only* the best evidence bearing on OBEs, or *only* the best evidence from mediumship, then we might well be inclined to ignore the belief in personal survival of death. After all, extraordinary claims require extraordinary evidence; and even though the evidence seems compelling in each of the above categories of research, we might not find the evidence in each category sufficiently compelling to warrant full-blooded conviction in personal survival.

The Evidence Viewed Collectively

But the force of the case for personal survival rests on the whole body of evidence viewed collectively as a *set* of arguments. Each argument from each category of research discussed and examined in these past pages is like a thread that, of itself, may well be incapable of carrying the full weight of the belief in some form of

255

personal survival. Bound together, however, they converge and make a strong cord that lifts the belief from the realm of superstition and thoughtless commitment in the absence of sound evidence. We have here support for a confirmed belief based purely on factual evidence. The *multiplicity* of the arguments provides the extraordinary evidence required for conviction. We have reached the point where a critical examination of *all* the evidence available makes such a commitment a good deal easier than it has ever been before. Certainly, we are considerably better off than was Plato in giving his reasons for believing in personal survival and reincarnation.

And the proponents of orthodox beliefs, such as Christianity, may well find the arguments herein congenial to their religious commitments. If so, that is a plus for them and something not intended by the author. Predictably, there will also be those who object on the grounds that such arguments may well undermine the virtuous necessity of faith. With a little bit of thought, however, one realizes that this objection need not be taken seriously. We do not always have the power to accept what we know to be true. Faith may well be that power in some way provided.

We must also remember that the evidence considered in this book on behalf of personal survival is also supportive of belief in reincarnation. It seems reasonably clear that the time has come for an earnest discussion of whether reincarnation is consistent with Christianity (or any other orthodox religion such as Judaism or Hinduism) and whether those with such orthodox attitudes could and should accept the evidence offered here.

In light of the present and other such contemporary studies, then, theologians may well have a good deal to think about as they examine the nature of religious activity. But this book makes no claims about God. Belief in personal survival of death neither requires nor precludes any particular beliefs about God. However, for those whose religious beliefs just happen to include belief in some form of life after death, this book should serve to indicate that the belief in question is capable of serious rational support totally independent of any particular religious doctrine.

But in the interest of completeness, we still need to examine a few more basic objections that have been raised in the past and that we have not yet confronted.

Three Basic Sceptical Objections

There are three fairly common sceptical objections to the belief in some form of personal survival after death—objections we have not yet considered in detail. Now that we have considered the separate categories of evidence and objections, we are in a position to address these three most fundamental responses of the sceptic. The first objection asserts that personal survival after death is impossible either because we cannot even imagine what a disembodied spirit would be like, or because the very idea of such survival is conceptually incoherent. The second objection is that, even if some form of personal survival were possible, we certainly do not yet have any experimental evidence (and hence no scientific knowledge) of anyone's surviving death. The third objection is related to the second and consists in asserting that the ever-present possibility of fraud or hoax in the evidence offered here for personal survival can only be excluded by insisting on the kind of robust confirmation required in experimental science—and we have nothing like that at present. All three of these objections are fairly common; but, as we shall now see, all rest equally on crucial misconceptions.

The Logical Impossibility of Personal Survival

Sceptics who assert the impossibility of personal survival usually do so on the grounds that the very idea of a human being's personality existing independently of his or her body is just inconceivable or incoherent. In their view, it makes no sense even to talk about personal survival after death either because we cannot imagine what a human personality is if it is not at least partially identifiable with a human body, or else because the very idea of surviving one's death is conceptually incoherent.

Let us consider the first disjunct here: that our very concept of a person is so firmly tied to our understanding of bodily existence and activities that we cannot even imagine what a person is like if it does not possess such characteristics. Just think of it. A disembodied person would need to perceive events clairvoyantly in some

way, without any sense organs such as eyes and ears. A disembodied person would need to act upon other things and other persons
in some way without using limbs and without the usual feelings
of stress and strain that come from the skin, the joints, and the
muscles. And a disembodied person would need to communicate
with others telepathically without using vocal organs and emitting
audible sounds. All this, as C. D. Broad has noted, is *conceivable*
as long as we keep it in the abstract; but when we try to think
"what it would be like" in concrete detail, we do not seem to have
any clear or definite ideas at all.[1]

In urging this objection, however, the sceptic makes a crucial
mistake. The mistake consists in thinking that, just because we
cannot imagine what a disembodied spirit must be like, there
cannot be any. Indeed, an adequate reply to the sceptic is that our
inability to imagine fully any particular state of affairs should not
be taken as evidence for its nonexistence. We may not be able to
imagine an infinite series of numbers, or what it would be like to
walk on the moon; still, there are infinite series of numbers, and
some people have walked on the moon. In short, the sceptic makes
the mistake of inferring the nonexistence of spirits simply because
we cannot imagine them as some sort of physical objects. The
sceptic might just as well object to belief in the existence of God
because we cannot imagine what God looks like. If one believes in
the existence of disembodied persons, then one believes in beings
who are by definition not understandable in *purely* physical terms.
Obviously, our belief or disbelief in such beings should be a
function of whether we have sufficient evidence for thinking that
some such beings must exist, and not whether we can imagine
them as we would a physical object.

Besides, even if we cannot fully imagine what a disembodied
person must be like, we can still say a good deal about what
human personality *must* be like if it is to survive bodily death. On
this last point, C. D. Broad once sought to answer the question
"Is survival possible, and, if so, in what possible sense or senses?"

> It seems to me that a *necessary*, though by no means a sufficient,
> condition for survival is that the whole or some considerable part
> of the *dispositional basis* of a human being's personality should

persist, and should retain at least the main outlines of its characteristic type of organization for some time after the disintegration of
his brain and nervous system. The crux of the question is whether
this is not merely conceivable, in the sense of involving no purely
logical absurdity (whether explicit or implicit), but is also factually
possible, i.e. not irreconcilable with any empirical facts or laws for
which the evidence seems to be overwhelming. . . .

[T]here seems to be only one view of human nature compatible
with the possibility of the *post-mortem* persistence of the whole, or
any part, of the dispositional basis of a human being's personality.
We must assume some variant of the Platonic–Cartesian view of
human beings. This is the doctrine that every human being is some
kind of intimate *compound* of two constituents, one being his ordinary everyday body, and the other something of a very different
kind, not open to ordinary observation. Let us call this other
constituent in this supposed compound a "x-component." It would
be necessary to suppose that the x-component of a human being
carries some part at least of the organized dispositional basis of his
personality, and that during his life it is modified specifically and
more or less permanently by the experiences which he has, the
training which he receives, his habitual practical and emotional
reactions towards himself and others, and so on.[2]

Broad hastens to add that there are two traditional features of
the classical Platonic–Cartesian doctrine that we need not, and
ought not, accept. The first is that the x-component is *by itself* the
person. It might well be that personality (and even the lowest form
of actual experience) requires the association of an x-component
with an appropriate living organism. The known facts about the
intimate dependence of a human being's personality on his or her
body and its states would seem strongly to support this version of
the doctrine. The second traditional feature is that the x-component is unextended and unlocated and has none of the properties
of the physically existent. On this last point, Broad notes that, if
we gratuitously assume that the x-component has none of the
characteristics of the physically existent, then the x-component
could not be supposed to have a minute structure or to be the seat
of recurrent internal processes (which is what is needed if it is to
carry traces and dispositions), and the x-component could not be

conceived to be united with a particular living body to constitute an ordinary human being.

> If we are to postulate a "ghost-in-the-machine"—and that seems to me to be a *conditio sine qua non* for the barest possibility of the survival of human personality—then we must ascribe to it some of the quasi-physical properties of the traditional ghost. A mere unextended and unlocated Cartesian "thinking substance" would be useless and embarrassing for our purpose; something more like primitive animism than refined Cartesianism is what we need.[3]

Certainly we might disagree with Broad on some of the specifics of this proposal. His argument that the x-component cannot be the person, for example, seems problematic in light of an argument he once offered to the effect that we need not suppose that a mind be made up of any physical (or quasi-physical parts) in order to make sense of a causal interaction between minds and bodies.[4] Moreover, given what we said in Chapter 2 about apparitions of the dead (and F. W. H. Myers's view about the nature of such apparitions),[5] we need not suppose that ghosts have any physical parts at all. But it seems clear that, under the conditions Broad specifies, we can conceive of a form of dualism (and personal disembodied existence) not inconsistent with the known facts of physics, physiology, and psychology. Such a dualism would make it possible for the dispositional basis of a human personality to persist after the biological death of the human being who had possessed that personality. Thus it is neither logically inconceivable nor factually impossible that the dispositional basis of one's personality (or at any rate some part of it) might continue to exist and to be organized in its former characteristic pattern— for a time at least—after the death of one's body, without being associated with any other type of physical organism.[6] Even at that, however, the surviving personality would need to share some features in common with physical objects.

Moreover, the view that it is inconceivable that one could survive one's death is vaguely reminiscent of the traditional attack on the possibility of mind–body causal interaction. The familiar attack is parasitic on the claim that we cannot imagine how minds and bodies could possibly interact, and so they cannot. In facing this attack, however, Broad elsewhere encourages us to see first whether there is any evidence for such causal interaction, rather than deny the very possibility of it on the grounds that we cannot understand how two so different principles could be causally related.[7] That is, instead of saying something or other cannot occur because we cannot imagine how it could, we should look for independent evidence of its occurrence and, if and when we find it, either admit that we do not know how it occurs or seek new ways of trying to understand how it occurs.[8] This same procedure seems advisable with regard to disembodied persons: first, see if there is evidence for the existence of some such being not reducible to mere physicalistic terms; and second, if there is such evidence, admit that some such being exists but that we do not fully understand its nature and cannot imagine its properties in purely physicalistic terms.

What about the second part of the first objection: that the very idea of a person's surviving biological death is incoherent? This argument was offered at one time by Anthony Flew,[9] among others, and seems to have been inspired by the belief that our whole concept of a person is so rooted in the physical that it makes no sense to suggest anybody could survive biological death. There would be nothing to survive. Flew points to numerous instances of ordinary discourse wherein the logic of the usage seems to require that human personality does not survive biological death. We often say, for example, after a shipwreck or a tragedy of some sort, "There were no survivors" or "There was only one survivor." And what does this mean except that, by definition, one does not survive biological death. The ordinary concept of "death" just *means* no survival after biological death. Hence it is simply incoherent to suggest that anybody could possibly survive death.

And how does one answer this sort of argument? The short answer is to say that it is dogmatic. For scepticism of this ilk, it is simply a conceptual truth that human personality—whatever this may be—does not survive physical death. Apart from the question of whether there are such conceptual truths and, if there are, whether they can be derived from the logic of ordinary usage, this particular argument carries with it the unfortunate implication that no matter what happens in the future, no matter what facts ultimately come to light, it is simply not possible that we shall ever get empirical evidence for personal survival. How is such an argument any different from a dogmatic refusal to regard anything as evidence for the thesis? Besides, even on its own terms, this argument is not very persuasive. After all, why can we not mean—when we say, "Nobody survived the accident"—nothing more than that everybody suffered biological death? And if so, this only *raises* the question of whether people ever suffer biological death and survive it in some way. It does not settle it. Which raises the further question as to what human personality consists in, and what evidence there may be for the view that human personality is not simply reducible to the physical in such a way as to make the suggestion of surviving biological death incoherent.

Similar to Flew's argument (because based on the idea that the body is essential to human personality) is the objection once raised by James Wheatley.[10] For Wheatley, one cannot possibly survive as a person if nobody would be able to identify the survivor; and since without a body nobody would be able to identify the survivor, it follows that nobody could possibly survive death. The fairly obvious question-begging nature of such an argument has (to steal a phrase from Bertrand Russell) all the merits of theft over hard toil. This same sort of fallacy is committed equally well by those who insist on the *social nature* of human personality (i.e., social relationships as a necessary condition for human personality), and then insist that without a body one cannot have much of a social life.[11]

At any rate, if we are to avoid being dogmatic, we must disown the claim that nothing could possibly count as evidence for the view that human personality survives biological death. If we are to avoid question begging, we must not smuggle into our discussions the moot point that having a body is a necessary condition for human personality.

The Scientific Improbability of Personal Survival

As we saw above, the second common sceptical objection to belief in personal survival consists in arguing that even if personal survival is logically and factually possible, still we have no scientific knowledge of anybody's ever surviving biological death, because we have no experimental evidence that will hold up under serious scientific scrutiny. This sort of objection feeds on the belief that all the evidence offered for personal survival (whether it be from reincarnation studies, apparitions of the dead, ostensible possessions, OBEs, or mediumship) is not publicly repeatable in experimental contexts under controlled conditions. We cannot, so the objection goes, generate at will compelling case studies. We cannot, for example, scientifically control disembodied spirits so as to make them appear under empirically desirable conditions. Because the evidence for personal survival lacks this characteristic, the evidence is not, the sceptic asserts, repeatable under the experimental method. For this often-cited reason (which we discussed briefly in Chapter 1), some scientists tend to consider the case studies offered in the preceding chapters as "anecdotal" rather than as solid scientific evidence. And some sceptics are downright insistent that, unless a belief is established by the experimental methods of the natural sciences, the belief cannot be an item of human knowledge.

In replying to this objection, we may reflect on at least two basic points. The first point is that although *much* of the evidence for personal survival is not repeatable and accessible in the usual way that, for example, the evidence for the law of gravity is public and repeatable, it is a mistake to think that all knowledge requires experimental evidence that is public and repeatable in the way just suggested. Such repeatability is necessary only when, in the interest of prediction and control, we require causal explanations, or statements of the causes of the nomic phenomena in question. But such causal explanations are not necessary to establish *that* something or other occurs, rather than *why* it occurs. We might, for example, establish *that* dinosaurs existed sometime in the past without having to establish the reasons *why* dinosaurs happened to appear. While there is a kind of repeatability that is necessary for reliability in establishing mere existence or occurrence, it is quite a different kind of repeatability from the experimental repeatability necessary for causal explanations of nomic phenomena. The latter, but not the former, typically require our being able to show at will the conformity of controlled experiment to causal hypothesis, thereby producing at will the data that confirm the hypothesis. However, there is a good deal of legitimate scientific knowledge that does not require the experimentally repeatable kind of evidence. Once again, for example, the evidence for the past existence of dinosaurs is not experimentally repeatable or reproducible at will. The facts that confirm the hypothesis cannot be produced at will and so repeated in the way suggested. What makes the "dinosaur hypothesis" scientifically acceptable is its simplicity, or the fit between the existing data and the hypothesis; also, we know what sensory experiences would refute the hypothesis. The only plausible explanation for the data requires believing in the past existence of dinosaurs.

It is not a necessary condition for empirical knowledge, then, that the evidence be experimentally repeatable at will in the way dictated by laboratory science to provide causal explanations for observed nomic regularities. This type of evidence is necessary for causal explanations of a certain sort, but not necessary for empirically reliable explanations to the effect that something or other has occurred. This basic point has already been well argued and discussed by Stephen Braude in the first chapter of his book *The Limits of Influence*.[12] There is an appropriate sense in which the evidence for belief in the past existence of dinosaurs, say, is repeatable and needs to be repeated, but it is not the same sense in which an experiment is said to be repeated and repeatable in lab science. So much seems fairly obvious.

Also, I know what my father said to me just before he died. The evidence for my knowledge claim—his spoken words—is not experimentally repeatable or publicly accessible. And even if there had been 5,000 people in the room with me when my father spoke his dying words, the evidence would still not be experimentally repeatable in the sense specified by the sceptic. But surely, I (and the 5,000 who may have been with me in the room) know what my father said on that day. His diction was impeccable and his voice loud and clear. In other words, even if all the evidence for personal survival were not experimentally repeatable in the way suggested, it would by no means follow that the belief is not an item of human public knowledge. Do unique historical events need to be repeated in that way in order for us to be justified in believing that they occurred? Or, ceteris paribus, do we accept eyewitness testimony of a sufficiently large number of honorable and generally reliable people?

It is distinctly possible that the methods of the natural sciences, including the requirement of experimental repeatability, make sense only when we seek causal explanations of subject matter understood to be physical and nomic in its behavior. By definition, however, minds or human personalities will not be physical in any usual sense. Thus, not only is the requirement of experimental repeatability not necessary for human or scientific knowledge; it also sometimes seems to argue against the very existence of minds by requiring that they be physical and nomic in the usual sense. Why would anyone assume that the same scientific method, especially when it comes to experimental repeatability, is appropriate for understanding a subject matter so different in fundamental ways? Coherence of the subject matter aside, this is very much like asking the theist for scientifically demonstrable knowledge of the existence of God after she or he has noted that God is not a physical object conforming to nomic regularities.

The second point in our reply to the objection that personal survival is not scientifically evidenced is that, notwithstanding the above considerations, we do in fact have repeatable, and repeated, evidence of personal survival. The trouble is that we cannot produce at will the phenomena necessary for acquiring the repeatable evidence. Let me explain.

Empirically repeatable evidence for personal survival is certainly provided by the evidence we offered earlier for reincarnation. As suggested in Chapter 1, in order to verify the belief in reincarnation we need only study an indefinitely large number of suitable subjects until we secure an interesting number of them with the appropriate memory claims and the appropriate skills not learned in their present life. Other researchers, such as Ian Stevenson, have already done this, and continue to do so, and there is no more plausible explanation of the results than to suppose that some persons reincarnate. On any given day, of course, one might get no good evidence from one's searching use of the regression technique; just as on any given day, digging deeply into a particular desert spot will not produce any evidence confirming the hypothesis that there were dinosaurs.

Stevenson himself is quick to admit that the methodology of regression as a way of confirming reincarnation does not provide the best cases to date and that, most of the time, most of the regressions conducted are worthless as evidence.[13] Even so, if the hypothesis of reincarnation is true, then by use of regression techniques we should sooner or later produce some rich cases; and that would count for experimental repetition. However, this test would not be unique or even necessary because, as Stevenson has noted,[14] we have some very strong cases that are the product of spontaneous and uninduced memories. Indeed, these seem to be the strongest cases. So, failure to produce rich cases under regression would not falsify the thesis if there are—as indeed there are—rich cases not the product of memories induced under regression techniques. Thus, while the virtue of the regression technique is that it may well repeatedly produce some rich cases (like the Jensen case, the Gretchen case, or the Sharada case; see Chapter 1), failure to come up with such cases would not refute the hypothesis. Using regression, we would be actively seeking to generate cases instead of waiting for those based on spontaneous past-life memories. What would refute the reincarnation hypothesis, it seems, is a failure to come up with any more cases under the regression techniques *and* a failure to come up with any more well-documented rich cases based on memories that are spontaneous and not induced by regression techniques. Certainly, the evidence for reincarnation is repeatable under the regression technique, and it has in fact been repeated. But, unlike repeatability in lab science, the confirming evidence does not emerge with each use of the technique. For all the reasons noted in discussing the first point above, the kind of repeatability appropriate in lab science should no more be required for legitimizing belief in reincarnation than it should for legitimizing belief in the past existence of dinosaurs.

Moreover, we argued in Chapter 4 that the controlled OBE experiment conducted by Charles Tart with Ms. Z was in fact repeated in the experiments conducted by Karlis Osis and Donna McCormick with Alex Tanous. If we were to repeat again (and again) the results of the Osis–McCormick experiments, this would provide very strong evidence for personal survival. These experiments more rigidly satisfy the requirements of repeatability as practiced in lab science. So too does the mediumship experimental design offered by Arthur Berger—see Chapter 5—although in each case following his design one must have a suitable subject and, of course, we cannot produce such subjects at will. Whether the Berger experiment will produce solid results in the future remains to be seen.

Admittedly, none of this would tell us what human personality is, how it reincarnates, how long it reincarnates, whether it disappears after a series of reincarnations, or even why it reincarnates. But such experimentally repeated and confirmed tests would quite clearly provide us with knowledge that the whole of human personality cannot be identified with the human body, that human personality sometimes survives for some time after death, and that it sometimes reincarnates.

The Long Shadow of Hoax and Fraud

The third common sceptical objection to belief in personal survival seems to be the most persistent, and this is the assertion that the evidence is persuasive only if the ever-present possibility of fraud can be clearly excluded. This possibility can be excluded, it is argued, only when the thesis is robustly verified in the way specified for experimental theses in the natural sciences. Because we do not yet have that sort of verification for personal survival, the burden of proof is still on the proponent to show that the evidence offered is free from hoax and fraud.

This sort of objection is based on the acceptable principle that extraordinary claims require extraordinary evidence, and extraordinary evidence needs to be fraud-proof—especially in an area of inquiry where extensive fraud and trickery has been richly documented. Given this objection, however, even the best cases for survival cannot be accepted as good evidence, because in each case we cannot exclude the real possibility of fraud in the way that the experimental method excludes such fraud. For example, how do we know that Stevenson and his associates did not fabricate both the claim that Bishen Chand Kapoor demonstrated knowledge of where Laxmi Narain had secretly hidden gold before he died, and the claim that Bishen played the drums skilfully without ever having played them before? (See Chapter 1.) And so on. This is not to say that Stevenson and his associates in fact did so. Rather, it is to raise a real possibility that must be excluded before we can accept such cases as our best evidence; and the use of the experimental method seems to be the only way we could detect such fraud if it were present. This general objection is one that Patrick Grimm raises in his review of Braude's book *The Limits of Influence*.[15] But is this third sceptical objection any better than the first two?

Perhaps the strongest reply to this pointed objection is that we really do not need the experimental method to exclude the possibility of fraud. The same effect can be achieved simply by pointing to the best cases and the fact that the number of cases is not fixed or historically isolated—that such cases are always occurring in different places, and what makes the best cases persuasive (and unlikely to be instances of fraud) is that many logically identical cases occur regularly although not predictably.

Analogously, if only a few people in Idaho in 1981 claim to have seen UFOs and we cannot prove fraud or hoax, we still have a right to be sceptical. However, if the number of sightings that we cannot prove fraudulent increases dramatically over the years and in different places (in contexts where we can establish that people have no reason to perpetrate a fraud), this increases the credibility of the first sightings and (by implication) the thesis that there are UFOs, precisely because the likelihood of fraud decreases dramatically as a result of there being an enhanced likelihood of detecting fraud the more frequently the sightings occur.

Thus the fact that there are many past and current ideal cases of the reincarnation type, in many different lands, offered by many different researchers from differing parts of the world and with strong reasons to avoid fraud or hoax, seems to serve the same purpose as repeatability in experimental science: it excludes any real likelihood of fraud or hoax. Add to this the fact that such cases continue to appear frequently and widely (as we would expect if the hypothesis were true), and we have reason for thinking that we are dealing with a robustly confirmed hypothesis.

In addition, as we saw in the preceding section, reincarnation is indeed an experimental hypothesis that admits of conclusive verification and falsification. True, if we were to regress a large number of people and never get the sorts of memories or unlearned skills that only reincarnation could plausibly explain, or if—for any reason whatever—we were never to come across any more spontaneous cases like the ideal cases, we would need to reject the hypothesis. However, the cases do keep coming, and the attempts to prove fraud in the best ones fail. This is also true in the best cases of spirit apparition, ostensible possession, OBE, and mediumship.

So, our reply to the third sceptical objection is, first, that we do not need the experimental method to exclude the real possibility of fraud in the best cases; we only need the continual widespread appearance of cases that have the same logical characteristics as the ideal cases. When enough such cases continue to occur and are examined by many different researchers who are incapable of finding any fraud, the probability of fraud becomes remote just because such cases are repeating themselves in widely differing contexts and in the hands of different researchers. Second, if this reply is not enough, then there is also—for all the reasons mentioned above—a very strong case to be made for the claim that not only is belief in reincarnation and personal survival an experimentally viable hypothesis; it is a strongly confirmed one, as well.

Notes

1. C. D. Broad, *Lectures on Psychical Research* (New York: Humanities Press, 1962), p. 409. For a similar argument, see Anthony Flew's "Can a Man Witness His Own Funeral?" *Hibbert Journal* 54 (1956); and William James, "Human Immortality: Two Supposed Objections to the Doctrine," in Gardner Murphy and Robert Ballou, eds., *William James on Psychical Research* (New York: Viking Press, 1960), pp. 279ff.
2. Broad, *Lectures*, pp. 414–15.
3. Ibid., p. 416.

4. C. D. Broad, *Mind and Its Place in Nature* (London: Routledge and Kegan Paul, 1962), pp. 96ff.

5. F. W. H. Myers, *Human Personality and Its Survival of Bodily Death* (New Hyde Park, N.Y.: University Books, 1961; originally published 1903).

6. Broad, *Lectures,* p. 417. A view quite similar to C. D. Broad's appears in Anthony Quinton's "The Soul," *Journal of Philosophy* 59, no. 15 (July 19, 1962), pp. 393–404; and more recently in James M. O. Wheatley's "Reincarnation, 'Astral Bodies,' and 'Components,' " *Journal of the American Society for Psychical Research* 73, no. 2 (April 1979), pp. 109–22.

7. Broad, *Mind,* pp. 97ff.

8. Ibid., p. 99.

9. Flew, "Can a Man Witness?" More recently these same arguments occur in Flew's Gifford Lectures published as *The Logic of Mortality* (Oxford, England: Blackwell, 1987).

10. Wheatley, "Reincarnation," p. 112.

11. See H. H. Price in J. R. Smythies, ed., *Brain and Mind* (New York: Humanities Press, 1965), pp. 29–31.

12. Stephen Braude, *The Limits of Influence: Psychokinesis and the Philosophy of Science* (New York: Routledge and Kegan Paul, 1986), pp. 57ff; and also, Stephen Braude, *ESP and Psychokinesis: A Philosophical Examination* (Philadelphia: Temple University Press, 1979), pp. 41ff.

13. Ian Stevenson, *Children Who Remember Previous Lives* (Charlottesville: University Press of Virginia, 1987), p. 45.

14. Ibid., pp. 46ff.

15. Patrick Grimm, "Review of *The Limits of Influence* (by Stephen Braude)," *Nous* 23 (March 1989), p. 129.

Selected Bibliography

1   Reincarnation

Alexander, V. K. "A Case of a Multiple Personality." *Journal of Abnormal and Social Psychology* 52 (1956), pp. 272–76.

Almeder, R. *Beyond Death: Evidence for Life after Death*. Springfield, Ill.: Charles C Thomas, 1987.

———. "Response to 'Past Tongues Remembered.' " *Skeptical Inquirer* 12 (Spring 1988), pp. 321–23ff.

———. "Reincarnation." In *What Survives Death?* edited by John Dore. Los Angeles: J. B. Tarcher, 1990.

———. "Review of I. Stevenson's *Children Who Remember Previous Lives*." *Journal of the American Society for Psychical Research* (January 1990).

———. "Against 'Against Reincarnation.' " *Free Inquiry* (forthcoming).

Ayer, A. J. *The Problem of Knowledge*. Baltimore: Penguin Books, 1962; and London: Penguin Classics PB, 1964, ch. 5.

Braude, Stephen E. *ESP and Psychokinesis: A Philosophical Examination*. Philadelphia: Temple University Press, 1979.

———. *The Limits of Influence*. London: Routledge and Kegan Paul, 1986.

———. "Evaluating the Super-psi Hypothesis." In *Exploring the Paranormal: Perspectives on Belief and Experience,* edited by George K. Zollschan, John F. Schumaker, and Greg F. Walsh. Dorset, England: Prism Press, 1989.

Brennan, J. H. *Reincarnation: Five Keys to Past Lives*. Wellingborough, Northants, England: Aquarian Press, 1981.

Chadwick, L. *Early Christian Thought and the Classical Tradition*. New York: Oxford University Press, 1966.

Chari, C. T. K. "Regression 'Beyond Birth.' " *Tomorrow* 6 (1958), pp. 89–94.

———. "How Good Is the Evidence for Reincarnation?" *Tomorrow* 10 (1962), pp. 89–98.

———. "Reincarnation Research: Method and Interpretation." In *The Signet Handbook of Parapsychology*, edited by Martin Ebon. New York: New American Library, 1978, pp. 313–24.

Congdon, M. H., Hain, J., and Stevenson, I. "A Case of Multiple Personality Illustrating the Transition from Role-playing." *Journal of Nervous and Mental Disease* 132 (1961), pp. 497–504.

Dalai Lama. *My Land and My People*. New York: McGraw-Hill, 1962.

Daniélou, Jean Cardinal. *Origène*. Paris: La Table Ronde, 1948; and translated by W. Mitchell. New York: Sheed and Ward, 1965.

Ducasse, C. J. "The Doctrine of Reincarnation in the History of Thought." *International Journal of Parapsychology* 2 (Summer 1960), pp. 61–80.

———. *A Critical Examination of the Belief in Life after Death*. Springfield, Ill.: Charles C Thomas, 1961.

Ebon, M., ed. *Reincarnation in the Twentieth Century*. New York: Signet Books, 1969.

———, ed. *The Signet Handbook of Parapsychology*. New York: New American Library, 1978.

Eisenbud, Jule. *Parapsychology and the Unconscious*. Berkeley, Calif.: North Atlantic Books, 1983, ch. 14.

Franz, S. I. *Persons One and Three: A Study in Multiple Personality*. New York: McGraw-Hill, 1974.

Gallup, George Jr., with Proctor, W. *Adventures in Immortality*. New York: McGraw-Hill, 1982.

Guirdham, Arthur. *The Cathars and Reincarnation*. London: Spearman Press, 1970.

Gupta, L. D., Sharma, N. R., and Mathur, T. C. *An Inquiry into the Case of Shanti Devi*. Delhi: International Aryan League, 1936.

Harris, Melvin. "Are Past-life Regressions Evidence of Reincarnation?" *Free Inquiry* (Fall 1986).

Hintze, N., and Pratt, J. G. *The Psychic Realm: What Can You Believe?* New York: Random House, 1975.

Lewis, H. D. *Persons and Life after Death*. New York: Barnes and Noble, 1978.

MacGregor, Geddes. *Reincarnation in Christianity: A New Vision of the Role of Rebirth in Christian Thought*. New York: Barnes and Noble, 1978.

———. *Reincarnation as a Christian Hope*. New York: Barnes and Noble, 1982.

Mills, Antonia. "Making a Scientific Study of Reincarnation." Currently unpublished paper presented at the Canadian Ethnology Society Meeting, 1988.

———. "A Replication Study: Three Cases of Children in Northern India Who Are Said to Remember a Previous Life." *Journal of Scientific Exploration* 3, no. 2 (1989), pp. 133–84.

Origen. *Contra Celsum,* translated by L. Chadwick. Cambridge, England: Cambridge University Press, 1965.

———. *On First Principles (De Principiis)*, translated by G. W. Butterworth. New York: Harper and Row, 1966.

"Origen." In the *New Encyclopaedia Britannica*, Volume 8. Chicago: Encyclopaedia Britannica, 1988, pp. 997–99.

Parrinder, E. G. "Varieties of Belief in Reincarnation." *Hibbert Journal* 55 (1956), pp. 260–67.

Penelhum, Terence. *Survival and Disembodied Existence*. New York: Humanities Press, 1970.

———. *Religion and Rationality*. New York: Random House, 1971.

Rhine, Louisa E. "Review of Ian Stevenson, *Twenty Cases Suggestive of Reincarnation.*" *Journal of Parapsychology* 30, no. 4 (December 1966), pp. 263–72.

Shirley, R. *The Problem of Rebirth: The Basis of the Reincarnation Hypothesis*. London: Rider, 1936.

Shoemaker, Sidney. "Persons and Their Pasts." *American Philosophical Quarterly* (October 1970).

Smart, Ninian. *The Long Search*. Boston: Little, Brown, 1978.

Stevenson, Ian. "Some New Cases Suggestive of Reincarnation: The Case of Bishen Chand Kapoor." *Journal of the American Society for Psychical Research* (October 1972), pp. 375–400.

———. *Twenty Cases Suggestive of Reincarnation,* 2nd edition, revised. Charlottesville: University Press of Virginia, 1974.

————. *Xenoglossy: A Review and Report of a Case.* Charlottesville: University Press of Virginia, 1974.

————. "The Explanatory Value of the Idea of Reincarnation." *Journal of Nervous and Mental Diseases* 164 (1977), pp. 305–26.

————. "American Children Who Claim to Remember Previous Lives." *Journal of Nervous and Mental Disease* 171, no. 12 (1983), pp. 742–48.

————. "Cryptomnesia and Parapsychology." *Journal of the Society for Psychical Research* 52 (1983), pp. 1–30.

————. *Unlearned Language: New Studies in Xenoglossy.* Charlottesville: University Press of Virginia, 1984.

————. *Children Who Remember Previous Lives.* Charlottesville: University Press of Virginia, 1987.

————. *Birthmarks and Birth Defects: A Contribution to Their Etiology.* New York: Paragon House Publishers, 1992.

Stevenson, Ian, et al. "A Preliminary Report of a New Case of Responsive Xenoglossy: The Case of Gretchen." *Journal of the American Society for Psychical Research* 70 (1976), pp. 65–77.

Stevenson, Ian, and Chadha, Narender K. "Can Children Be Stopped from Speaking about Previous Lives? Some Analyses of Features in Cases of the Reincarnation Type." *Journal of the Society for Psychical Research* (1989).

Stevenson, Ian, and Pasricha, S. "A Preliminary Report on an Unusual Case of the Reincarnation Type with Xenoglossy." *Journal of the American Society for Psychical Research* 74 (1980), pp. 331–48.

Stevenson, Ian, Pasricha, S., and McClean-Rice, N. "A Case of the Possession Type in India with Evidence of Paranormal Knowledge." *Journal of Scientific Exploration* 3, no. 1 (1989), pp. 81–101.

Stevenson, Ian, and Samararatne, G. "Three New Cases of the Reincarnation Type in Sri Lanka with Written Records Made before Verifications." *Journal of Scientific Exploration* 2, no. 2 (1988), pp. 217–38.

Thigpen, C. H., and Cleckley, H. M. *The Three Faces of Eve.* New York: McGraw-Hill, 1957.

Thomason, Sarah. "Past Tongues Remembered." *Skeptical Inquirer* 11 (Summer 1987).

————. "Reply to 'Response to Past Tongues Remembered.' " *Skeptical Inquirer* 12 (Spring 1988), pp. 323–24.

Toynbee, A. *Life after Death.* New York: McGraw-Hill, 1976.

Tregg, J. W. *Origen*. Atlanta, Ga.: John Knox Press, 1949.

Walker, E. D. *Reincarnation: A Study of Forgotten Truth*. New Hyde Park, N.Y.: University Books, 1965.

Weatherhead, Leslie. *The Christian Agnostic*. London: Hodder and Stoughton, 1965.

Wilson, Ian. *Mind Out of Time: Reincarnation Investigated*. London: Victor Gollancz, 1981.

2   Apparitions of the Dead

Bayless, R., and McAdams, E. E. *The Case for Life after Death: Parapsychologists Look at the Evidence*. Chicago: Nelson–Hall, 1981.

Bennett, Ernest. *Apparitions and Haunted Houses: A Survey of Evidence*. London: Faber and Faber; reprinted, Ann Arbor, Mich.: Gryphon Books, 1971.

Braude, Stephen. *The Limits of Influence*. London: Routledge and Kegan Paul, 1986.

Broad, C. D. *Lectures on Psychical Research*. New York: Humanities Press, 1962.

———. *Religion, Philosophy, and Psychical Research*. New York: Humanities Press, 1969, p. 100. Originally published 1953.

Collins, B. Abdy. *The Cheltenham Ghost*. London: Psychic Press, 1948.

Cummings, Abraham. *Immortality Proved by the Testimony of the Senses*. Bath, England: Torrey, 1826.

Dommeyer, Frederick. "Body, Mind, and Death." *Pacific Forum* (1963).

Ducasse, C. J. *A Critical Examination of the Belief in Life after Death*. Springfield, Ill.: Charles C Thomas, 1961.

Fuller, John. *The Ghost of Flight 401*. New York: Berkeley Press, 1978.

Gauld, Alan. "Discarnate Survival." In *Handbook of Parapsychology*, edited by B. B. Wolman. New York: Van Nostrand Reinhold, 1977, pp. 577–630.

———. *Mediumship and Survival*. London: Heinemann, 1982.

Green, C., and McCreery, C. *Apparitions*. London: Hamish Hamilton, 1975.

Gurney, E., Myers, F. W. H., and Podmore, F. *Phantasms of the Living*, 2 volumes. London: Trubner, 1886.

Hart, H. "Do Apparitions of the Dead Imply Any Intention on the Part of the Agent? A Rejoinder to Louisa Rhine." *Journal of Parapsychology* 22 (March 1958), pp. 59–63.

———. *The Enigma of Survival: The Case for and against an After Life.* Springfield, Ill.: Charles C Thomas, 1959.

Hart, H., and collaborators. "Six Theories about Apparitions." *Proceedings of the Society for Psychical Research* 50 (1956), pp. 153–239.

Hart, H., and Hart, E. "Visions and Apparitions Collectively and Reciprocally Perceived." *Proceedings of the Society for Psychical Research* 41 (May 1933), pp. 205–49.

Jaffé, Aniela. *Apparitions and Precognition.* New Hyde Park, N.Y.: University Books, 1963.

MacKenzie, Andrew. *The Unexplained: Some Strange Cases in Psychical Research.* London: A Barker, 1966.

———. *Apparitions and Ghosts.* London: A Barker, 1971.

———. *Hauntings and Apparitions.* London: Heinemann, 1982.

Morton, R. C. "Record of a Haunted House." *Proceedings of the Society for Psychical Research* 7 (1892), pp. 311–32.

Myers, F. W. H. *Human Personality and Its Survival of Bodily Death,* abridged and edited by S. Smith. London: Longmans Green, 1954; and New Hyde Park, N.Y.: University Books, 1961, esp. the chapter, "Phantasms of the Dead," in Volume 2, pp. 277–321, which is also reprinted in *The Signet Handbook of Parapsychology,* edited by M. Ebon. New York: New American Library, 1978, pp. 273ff. Originally published 1903.

Paranormal Phenomena, Science, and Life after Death. Parapsychological Monographs, no. 8. New York: Parapsychology Foundation, 1969.

Price, H. H. "Apparitions: Two Theories." *Journal of Parapsychology* 24 (1960).

Rhine, L. E. "Hallucinatory Psi Experiences II. The Initiative of the Percipient in Hallucinations of the Living, the Dying, and the Dead." *Journal of Parapsychology* 21 (March 1957), pp. 13–46.

———. "Hallucinatory Psi Experiences III. The Intention of the Agent and the Dramatising Tendency of the Percipient." *Journal of Parapsychology* 21 (September 1957), pp. 186–226.

Salter, W. H. *Ghosts and Apparitions.* London: G. Bell, 1938.

Stevenson, Ian. "Are Poltergeists Living or Are They Dead?" *Journal of the American Society for Psychical Research* 66 (1972), pp. 233–52.

———. "The Contribution of Apparitions to the Evidence for Survival." *Journal of the American Society for Psychical Research* 76 (October 1982), pp. 341–58.

———. "Do We Need a New Word to Supplement 'Hallucination'?" *American Journal of Psychiatry* 140, no. 12 (December 1983), pp. 1609–11.

Thouless, R. H. *Psychical Research Past and Present.* London: Society for Psychical Research, 1952.

Turner, Paul. "The Grey Lady: A Study of a Psychic Phenomenon in the Dying." *Journal of the Society for Psychical Research* 40 (1959), pp. 124–29.

Tyrrell, G. N. M. *Apparitions,* revised edition. London: Society for Psychical Research, 1973. Originally published 1953.

Underwood, P. *Gazetteer of Scottish and Irish Ghosts.* London: Souvenir Press, 1973, p. 102.

3   Possession

Anderson, Rodger. "The Watseka Wonder: A Critical Reevaluation." *Theta* 8, no. 4 (Fall 1980).

———. In "The End of the Watseka Wonder." *Theta* 9, no. 4 (Autumn 1981), pp. 21–22.

———. In "Final Comments on the Watseka Wonder." *Theta* 10, no. 1 (Spring 1982), pp. 23ff.

Bourguignon, E. *Possession.* San Francisco: Chandler and Sharp, 1976.

Chari, C. T. K. In "The End of the Watseka Wonder." *Theta* 9, no. 4 (Autumn 1981), pp. 21ff.

Dommeyer, Frederick. "Body, Mind, and Death." *Pacific Forum* (1963).

Ducasse, C. J. "Response to Dommeyer." *Pacific Forum* (1963).

Hodgson, R. "The Watseka Wonder—Additional Evidence." *Religio-philosophical Journal,* Chicago (December 1890), pp. 469–70.

Lewis, I. M. *Ecstatic Religion: An Anthropological Study of Spirit Possession and Shamanism.* Harmondsworth, Middlesex, England: Penguin Books, 1971.

Martinez-Toboas, A. In "The End of the Watseka Wonder." *Theta* 9, no. 4 (Autumn 1981), pp. 20–21.

————. In "Final Comments on the Watseka Wonder." *Theta* 10, no. 1 (Spring 1982), pp. 23ff.

Myers, F. W. H. *Human Personality and Its Survival of Bodily Death,* Volume. 1. London: Longmans Green, 1954; and New Hyde Park, N.Y.: University Books, 1961.

Pattison, E. M., Kahan, J., and Hurd, G. S. "Trance and Possession States." In *Handbook of States of Consciousness,* edited by B. B. Wolman and M. Ullman. New York: Van Nostrand Reinhold, 1986.

Salter, W. H. *Zoar: Or the Evidence of Psychical Research concerning Survival.* London: Sidgwick and Jackson, 1961.

Stevens, E. W. "The Watseka Wonder: A Narrative of Startling Phenomena Occurring in the Case of Mary Lurancy Vennum." *Religio-philosophical Journal,* Chicago (1887), pp. 286–316.

Stevenson, Ian. *Birthmarks and Birth Defects: A Contribution to Their Etiology.* New York: Paragon House Publishers, 1992.

Stevenson, Ian, Pasricha, Satwant, and McClean-Rice, Nicholas. "A Case of the Possession Type in India with Evidence of Paranormal Knowledge." *Journal of Scientific Exploration* 3, no. 1 (1989), pp. 81–101.

4   Out-of-Body Experiences

Alvarado, C. "The Physical Detection of the Astral Body: An Historical Perspective." *Theta* 8, no. 2 (1980).

Blackmore, Susan. *Beyond the Body: An Investigation of Out-of-the-body Experiences.* London: Heinemann, 1982.

————. "Are Out-of-body Experiences Evidence for Survival?" *Anabiosis* 3, no. 2 (December 1983), pp. 137–55.

————. "A Psychological Theory of the Out-of-body Experience." *Journal of Parapsychology* 48 (September 1984), pp. 201–18.

————. *The Adventures of a Parapsychologist.* Buffalo, N.Y.: Prometheus Books, 1986.

————. "Susan Blackmore Responds." *Journal of Near Death Studies* 7, no. 1 (Fall 1988).

Cook, Emily Williams. "Review of *Beyond the Body: An Investigation of Out-of-the-body Experiences* (by Susan Blackmore)," *Anabiosis* 4, no. 1 (Spring 1984), pp. 97–104.

Crookall, Robert. *The Study and Practice of Astral Projection*. New Hyde Park, N.Y.: University Books, 1966.

————. *Out-of-the-body Experiences: A Fourth Analysis*. New Hyde Park, N.Y.: University Books, 1970.

Drab, K. J. "The Tunnel Experience: Reality or Hallucination?" *Anabiosis* 1 (1981), pp. 126–52.

Ducasse, C. J. *A Critical Examination of the Belief in Life after Death*. Springfield, Ill.: Charles C Thomas, 1961.

Gallup, George Jr., with Proctor, W. *Adventures in Immortality: A Look beyond the Threshold of Death*. New York: McGraw-Hill, 1982.

Greyson, B. "A Typology of Near-death Experiences." *American Journal of Psychiatry* 142 (1985), pp. 967–69.

Greyson, B., and Flynn, C., eds. *The Near-death Experience*. Springfield, Ill.: Charles C Thomas, 1984.

Greyson, B., and Stevenson, I. "The Phenomenology of Near-death Experiences." *American Journal of Psychiatry* 137 (1980), pp. 1193–96.

Hartwell, J., Janis, J., and Harary, B., et al. "A Study of the Physiological Variables Associated with Out-of-body Experiences." In *Research in Parapsychology 1974*, edited by J. D. Morris, W. D. Roll, and R. L. Morris. Metuchen, N.J.: Scarecrow Press, 1975, pp. 127–29.

Irwin, H. J. *Flight of Mind: A Psychological Study of the Out-of-body Experience*. Metuchen, N.J.: Scarecrow Press, 1985.

————. "Out-of-body Experiences and Attitudes to Life and Death." *Journal of the American Society for Psychical Research* 82 (1988), pp. 237–52.

Irwin, H., and Bramwell, B. "The Devil in Heaven: A Near-death Experience with Both Positive and Negative Facets." *Journal of Near-death Studies* 7, no. 1 (Fall 1988), pp. 38–43.

Isaacs, Julian. "On Kinetic Effects during Out-of-body Projection." *Journal of the American Society for Psychical Research* 75 (1981), pp. 192–94.

Kurtz, Paul. "Brushes with Death." *Psychology Today* 22, no. 9 (September 1988), pp. 14–17.

Mitchell, John. "Out-of-body Vision." *Psychic* (April 1973), pp. 44–47.

Monroe, Robert. *Journeys out of the Body*. Garden City, N.Y.: Doubleday, 1971.

Moody, Raymond. *Life after Life*. Covington, Ga.: Mockingbird Books, 1975.

————. *Reflections on Life after Life*. New York: Bantam Books, 1978.

Moody, Raymond, with Perry, Paul. *The Light Beyond*. New York: Bantam Books, 1988.

Morris, R. L., Harary, S. B., Janis, J., Hartwell, J., and Roll, W. G. "Studies of Communication during Out-of-body Experiences." *Journal of the American Society for Psychical Research* 72 (1978), pp. 1–21.

Morris, Robert. "PRF Research on Out-of-body Experiences 1973." *Theta*, no. 41 (Summer 1974), pp. 1–3.

Muldoon, S., and Carrington, H. *The Projection of the Astral Body*. London: Rider, 1956; second printing, New York: Samuel Weiser, 1970.

Osis, Karlis. "Perspectives for Out-of-body Research." In *Research in Parapsychology 1973,* edited by W. G. Roll, R. L. Morris, and J. D. Morris. Metuchen, N.J.: Scarecrow Press, 1974, pp. 110–13.

Osis, Karlis, and Haraldsson, E. *At the Hour of Death*. New York: Avon, 1977.

Osis, Karlis, and McCormick, Donna. "Kinetic Effects at the Ostensible Location of an Out-of-body Projection during Perceptual Testing." *Journal of the American Society for Psychical Research* 74 (1980), pp. 319–29.

————. "The Authors Reply to Mr. Issacs." *Journal of the American Society for Psychical Research* 75 (1981), pp. 367–68.

Pasricha, S., and Stevenson, I. "Near-death Experiences in India: A Preliminary Report." *Journal of Nervous and Mental Disease* 174 (1986), pp. 165–70.

Ring, Kenneth. *Life at Death: A Scientific Investigation of the Near-Death Experience*. New York: Coward, McCann, and Geogheghan, 1980.

Saavedra-Aguilar, J. C., and Gomez-Jeria, J. S. "A Neurobiological Model for Near-death Experiences." *Journal of Near-death Studies* 7, no. 4 (Summer 1989), pp. 205–22.

Sabom, Michael. *Recollections of Death: A Medical Investigation*. New York: Harper and Row, 1981, p. 126.

Siegel, Ronald. "Hallucinations." *Scientific American,* no. 237 (1977), pp. 132–40.

————. "The Psychologgy of Life after Death." *American Psychologist* 35 (1980), pp. 911–31.

————. "Accounting for 'Afterlife' Experiences." *Psychology Today* (January 1981), pp. 65–75.

Stuckey, William. "Psychic Power: The Next Superweapon." *Harpers* (January 1977).

Tart, Charles T. "A Psychophysiological Study of Out-of-body Experiences in a Selected Subject." *Journal of the American Society for Psychical Research* 62, no. 1 (January 1968), pp. 3–27.

———. *Psi: Scientific Studies of the Psychic Realm.* New York: Dutton, 1977.

Woodhouse, Mark. "Near-death Experiences and the Mind–Body Problem." *Anabiosis* (July 1981), pp. 57–65.

———. "Five Arguments regarding the Objectivity of NDEs." *Anabiosis* (June 1983), pp. 63–75.

5 Communications from the Dead

Baird, A. T. *One Hundred Cases for Survival after Death.* New York: Bernard Ackermann, 1944.

Berger, Arthur S. *The Aristocracy of the Dead: New Findings in Post-mortem Survival.* Jefferson, N.C.: McFarland, 1987.

Braude, Stephen. "Mediumship and Multiple Personality." *Journal of the Society for Psychical Research* 55, no. 813 (October 1988), pp. 177–93.

Broad, C. D. *Lectures on Psychical Research.* New York: Humanities Press, 1962.

———. *Mind and Its Place in Nature.* London: Routledge and Kegan Paul, 1962.

Cook, Emily Williams. "Review of *The Aristocracy of the Dead* (by Arthur Berger)." *Journal of Parapsychology* 53 (1989), pp. 72–78.

Edmonds, J. W. *Speaking in Many Tongues.* New York: 1858.

Eisenbud, Jule. *Parapsychology and the Unconscious.* Berkeley, Calif.: North Atlantic Books, 1983, ch. 14.

Finucane, R. C. *Appearances of the Dead.* London: Junction Books, 1982.

Flew, Anthony. "Can a Man Witness His Own Funeral?" *Hibbert Journal* 54 (1956), pp. 242–50.

Gauld, A. "The 'Super-ESP' Hypothesis." *Proceedings of the Society for Psychical Research* 53 (1961), pp. 226–46.

———. *Mediumship and Survival: A Century of Investigation.* London: Heinemann, 1982.

Hart, Hornell. *The Enigma of Survival.* New York: Rider Press, 1959.

Hodgson, Richard. "A Record of Observations of Certain Phenomena of Trance." *Proceedings of the Society for Psychical Research* 8 (1892), pp. 1–167.

———. "A Further Record of Observations of Certain Phenomena of Trance." *Proceedings of the Society for Psychical Research* 13 (1898), pp. 284–582.

Hope, C. "Report on Some Sittings with Valiantine and Phoenix in 1927." *Proceedings of the Society for Psychical Research* 40 (1932), pp. 411–27.

Irwin, H. J. *Flight of Mind*. Metuchen, N.J.: Scarecrow Press, 1985.

James, William. "Report on Mrs. Piper's Hodgson Control." *Proceedings of the Society for Psychical Research* 23 (1909), pp. 2–121.

———. "Human Immortality: Two Supposed Objections to the Doctrine." In *William James on Psychical Research,* edited by Gardner Murphy and Robert Ballou. New York: Viking Press, 1960, pp. 279–308.

Litvag, Irving. *Singer in the Shadows*. London: Macmillan, 1972.

Murphy, Gardner. "An Outline of Survival Evidence." *Journal of the American Society for Psychical Research* 39 (January 1945), pp. 2–34.

———. "Difficulties Confronting the Survival Hypothesis." *Journal of the American Society for Psychical Research* 39 (July 1945), pp. 67–94.

———. "Field Theory and Survival." *Journal of the American Society for Psychical Research* 39 (October 1945), pp. 181–209.

Murphy, Gardner, and Ballou, Robert, eds. *William James on Psychical Research*. New York: Viking Press, 1960.

Prince, W. F., ed. *The Case of Patience Worth*. New Hyde Park, N.Y.: University Books, 1964.

Salter, H. "The History of George Valiantine." *Proceedings of the Society for Psychical Research* 40 (1932), pp. 389–410.

———. *Zoar*. London: Sidgwick and Jackson, 1961.

Sidgwick, Mrs. Henry. "A Contribution to the Study of the Psychology of Mrs. Piper's Trance Phenomena." *Proceedings of the Society for Psychical Research* 28 (1915), pp. 1–645.

Stevenson, I. *Xenoglossy*. Charlottesville: University Press of Virginia, 1974, pp. 2–3.

Whymant, N. *Psychic Adventures in New York*. London: Morley and Kennerly, 1931.

Yost, Casper. "The Evidence in Telka." In *The Case of Patience Worth,* edited by W. F. Prince. New Hyde Park, N.Y.: University Books, 1964, pp. 356–69.

Index

postmortem survival,
  basic objections against, 257ff
  C. D. Broad's assessment of the
    thesis, 257–60
  empirical repeatability of evidence
    for, 263–65
  evidence in general for, 255–57,
    264
  and hoax and fraud, 267

reincarnation, 1–95
  based on ESP, 42ff
  based on memory evidence and
    acquired skills, 5–12
  based on memory evidence and
    recognition, 22–25
  based on responsive xenoglossy,
    12–22
  and birthmarks, 157–58, 160n29
  bypassing ESP, 26–42
  and Christianity, 66–81
  and clairvoyance, 42
  core features of ideal case, 3–4, 58–
    62
  and ESP, 45–47
  evidential cases of,
    Bishen Chand Kapoor, 5–8
    Gretchen, 14
    Lydia Johnson, 13–14
    Mrs. Smith, 8–12
    Shanti Devi, 19–21
    Swarnlata, 22–25, 37, 90n24
  and Gallup poll, 1
  history of in the West, 64
  and personal survival, 2
  and possession, 53–55, 135–61
  and the problem of personal
    identity, 83–89
  and repeatability of evidence, 55–
    58
  sceptical responses to evidence for,
    26–58

and scientific evidence, 81–83
Stevenson's arguments for, 1–85
and subconscious impersonation,
  47
and super-psi, 50–53
super-psi, role in reincarnation,
  117–21
universality of, 63–64, 93n76
Reinée Passarow, 170
Repeatability objection, 55
Repeatability of evidence for reincarnation, 83ff

Sabom, Michael, on autoscopic
  hallucinations in NDEs, 182,
  192
Shoemaker, Sidney, and personal
  identity, 83–86, 95n103
Sidgwick, Mrs. Henry, 250n1, 252n36
Siegel, Ronald, on OBEs and NDEs,
  176ff
sloppy methodology, as a reply to
  reincarnation evidence, 32–
  33, 95n103
Stevenson, Ian, 1–85, 91n30, 91n34,
  91n35, 91n52, 93n71,
  133n65, 234, 266

Tart, Charles, experiments with Ms.
  Z, 167

unlearned languages, 90n15

Valiantine, George, 234ff

Watseka Wonder, the, 136–43
  discussion of case of, 137–43
  sceptic's response to, 138–43
Wheatley, James, 262

Xenoglossy, responsive and recitative,
  12–14, 90n14, 90n16

About the Author

Dr. Robert Almeder received his Ph.D. in philosophy from the University of Pennsylvania and, as a Fellow of the Council for Philosophical Studies, did postdoctoral work in logic and philosophy of science at Stanford University. Recipient of the Outstanding Educator of America Award in 1974 and of the Georgia State University Alumni Distinguished Professor Award in 1984, Dr. Almeder has published more than 50 philosophical essays in such journals as *Philosophy of Science, Synthese, American Philosophical Quarterly, Philosophia, Erkenntnis, Philosophical Quarterly, Australasian Journal of Philosophy*, and *History of Philosophy Quarterly*. He has published, or copublished, 16 other books including *The Philosophy of Charles Peirce: A Critical Introduction* (Basil Blackwell, 1990) and *Blind Realism: An Essay on Human Knowledge and Natural Science* (Rowman & Littlefield, 1991).